Contemporary Plays from Iraq

Contemporary Plays from Iraq

The Takeover
A Cradle
Ishtar in Baghdad
Summer Rain
Romeo and Juliet in Baghdad
Me, Torture, and Your Love
A Strange Bird on our Roof
Cartoon Dreams
The Widow

Edited and translated by
A. AL-AZRAKI *and* JAMES AL-SHAMMA

with an introduction by the editors
and a foreword by MARVIN CARLSON

Bloomsbury Methuen Drama
An imprint of Bloomsbury Publishing Plc

B L O O M S B U R Y
LONDON · OXFORD · NEW YORK · NEW DELHI · SYDNEY

Bloomsbury Methuen Drama

An imprint of Bloomsbury Publishing Plc

Imprint previously known as Methuen Drama

50 Bedford Square
London
WC1B 3DP
UK

1385 Broadway
New York
NY 10018
USA

www.bloomsbury.com

BLOOMSBURY, METHUEN DRAMA and the Diana logo are trademarks of Bloomsbury Publishing Plc

This collection first published 2017 and the plays published for the first time in the English language in this volume.

The Takeover © Hoshang Waziri, A.Al-Azraki and James Al-Shamma 2017
A Cradle © Abdul-Kareem Al-Ameri, A.Al-Azraki and James Al-Shamma 2017
Ishtar in Baghdad © Rasha Fadhil, A.Al-Azraki and James Al-Shamma 2017
Summer Rain © Abdel-Nabi Al-Zaidi, A.Al-Azraki and James Al-Shamma 2017
Romeo and Juliet in Baghdad © Monadhil Daoud Albayati,
A.Al-Azraki and James Al-Shamma 2017
Me, Torture, and Your Love © Awatif Naeem, A.Al-Azraki and James Al-Shamma 2017
A Strange Bird on our Roof © Abdul Razaq Al-Rubai,
A.Al-Azraki and James Al-Shamma 2017
Cartoon Dreams © Kareem Sheghaidil, A.Al-Azraki and James Al-Shamma 2017
The Widow © A. Al-Azraki 2017

Introduction copyright © Bloomsbury Methuen Drama 2017
Foreword copyright © Marvin Carlson 2017

The authors have asserted their right under the Copyright, Designs and Patents Act, 1988, to be identified as author of this work.

British Library Cataloguing-in-Publication Data
A catalogue record for this book is available from the British Library.

ISBN: HB: 978-1-4742-5330-7
        PB: 978-1-4742-5329-1
        EPDF: 978-1-4742-5331-4
        EPUB: 978-1-4742-5332-1

Library of Congress Cataloging-in-Publication Data
A catalog record for this book is available from the Library of Congress.

Typeset by RefineCatch Limited, Bungay, Suffolk

Contents

Foreword vi
Biographies viii
General Introduction xi

Introduction to *The Takeover* 1
The Takeover by Hoshang Waziri 3

Introduction to *A Cradle* 23
A Cradle by Abdul-Kareem Al-Ameri 25

Introduction to *Ishtar in Baghdad* 35
Ishtar in Baghdad by Rasha Fadhil 37

Introduction to *Summer Rain* 51
Summer Rain by Abdel-Nabi Al-Zaidi 53

Introduction to *Romeo and Juliet in Baghdad* 71
Romeo and Juliet in Baghdad by
Monadhil Daoud Albayati 73

Introduction to *Me, Torture, and Your Love* 107
Me, Torture, and Your Love by Awatif Naeem 109

Introduction to *A Strange Bird on our Roof* 121
A Strange Bird on our Roof by
Abdul Razaq Al-Rubai 123

Introduction to *Cartoon Dreams* 143
Cartoon Dreams by Kareem Sheghaidil 145

Introduction to *The Widow* 169
The Widow by A. Al-Azraki 171

Foreword

During the twentieth century, Iraq developed a significant modern theatre, one of the most successful and productive in the Arab world. In more recent times, however, the sufferings under a brutal authoritarian rule, a series of devastating wars, an occupation and ongoing civil strife have exacted a tremendous toll on that theatre, as they have on every aspect of Iraqi society and culture. Nevertheless, a dedicated community of artists and public has continued under the most adverse conditions to keep the Iraqi theatre tradition alive. The present volume provides heartening evidence of that ongoing commitment, gathering a group of nine powerful dramatic expressions arising out of these dark years. These works singly and together show the power of theatre to provide a voice of humanity and hope even in the ongoing tragic circumstances of this long-suffering country.

The key event in modern Iraqi history is, of course, the U.S.-led invasion of 2003, which toppled the long-standing and highly repressive dictatorship of Saddam Hussein, but replaced it with a weak and often corrupt central government and a continuing many-faceted insurgency against both the government and the American occupation that established and supported it. The majority of the works collected here were created after that invasion, although two represent the Iraqi society of the years just before it.

The earliest play in the collection is Hoshang Waziri's *The Takeover*, created in the late 1990s in the final years of the Hussein regime, where the country was struggling not only under a cruel authoritarian regime, but the exhaustion of years of war and international sanctions. The play is a kind of dance of death, suggesting some of the dark, quasi-allegorical works of Strindberg or Genet, set in a decaying and seemingly haunted house where a group of mad and half-mad women (the male figures, primarily military, are dead or absent) plot against one another for the decaying remains of a once-elegant mansion. Now based in Erbil, in the Kurdish area of Iraq, Waziri is a political researcher and writer. *The Takeover*, his first play, has received several productions in Iraq in recent years as a certain amount of theatre activity has resumed in Baghdad and elsewhere. *The Takeover* was presented at the National Theatre in Baghdad in 2014. This theatre, closed during the 2003 war, reopened in 2009 with reinforced blast walls to protect against terrorist attacks.

The other pre-2003 work in this collection is *A Cradle* by Abdul-Kareem Al-Ameri, which was premiered in 2001 at Baghdad's elegant Al-Rashid Theatre. Like *The Takeover*, it depicts a group of semi-allegorical characters trapped in a Doomsday environment of choking dust and roofs collapsing from bombing where the carpenter protagonist divides his work between cradles and coffins and the most articulate voice is that of a madman. Two years after this prescient vision of disaster, the 2003 invasion came, bringing tremendous loss to human life and to the Iraqi culture. The Al-Rashid Theatre was reduced to ruins and several other major theatres were swallowed up in the heavily guarded green zone, the center of occupation, where they still today remain inaccessible to most Baghdad citizens. Happily, thanks to the efforts of Najeen (Survivors), a group of artists and film-makers formed in 1991 to work underground during the Saddam regime, Al-Rashid has been repaired and reopened, despite continuing unrest in the city, in May of 2016—a testimony to the resilience of Iraqi theatre.

Me, Torture and Your Love by Awatif Naeem, *Summer Rain* by Ali Abdel-Nabi Al-Zaidi, *Ishtar in Baghdad* by Rasha Fadhil and *A Strange Bird on our Roof* by Abdul Razaq Al-Rubai reflect the turmoil and tensions in Iraq in the immediate aftermath of the U.S.-led invasion and occupation. The two characters in the Naeem play, one wealthy and one poor before the new order and now reduced to a common plight, find hope in their desperate situation by recognizing their common roots in their suffering country. *Cartoon Dreams* by Kareem Sheghaidil approaches this turbulent period in a more lighthearted way, assembling a group of Iraqis, male and female, secular and religious, first in a dreamlike airport lounge and then on an equally dreamlike plane, where their fears and their frustrated desire to escape their current home situation are developed in a dark surrealistic vision.

In the plays *Ishtar in Baghdad* and *Strange Bird* the invading Americans make a significant appearance. *Ishtar* is by far the darker of the two plays, clearly created in the shadow of the shocking revelations from Abu Ghraib. The Mesopotamian gods Ishtar and Tammuz, representing the ancient culture of Iraq, appalled by the current destruction and suffering, come down to earth to restore life and beauty. However, they are captured, imprisoned and tortured in an echo of Abu Ghraib and the play ends in a burst of explosions, which perhaps signals a return of hope, but perhaps (as has proven the case) only a continuation of the suffering and violence. *A Strange Bird on our Roof* presents a less cruel, but scarcely more hopeful, meditation upon the occupation and its aftermath. An American soldier, stationed on the roof of the home of an Iraqi the army is seeking, establishes a fragile bond of common humanity with the mother of the house, but at the end, the dynamics of the war and the occupation destroy all hope of such a humane outcome.

The Iraqi National Theatre in Baghdad reopened in 2009 and has bravely struggled since then to restore a central theatrical presence to the capital. In 2012, the author Monadhil Daoud Albayati, an exile for many years, premiered here *Romeo and Juliet in Baghdad,* which had been commissioned by the World Shakespeare Festival held in conjunction with the London Olympics that year. The play, in keeping with a long-standing practice in the Iraqi and in other heavily censored traditions, uses Shakespeare to comment on contemporary political and social concerns. To an Iraqi audience, the feuding families are clearly Shiite and Sunni and the play is full of clear current references—Paris becomes a clownish Al-Qaeda member wearing an explosive vest, an American general makes a brief appearance, and the rattle of machine guns is, from time to time, heard offstage. The play was well received in London, where reviewers praised both its timeless quality and the significance of its application to contemporary Iraq.

The final play in this collection and the most recent, *The Widow* by A. Al-Azraki, offers an important different perspective on contemporary Iraqi theatre, the theatre of exile. In this play, for the first time we move outside Iraq into the exile community. A central character in the play has fled the dangers of Iraq and become, like the play's author, an exile in Canada. Ashamed of abandoning a widow of the 2003 U.S.-led invasion whom he left pregnant, he at last returns to Iraq, only to become a victim of the violence he originally fled. The emphasis, however, is upon the oppressed women in the play and its picture of this oppression would make a presentation in the author's homeland almost impossible today. For such frank and open dramatic discussions of Iraq, we must now rely upon the increasingly important Iraqi theatre in exile, while hoping that the time is not too far distant when artists like A. Al-Azraki and plays like *The Widow* can be reunited with those brave artists who are continuing to keep the flame of theatre alive in the often desperate situation in Iraq itself.

Marvin Carlson,
Sidney E. Cohn Distinguished Professor of Theatre,
Comparative Literature and Middle Eastern Studies,
City University of New York

Biographies

Hoshang Waziri was born in Erbil, Iraqi Kurdistan. He studied Fine Arts and graduated with a Bachelor's in Theater Directing from the College of Fine Arts, Baghdad University, in 1990. His collection of political essays, *Between Two Iraqs* (*Bilad Mabayeen Iraqain*), was published by Noon Publishing House, United Arab Emirates, in 2014. His political, theatrical, and literary articles and essays have appeared in many Arabic-language newspapers, including *Alhayat* and *Assafir*, and in English-language publications such as *openDemocracy* and *ex Ponto Magazine*. He has written several plays and many essays about theatre. Mr. Waziri has conducted research for Oxford University and Artis International, and was the executive producer of the documentary *A Syrian Love Story*, which won the Grand Jury Prize at the Sheffield Documentary Festival, UK, in 2015. His play *Ismail's Places* won first place in the 2015 Arab Theatre Institute Contest held in the United Arab Emirates.

Abdul-Kareem Al-Ameri is a poet, playwright, and journalist. He was born in 1958 in Basra. He is editor-in-chief of the cultural and literary magazine *Basrayatha*. His plays include *A House Registry* (*Qaid Dar*; 1998), *Jaaban* (*Ja'aban*; 2015), and *A Cradle* (*Karouk*; 2001). He has published the novel *Anbar Saeed* (*A'nbar Sa'eed*; 2010) and two anthologies of poetry: *No One before Time* (*La Ahad Qabla al-Awan*; 1998) and *Hideouts* (*Makhab'*; 2000).

Rasha Fadhil is an award-winning short-story writer, novelist, playwright, and journalist. She was born in Basra in 1975 and spent her childhood there, attended college and lived for a time in Tikrit, and currently resides in Lebanon. She holds a B.A. in English from the University of Tikrit and was awarded a certificate in International Journalism and Media Studies from the Institute of Arab Strategy in Beirut in 2008. She has participated in numerous conferences, conventions, and literary and cultural events inside and outside of Iraq. Five of her books, consisting of collections of short stories, poetry, and criticism, have been published in Cairo and Syria. She is a member of the Federation of Writers in Iraq, the Advisory Board of the Palace of Culture and Arts in Salah al-Din, and the International PEN Club in Berlin. She has worked for the Red Crescent and the Red Cross in Iraq at the Department of Prisoners and Detainees as well as in health education addressing AIDS prevention. She was among the creative writers honored by the Iraqi Ministry of Culture in 2010 and has received several international awards in playwriting and short fiction. Her plays have been staged in Oman, Saudi Arabia, Morocco, and Iraq.

Ali Abdel-Nabi Al-Zaidi was born in Nasiriya in 1965, and graduated from the Teachers' Institute of that city in 1987. His play collections include *The Eighth Day of the Week* (*Thamin Ayam al-Usbu'*; 2000), *The Return of the Man Who Has Not Been Absent* (*Awda al-Rajul allthi lam Yaghib*; 2005), *A Show in Arabic* (*Ardh bil Arabi*; 2011), and *The Divine Plays* (*Al-ilahiyat*; 2014).

Monadhil Daoud Albayati is a theatre director, playwright, and actor. He was born in 1960 in Basra. He has a PhD in Performing Arts and a High Diploma in Theatre Directing from the Theatre Academy in Saint Petersburg, Russia, and a Diploma in Directing from the Fine Arts Institute, Baghdad. He was a program supervisor at Spectrum London from 1995 through 1997. He is currently a director in the Department of Cinema and Theatre in the Iraqi Ministry of Culture. As an actor, he has appeared in the plays *The Great Wall of China* (*Soor al-seen*), *The Court* (*Al-mahkama*), *The Dramatic Wedding* (*Al-zafaaf al-dirami*), *Joan of*

Arc (*Jan Dark*), *Hamlet's Conference* (*Mu'tamar Hamlet*), *Richard III*, and *Tartuffe* (*Tartuf*). He has written the plays *Here is Baghdad* (*Huna Baghdad*) and *Time of the Mill* (*Zamen al-Mat'hana*), and the play adaptations *Romeo and Juliet in Baghdad* (*Roemo wa Juliet fi Baghdad*) and *Forget Herostratus!* (*Insu Herostrat*). His directorial credits include *The Boy Mahran* (*Al-fata Mahran*) and *Cannibals* (*Akilat Luhoom al-Basher*). All of the above have been staged in Baghdad, and *Romeo and Juliet in Baghdad* received a production in Stratford, England, as well, at the World Shakespeare Festival in 2012.

Awatif Naeem is an award-winning TV and theatre actress, director, playwright, and critic, whose work has been presented locally and internationally. She was born in Baghdad in 1950 and has a PhD in Directing from the College of Fine Arts in Baghdad. She is the Director and Founder of the Children's Theatre of Baghdad, a cofounder in 1994 of the Theatre Critics' Association (which represents all theatre critics in Iraq), and the Vice-President of the Iraqi Union of Artists. She has written and directed more than 30 plays for the National Theatre Troupe and has represented Iraqi theatre at many international festivals. Her work as a playwright includes *Sorry Sir, I Didn't Mean That* (*A'tathir Ustadi, lam Aqsud thalik*; Tunisia, 2003) and *Oh My Son, Mutar!* (*Mutar Yuma*; Iraq, 1989), and she directed the play *Lorca's Women* (*Nisaa Lorca*) in Iraq in 2006. She wrote and directed *House of Sorrows* (*Bait al-Ahzan*; Jordan, 1997) and *Hardy Clay Stones* (*Hajar al-Sijeel*; Iraq, 2000). She has written the following TV dramas: *Me, Her, and Him* (*Ana wa hiya wa hua*), *Above the Clouds* (*Fawq al-Sahab*), *Eyes of Fear* (*Oyoon al-Khawf*), and *Hearts Inhabited by Love* (*Qiloob Taskunuha al-Mahaba*). She appeared as an actress in the films *Borders in Flames* (*Al-hudood al-Multahiba*; 1984) and *Another Day* (*Yawm Akhir*; 1977).

Abdul Razaq Al-Rubai was born in Baghdad in 1961 and received his B.A. in Arabic Language from Baghdad University. He has served as an editor for many cultural and literary magazines, and he is a well-known poet whose verse has been anthologized in numerous volumes, including *A Tribute to Her Laughter* (*Fi al-Thanaa ala Dhihkataha*; Muscat, 2015), *Speicher's Birds* (*Tiyour Speicher*; Baghdad, 2014), and *Nostalgia Diary* (*Yaoumiyat al-Hanin*; Muscat, 2012). His plays include: *A Strange Bird on Our Roof* (*Alla Sathuna Tair Ghraib*), published in Muscat in 2013; *Hell's Evangelists* (*Umraa al-Jahim*), produced in Auckland in 2007; and *Tramps Catching Stars* (*al-Sa'alik Yastadhoon al-Nijoom*) and *Planets of the Personal System* (*Kawakib al-Majmua al-Shakhsiya*), both produced in Cairo in 2004. He currently resides in Muscat, Sultanate of Oman, and works at the Studies and Research Centre, Oman Establishment for Press Publication and Advertising.

Kareem Sheghaidil is a playwright, poet, and journalist. He has a PhD in Arabic from Al-Mustansiriyah University and is currently a researcher in the Department of Civil Society and Human Rights Studies, Mustansiriyah Centre for Arabic and International Studies in Baghdad. His poetry collections include *Manuscript of Pain* (*Makhtootat al-Alem*), published by *Dar al-Shi'oon al-Thaqafiyah al-A'ama* (The General House of Cultural Affairs), Baghdad, 2005; *Sins Are Its Fruits* (*Thimaraha al-Ma'asi*), published by *al-Marqaz al-Arabi al-Thaqafi al-Suweesri* (The Swiss-Arab Cultural Center), Zürich, 2006; and *Care about Ash* (*Al-A'naya bil Ramad*) published by *al-Suwaida*, Syria, 2015. Productions of his plays include *The Ringing* (*Al-Raneen*), at *Muntada al-Masrah* (Theatre Forum) in Baghdad in 1995; *Air-to-Ground* (*Ardh Jaw*), at the Department of Cinema and Theatre, Baghdad, in 2009; *Out of Coverage Area* (*Kharij al-Taghtiyah*) at the Department of Cinema and Theatre, Baghdad, 2009; and *Cartoon Dreams* (*Ahlam Cartoon*), at the Jordan Theatre Festival, Amman, 2014.

A.Al-Azraki is an Iraqi playwright who wishes to remain anonymous.

James Al-Shamma is Assistant Professor of Theatre at Belmont University, where he started teaching in 2007. He teaches theatre history and literature, scriptwriting, improvisation, and other courses. Dr. Al-Shamma's principal areas of research are contemporary women playwrights and Arabic, and specifically Iraqi, theatre. He has published two books on American playwright Sarah Ruhl and has published articles in the *Journal of Dramatic Theory and Criticism* and *The Eugene O'Neill Review*.

General Introduction

A. Al-Azraki and James Al-Shamma

To the best of our knowledge, only four plays by Iraqis have previously been translated from Arabic into English, representing just two dramatists.[1] They are *The Key* (1967–68) and the one-act *Where the Power Lies* (published in English in 2003) by Yusuf al-Ani, and *Forget Hamlet* (1994) and *Baghdadi Bath* (2005) by Jawad Al Assadi.[2] This volume will increase that number by eight plays translated from the Arabic, plus one written by an Iraqi in English. For this anthology, we have selected contemporary works, most written after the 2003 invasion. All have received at least one production with the exception of *Ishtar in Baghdad*, which was, nonetheless, granted an award in 2008 by the Ministry of Education in Iraq, and *A Strange Bird on Our Roof*, which has been published in Arabic.[3] We have sought to represent a cross-section of Iraqi theatre and, to this end, have included both male and female, and established and emerging, playwrights from Central and Southern Iraq, as well as one from Iraqi Kurdistan, written in-country and in exile.

The political drama represented in these pages is, to a great extent, a theatre of trauma, reflective of the Iraqi experience under invasion and occupation. Even the one comedy, *Cartoon Dreams*, addresses terrorism and hijacking. Nevertheless, a wide range of dramaturgical strategies are represented therein, expressed through any number of genres, inclusive of realism and absurdism. One playwright approaches the war through the mythology of ancient Mesopotamia, another addresses sectarian conflict through Shakespeare, and yet another applies science fiction to the problematics of identity and social instability. The plays exhibit any number of linguistic strategies, incorporating, as they do, poetic and realistic dialogue, in the heightened language of Modern Standard Arabic as well as the colloquial. Much energy is devoted to the apportioning of responsibility for the suffering of the Iraqi people. Candidates include Saddam Hussein, the United States and its military, sectarians and *jihadis*, Iraqi politicians, and in some cases, the Iraqi people themselves. Other themes include the plight of war widows, life in exile, and the degradation of civil society which has resulted after decades of hardship. The resiliency of the Iraqi people is celebrated as well although, more frequently than not, the plots race toward tragic conclusions.

In making these works available in English, we hope to offer Iraqi perspectives on a war and occupation that had, and will continue to have, a significant and long-lasting impact, not only on the Middle East, but on the world at large. Iraqi dramatists have long had much to say about political developments in their country. Indeed, these plays belong to a deep tradition dating back to at least the late nineteenth century, when Western-style theatre was introduced to Mosul, and even to antiquity if one includes performance practices such as oral storytelling and the scripted shadow puppet theatre of Ibn Daniyal of the medieval period, both of which were put to use, at times, to critique those in power. The development of modern Iraqi theatre since the late nineteenth century is most relevant to the plays included within these covers. In what follows, we will track that development as a response to the course of history in Iraq.

The modern history of Iraq has been a conspicuously violent one. Iraq entered the twentieth century under Ottoman rule; with the defeat of that empire in World War I, the occupation by Great Britain led to a British mandate in 1920, during which year Sunni, Shia, and Kurds united in a revolt that persuaded the British to install an Arabic monarchy. In 1932, Iraq achieved sovereignty and continued as a monarchy under a Hashemite family originally from western Arabia until a coup in 1958 installed a Republican regime led by Brigadier General Abdul-Karim Qasim. The next coup, in 1963, established the government of Colonel Abdul-Salam

Aref. His brother took over the presidency in 1966 after Abdul-Salam died in a helicopter crash; the Baathists firmly seized control in the July 1968 coup. Saddam rose within the party to emerge as the supreme leader in 1979. Throughout his reign, Saddam's intelligence officers routinely imprisoned, tortured, and executed his political opponents, and additionally he committed genocide against Kurdish and Shiite populations. The brutal dictator entangled Iraq in a devastating war with Iran from 1980 through 1988, gassed the Kurdish population at Halabja in 1988, invaded Kuwait in 1990 from whence he was expelled in 1991 by U.S.-led forces in the first Gulf War, and crushed the Shiite uprisings in 1991 and 1998. Sanctions further impoverished the country. Based on dubious evidence that Saddam was stockpiling weapons of mass destruction and supported Al Qaeda, U.S.-led forces under the Bush administration invaded in March 2003, replaced Saddam's dictatorship with a democracy, and occupied the country through 2011. Since then, terrorism perpetrated by Al Qaeda and sectarian violence have continued to plague Iraq, inclusive of the capture of Mosul, the second-largest city in Iraq, in June, 2014 by the Islamic State of Iraq and Syria (ISIS; also referred to as the self-proclaimed Islamic State and the Islamic State of Iraq and the Levant [ISIL]).

Although often produced under difficult circumstances, Iraqi theatre has responded to these violent and often rapid political transformations. Modern Iraqi political theater can be subdivided into the following phases, which are, in most cases, demarcated by political events:

Early theatre (1880–1908);
Forum and club theatre (1908–1932);
Revolutionary theatre (1932–1958);
Theatre that depicts the tension between nationalism and communism (1958–1979);
Theatre under Saddam (1979–2003);
Theatre under American occupation (2003–2011);
Theatre after occupation (post-2011).

Throughout this history, dramatists were acutely aware of censorship and the sensitivity of the ruling regime of the moment to criticism, as retaliation could be severe. Indeed, theatre expanded and thrived when government controls were relatively light, and when it was allowed to partake in the debate over the best form of governance, during the 1950s and 1960s, and shrunk under the weight of Saddam Hussein's dictatorship from 1979 through 2003. Comparisons will be made below to the development of theatre in Egypt, considered to be the leader in the Arab world in this arena, as a useful gauge to that in Iraq.

Early theatre (1880–1908)

Western-style theatre or, as it might also be called, modern theatre, was introduced to the Middle East in the middle of the nineteenth century in Syria, and from there spread to Egypt. Indeed, Egypt and Syria have served as the centers of modern Arabic drama. Its beginnings may be traced to Marun Al-Naqqash, a Maronite businessman who wrote and staged his play *al-Bakhil* (*The Miser*) in his house in Beirut in 1847. Although inspired by Molière's play of the same name, his work is original rather than an adaptation and was quite possibly set entirely to music, in which case it would qualify not only as the first Arabic play, but also the first Arabic opera.[4]

In the introduction to his excellent study of one of Iraq's premier dramatists, "The People's Theatre of Yusuf Al-Ani" (1997), Salaam Yousif delineates the factors that contributed to theatre developing more slowly in Iraq than it did in Egypt and Syria. These include "high illiteracy, limited contacts with the West," the late adoption of "modern ideas and the *Nahdha*

(Arab Renaissance)" and the conservativism of Iraqi society. Iraqi theatre was created by untrained amateurs and acting focused on oratory and reading of the text as a literary rather than dramatic work. Playwrights were unskilled and developed characters and plot poorly, were given to "ornate language and flights of rhetoric," and at times inserted long poems into the dialogue.[5] A professional theatre emerged in Iraq only during the 1940s and this was due in large part to government support. The Iraqi monarchy at this time, indeed, was supportive of literature and the arts in general, inclusive of poetry and the fine arts.[6] It "provided financial incentives for troupes and established a theatre department at the Institute of Fine Arts in Baghdad in 1940."[7] Despite the amateurish quality of early Iraqi theatre, it nevertheless deserves study within its sociopolitical and historical context and as the forerunner of later developments.

Although the first Iraqi playwrights were primarily concerned with religion, interest in politics grew as the country entered the twentieth century. Most of the playwrights working in the period from 1880 through 1920 were residents of Mosul, adept at foreign languages, and in closer contact with the West, by way of Turkey and Syria, than those living elsewhere in Iraq, and many were members of the clergy. Early Iraqi efforts included translations and adaptations of Western plays and novels from French, Turkish, and English into Arabic; these include plays by Molière. Some of these translations supported Ottoman rule, such as those of Shakespeare's tragedies that depict the negative consequences of challenging the ruling regime, including *Hamlet, Macbeth*, and *Julius Caesar*.[8]

The first play scripted by an Iraqi is purportedly a trilogy composed by the Dominican priest and poet Hanna Habash (1820–1882) in 1880, which appear to be inspired by medieval morality plays.[9] Some 12 years later, the first Iraqi play to be printed would herald a shift in focus in Iraqi theatre from primarily religious concerns to sociopolitical ones. Naʿoum Fathalla Sahhaar (1855–1900) adapted *Lateef and Houshaaba* (*Lateef Wa Houshaaba*) from the French, and had it printed in 1892.[10] Hoping to reform his spoiled son, Lateef, a wealthy landlord tricks him into believing that he is actually the son of a poor tenant farmer. The ploy works too well, and Lateef comes to reject his father and his wealth. Through its central action, the play implicitly criticizes the class system.

Forum and club theatre (1908–1932)

The Young Turk revolution of 1908 allowed for greater freedom of expression across the Ottoman Empire even as it led to the implementation of unpopular policies. The Young Turk movement began in the late nineteenth century in opposition to the autocratic rule of Sultan Abdulhamid II and culminated in the revolution of 1908, led by army officers. Although the Young Turks disappointed Arab hopes for a more liberal Ottoman governance and instead imposed stricter controls, they did loosen censorship and, in Iraq, this led to a proliferation of journals and newspapers as well as societies, groups, and clubs.[11] The clubs provided a venue for the expression of pro-Arabic nationalistic sentiment in opposition to the Empire and theatre proved a useful medium through which to do so. Touring Arab and Turkish theatre troupes (such as those of George Abyad, Artughrul Bik, and Yusuf Wahbi) provided inspiration, as did Iraqi theatre scholars (such as Haki Shibli) who returned home with Western diplomas. Although Iraqi scholars founded the first clubs in Istanbul, the rest were located primarily in the three main cities of Iraq: Basra, Baghdad, and Mosul. Although at this time theatre was already firmly established in Egypt, in Iraq it was still an amateur endeavor. At these clubs, local practitioners staged low-budget productions and eventually wrote and produced short original works.

The 1920 Revolution (*Thawra al-Eshreen*) led to the establishment of the Iraqi monarchy and opened the door to widespread expressions of resistance against British oppression, in the theatre as elsewhere. The British wrested control of Iraq from the Ottomans during World War I. In 1920, various Iraqi factions, including Sunnis and Shias, revolted in unison. Although the uprising was suppressed, there were many casualties on both sides and the conflict proved quite expensive to the occupiers. As a result, they acquiesced to Iraqi demands for an Arabic Islamic state in the form of a constitutional monarchy. Although Faisal bin al-Hussein assumed the throne in 1921, the Iraqi state remained a British mandate until independence was granted in 1932.

After the 1920 Revolution, Iraqi theatre turned to Arabic history in search of glorious and chivalric themes to promote Arab and Islamic unity and also raise awareness of the oppression suffered by Iraqis, first under the Ottoman Empire and then the British. The growth of political theatre in Iraq owes much to the expansion of the Iraqi bourgeoisie, who had the privilege to travel and witness politics and culture abroad, including Western theatrical practices. Itinerant troupes from Lebanon, Syria, and Egypt also informed and advanced theatre practice in Iraq during the 1920s. Egyptian troupes influenced the development of theatre in other Arab regions as well; from the 1910s through the 1930s, for example, they inspired the formation of theatre companies first in Tunisia and Algeria, and then Morocco.[12]

Most Iraqi plays during this period were based on historical events and meant to promote Arab nationalism and Islamic glory against Turkish and British hegemony, and staged in defiance of government disapproval and censorship. The spread of nationalist sentiment and a call for armed struggle against the occupiers and colonizers pushed young Iraqis toward theatre as a means of raising nationalist, political, and cultural awareness. Poets recited nationalistic poems on opening nights, in the tradition of the *Nahdha* theatre movement, and adapted stories for the stage.[13] Generally speaking, the political plays of this phase were immature, performed by amateurs and students in clubs and schools. In contrast, in Egypt the government had begun to support theatre in the late 1920s and established a school of drama in 1930 and, during that decade, the status of theatre was improved due to the involvement of well-educated practitioners.

Revolutionary theatre (1932–1958)

The next phase of Iraqi theatre begins with the establishment of Iraqi independence in 1932, which continued as a constitutional monarchy as had been established in 1921 under the British, and extends through the termination of the monarchy by means of the Revolution of 1958. Political theatre began to mature during this period, especially during the 1940s and 1950s. The pioneers were mostly leftists and Marxists who attempted to incite revolutionary violence against the monarchy by depicting it on the stage. In 1948, *al-Firqa al-Shabia lil Tamtheel* (Popular Troupe for Performance) staged *Patrie!* at *Masrah al-Malik Faisel* (King Faisal Theatre) under the direction of one of the best-known pioneers of Iraqi theatre, Ibrahim Jalal. Many critics consider the production a turning point in Iraqi theatre for both its content and presentation. For the first time, a play referred to a current political event, in this case the Portsmouth Treaty, which had been implemented merely two months earlier. Signed in secret, the treaty forestalled the deadline for British withdrawal by 15 years, with a limitless extension in case of war. When details were made public, enraged Iraqis took to the streets; the shooting of protesters by Iraqi security forces only heightened the tension.[14] In addition to addressing this topical event, the production employed various new theatrical techniques in the areas of set design, lighting, and makeup.

**Theatre that depicts the tension between nationalism
and communism (1958–1979)**

The next phase extends from Qasim's revolution and the overthrow of the monarchy in 1958 through Saddam's consolidation of power in 1979. Much theatre at this time depicts the power struggle, both ideological and manifest, between the nationalists and communists that dominated state politics, and does so indirectly, through symbolism, folklore, mythology, and history, in order to evade Baathist retaliation. Indeed, this period witnessed the rise to power of the Sunni-dominated Baath party that culminated in Saddam's rule. Although social realism was the norm in theatre in Egypt during the 1950s, the Iraqi plays during this period present a range of approaches including the adoption of folk myths and the adaptation of historical events. In both countries, it was necessary to disguise political messages in order to avoid governmental retaliation.

The growing influence of communism on cultural and political life can be felt in what is perhaps the most influential play from this period, al-Ani's *I'm Your Mother, Shakir,* first produced in 1958 by *Firqet al-Masrah al-Fani al-Hadith* (Modern Artistic Theatre Troupe). The plot is based on an actual event. Umm Shakir has lost her elder son, Shakir, during the resistance against the British. Her second son, Sa'udi, is arrested and imprisoned for his subversive activity. The playwright pits those who collaborate with the unjust government against those who patriotically resist oppression and corruption, as represented, respectively, by the uncle and the doctor. The uncle asks Umm Shakir to persuade her imprisoned son to sign a statement renouncing all political activity. Rejecting the request, Umm Shakir asks rhetorically that if students, workers, and women refrain from politics, then who will liberate the country? At the end, Kawthar, her activist daughter, is captured by the police and Sa'udi is executed. Alone, the mother praises her revolutionary son and asks the audience to avenge his death. The play criticizes the defunct, British-influenced monarchy rather than Qasim's new regime, which was established by a coup which resulted in the massacre of most of the Hashemite royal family. Indeed, the play opened in December 1958 to great acclaim, received as a celebration of the revolution, and it cemented Al-Ani's reputation and established Umm Shakir as a household name. Additionally, as Yousif notes, the play celebrates the role of women in the period up to and including the revolution as personified in the three main characters, Umm Shakir, her daughter Kawthar, and her good neighbor Umm Sadiq.[15]

On February 9, 1963, the Baath Party deposed and executed Qasim, and Abdel-Salam Aref, his former close ally, assumed the leadership of Iraq. In contrast to Qasim, who advocated Iraqi nationalism, Aref was a Nasserite and Arab nationalist. During the first months of the coup the opposition, including members of the Iraqi Communist Party, was "indiscriminately arrested, imprisoned, and murdered"; not even "hapless" bystanders were safe. The newly-formed Baathist National Guard extended this into a one-year "regime of terror."[16] In *The Flood* (1964), one example from this period, Adil Kadhim employs the mythology of ancient Mesopotamia to indirectly criticize the political and economic situation in Iraq. Gilgamesh was the fifth king of Uruk, and an oppressive tyrant, who ruled 126 years after the Old Testament Flood. In the play, the people, after the unjust execution of a shepherd, revolt. Eventually, as Gilgamesh kills himself, he declares, "no one can end Gilgamesh but Gilgamesh."[17] Even as it stages an egomaniacal leader, the play posits revolution as hopeful and necessary.

During the 1960s, Iraqi playwrights followed theatrical developments in Syria, Egypt, and Morocco, and like practitioners in those countries attempted to develop a distinctly Arabic form of theatre. As in Egypt, they frequently employed a narrator as storyteller and dramatized stories from the *Turath,* or "cultural heritage and tradition, including *belles lettres,* history, folklore, and the fairytale."[18] European theatrical techniques were nevertheless incorporated into this effort. *Turath*, for example, was typically given a "provocative and subversive reading" and dramatists relied heavily upon the methods of Erwin Piscator, Peter Weiss, and Bertold Brecht. Within Iraqi theatre practice, Yusuf Al-Ani pioneered this approach with *The Key* (*Al-Miftah*), staged in 1968. It adapts an Arabic nursery rhyme that involves a nonsensical search for a key in order to impart a Marxist message that one must work hard in order to achieve one's goals. It includes a storyteller, rhymed prose, children's songs, and the occasional song and dance and utilizes Brechtian techniques, including film projection, to ironize the superstitious belief system embedded in the nursery rhyme.[19]

As in Egypt, the 1970s marked a decline of theatre in Iraq due to increased governmental oppression as the Baath Party disapproved of its predominantly leftist inclinations. The regime frequently intervened days or hours before an opening to ban or censor the play in question. The situation worsened toward the end of the decade as the government increased pressure on the left: "theatre professionals were imprisoned, troupes disbanded, and theatre houses closed."[20]

Theatre under Saddam (1979–2003)

Practitioners of theatre under Saddam's rule (1979–2003) of necessity exercised extreme caution in order to evade retaliation. Serious theatre consisted mostly of stagings of Western classics, such as Shakespeare, or adaptations of traditional Arabic tales presented in standard Arabic, and was tailored for a relatively small audience of theatre students and professors, actors, and directors. This select group was alert to indirect references to Saddam's regime; the populace at large was too intimidated to attend. Iraqi theatre during this period can be broken down into three stages:

1. **1979–1980**: After the Ba'athist regime liquidated its political rivals, Iraq became a slightly more open society, both culturally and economically. The government allowed the establishment of new theatres and formed national theatre groups in Baghdad and in other provinces. Theatrical producers dared not challenge the regime: their unwritten mandate was to bolster the spirit of Iraqi nationalism and Ba'athist ideology.

2. **1980–1988**: The War with Iran precipitated a political shift, and three types of theatre took the stage:
   a. Agit-prop theatre. These productions glorified the war against Iran; they urged citizens to participate in defending their country against what the state called *al-Furs al-majoos* or "The Invasion of the *Majoos*."[21]
   b. Commercial theatre. In the face of cultural oppression, a number of playwrights and directors resorted to producing light comedies and farces that featured dancing, singing, and joke-telling (e.g. *Bayeit al-Tin, Bin Mreidi wa London*, and *al-Mahata*). Nonetheless, during this period there were a few serious efforts such as Awni Karumi's staging of Brecht's *The Good Person of Szechwan* and Ghanim Hameed's 1984 production of Adnan al-Saegh's *The Bitter Hallucination of Memory* (*Hathayan al-Thakera al-Mur*). In the latter, an Iraqi soldier hunkered down in a trench fears for his life; when the sniper's bullet strikes, his hallucination begins.
   c. Academic theatre. Usually experimental in nature, these stagings dared to indirectly criticize the regime. These include Selah al-Kasab's productions of Zafir's *Sorrows of a Circus Clown* (*Ahzan Muharrij al-Sirk* [1986]) and Shakespeare's *King Lear*.

3. **1990–2003**: Iraq witnessed grave political and economic unrest during this time due to the invasion of Kuwait, the Gulf War, the Shiite uprising, and the imposition of

economic sanctions. Saddam's regime continued to imprison, torture, and execute its opponents, and all these factors discouraged the staging of political content. Nevertheless, playwrights continued to employ traditional and historical Arabic and Western stories and dramas to comment indirectly. Kasim Mohamed's *Once Upon a Time* (*Kan yama Kan*) draws on Arabic tradition, and director Selah al-Kasab regularly mounted Shakespeare that related thematically to the contemporaneous political situation. For example, he set his 1998 production of *Macbeth* in the garden of the Fine Arts College in Baghdad and deployed fireman's hoses, as were turned on protesting students, in the killing of Duncan.

Theatre under American occupation (2003–2011)

The plays in this volume were mostly written during, and address, this time period, encompassing the American-led invasion, which occurred in March, 2003, and ensuing occupation, which ended with the withdrawal of American troops in December, 2011. The characteristics of this period have been noted above. It deserves mention that university playwriting programs do not exist in Iraq. Although most of the dramatists included herein have received university training in theatre, they have taken courses in directing, acting, and/ or literature rather than studying playwriting directly. That said, a number of them possess advanced degrees in theatre.

Theatre after occupation (Post-2011)

Following the occupation, Iraqi dramatists have turned their attention towards their politicians, with greater frequency, as the fledgling democracy struggles with corruption and sectarianism. It is likely that, over time, a response to the catastrophic advances of ISIS will emerge as well. Although the nascent democratic government in Iraq is more tolerant of free speech than its historical, autocratic predecessors, playwrights must nonetheless be wary of the retaliation of sectarian militias, which wield considerable influence both on the street and in the houses of governance, as is dramatized in a number of the works in this anthology. Theatrical production is hindered by uncertain security in Baghdad and its environs, and most likely completely forbidden in the area controlled by ISIS, although some degree of normalcy has resumed in the relatively stable South. Historically, theatrical activity in Kurdish Iraq has been rather limited, and continues to be so. In any case, Iraqi dramatists will no doubt continue to respond to the changing political landscape in their country and to contextualize it within the deep history of a culture that traces its origins to the cradle of civilization.

Notes

1   Al-Azraki and Al-Shamma are working on a book-length study of Iraqi theatre since 2003, and the material presented in this introduction is adapted from that project. We would like to thank Catherine Cocks for her editorial input. Some of the section on Iraqi theatre from 1880 through 1908 was previously published as: Amir Al-Azraki and James Al-Shamma, "The Birth of Modern Iraqi Theatre: Church Drama in Mosul in the Late Nineteenth Century," *Arab Stages* 3 (Fall 2015), n.p., www.arabstages.org.

2   Yusuf Al-'Ani, "The Key", *Modern Arabic Drama: An Anthology*, eds. Salma Khadra Jayyusi and Roger Allen, Bloomington: Indiana University Press, 1995, 253–288. Yusuf Al-'Ani, "Where the Power Lies", *Short Arabic Plays: An Anthology*, ed. Salma Khadra Jayyusi, New York: Interlink

Books: 2003, 1–19. Jawad al-Asadi, *Forget Hamlet*, trans. Margaret Litvin, Brisbane: University of Queensland, 2006. Jawad Al Assadi, "Baghdadi Bath", trans. Robert Myers and Nada Saab, *PAJ: A Journal of Performance and Art* 30.2 (May 2008): 112–23, accessed April 28, 2016, https://muse.jhu.edu/. The two different transliterations of Al Assadi's name are as they appear in the publications. *Forget Hamlet* was first staged in Cairo in 1994 under the title *Ophelia's Window*.

3   Abdul Razaq al Rubai, *A Strange Bird on Our Roof and Other Plays* (*Ala Satehuna Ta'er Gherib wa Mesrahiyat Ukhra*) (Oman: Dar Alghsham, 2013).

4   Matti Moosa, "Naqqash and the Rise of the Native Arab Theatre in Syria", *Journal of Arabic Literature* 3 (1972): 111, accessed April 28, 2016, http://www.jstor.org/stable/4182894. M. M. Badawi, *Modern Arabic Drama in Egypt* (Cambridge: Cambridge UP, 1987), 45.

5   Salaam Yousif, "The People's Theater of Yusuf al-Ani", *Arab Studies Quarterly* 4.19 (Fall 1997): 66.

6   Hala Fattah, *A Brief History of Iraq*, with Frank Caso (New York: Checkmark Books, 2009), 185.

7   Yousif, "The People's Theater", 65.

8   Omar Al-Talib, *Al Tarjama Al Masrahia Wal Bidayat Al Masrahia Fi Al Iraq* (*Translation of Drama and the Beginnings of Drama in Iraq*) (Baghdad: Afaq Arabia, 1982), 35.

9   Hanna is a man's name in Arabic; Hannah is the female version.

10   Ahmad Fiyyaad al-Mufraji, et al, "Iraq", *The World Encyclopedia of Contemporary Theatre, Vol. 4: The Arab World*, ed. Don Rubin (London: Routledge, 1999): 104–5.

11   Charles Tripp, *A History of Iraq*, 2nd ed. (Cambridge: Cambridge UP, 2000), 22.

12   Marvin Carlson, Introduction, *Four Plays from North Africa*, ed. Marvin Carlson (New York: Martin E. Segal Theatre Center Publications, 2008): 8.

13   Ali Al-Zubaidi, *Al-Masrahia al-Arabia fi al-Iraq (Arabic Drama in Iraq)*, (Mahad al-Dirasat wal Buhuth al-Arabia: Baghdad, 1967), 121.

14   Fattah, *A Brief History*, 178–9.

15   Yousif, "The People's Theater", 72.

16   Fattah, *A Brief History*, 205.

17   Adil Kadhim, *Al-Tufan* (Baghdad: Maktab Babel lil Tarjama wal Tab', 1966), 49.

18   Yousif, "The People's Theater", 76.

19   Yousif, "The People's Theater", 74–9.

20   Yousif, "The People's Theater", 86.

21   *Majoos* translates as "Zoroastrian" and in Iraq is commonly used as a pejorative term applied to people who are magicians, superstitious, etc., employed in this instance as anti-Iranian propaganda.

Introduction to *The Takeover*
Hoshang Waziri

The author, talking about his or her text, acquires a mysterious power over the reader's imagination—he or she restricts the space of interpretation, confining it to the master's reading. I will therefore avoid writing about the play itself and instead look back to the time during which *The Takeover* was written, at the external political and social world that contributed to giving birth to the play.

This, my first play, was written in the late 1990s, during which Iraq was still under a brutal dictatorship—a regime that tried, and to a certain extent succeeded, in militarizing the entire society through several devastating wars. The political suppression the Iraqi people were suffering was compounded by unbearable economic misery caused by cruel international sanctions; these resulted in the collapse of the Iraqi currency and entire economic system. People lost the normalcy of their daily lives; it was an era of political terror and economic dearth. The questions that dominated the thoughts of most had to do with freedom: how to be free, how to survive this hellish homeland?

However, some—the Kurds, for example—had already gained their liberty, for which they had fought for decades. They were now busy figuring out what to do with all of this sudden freedom! They embarked on a long civil conflict, waging a fierce, suicidal war against themselves that endured for several years.

But these details are all irrelevant to the play, but for one essential question with which I have always been obsessed: that is, can you see, or imagine what is out there, beyond the dark room from which you have been trying to escape? Suffice it to say that after all this time I am still longing to know what happens when the Maid leaves the house!

The Takeover has been translated from Arabic into Kurdish and has been performed in Erbil, Sulaymaniyah, and Baghdad. It was first produced in February 2003 at Al-Shaab Theatre in Erbil and the play's most recent performance was at the Baghdad National Theatre in February of 2014.

The Takeover

Hoshang Waziri

Characters

The old woman
The maid
The crazy woman
The friend

Scene One

The stage is dimly lit. A few vintage pieces of furniture are scattered here and there, as if we are in the living room of a grand, old house. Stage left, a dim spotlight on an **Old woman** *sitting in a wheelchair, knitting, her back to the audience. Two crutches rest beside her, upon which she props herself when standing over her dead feet. Upstage, the* **Maid** *stands as still as a statue under a dim spotlight. She holds balls of yarn for the* **Old woman**. *Strands of yarn can be seen extending between them. Stage right, a portable clothes rack on which the General's military uniform and beret are hanging. The uniform is hung in such a way as to suggest a military man, standing upright. Several balls of yarn are scattered around the wheelchair. All these items look ghostly under the dim lighting. In the beginning, we hear only the* **Old woman** *mumbling scattered words and incomplete sentences, but her speaking gradually becomes intelligible as the light intensifies. She moves only her hands and shoulders.*

Old woman   But he died and left me alone, and I have to do all these things. The house also seems to grow old.

She lifts up her head. Pause.

Come closer.

The **Maid** *does not move.*

Old woman   Dust . . . dust . . . dust . . . dust is on the dishes, on the clothes, on the walls, and even on our faces. I don't know where it comes from. And I am the only one left to look after everything, the furniture, the paintings, the masterpieces, and the small sculptures. Come closer!

The **Maid** *does not move.*

Old woman   I have been living in this house for fifty years. Maybe sixty. What an old relationship!

The **Old woman** *laughs. The* **Crazy woman** *enters, creeping on her tiptoes and looking at the* **Old woman**. *The* **Old woman** *does not see her. The* **Crazy woman** *throws a ball of yarn at the* **Maid** *but misses. She throws another, more forcefully, and hits the* **Maid**. *The* **Old woman** *finally notices her.*

Old woman   Stop! What are you doing?

Crazy woman   I am . . . I am . . . playing.

Old woman   This is not playing. Go to your room.

The **Crazy woman** *sits on the floor. The* **Old woman** *resumes mumbling to herself. The* **Crazy woman** *stands up and starts wrapping strands of yarn around the* **Maid**'s *body.*

Old woman   I said go to your room. Don't you see I'm busy?

Crazy woman (*still wrapping*)   Busy?! You only talk. You only know talking. And I am playing.

Old woman (*furiously*)   Stop it! Stop and go to your room!

The **Crazy woman** *stops, then runs toward the door to the outside. The* **Maid** *removes the yarn from her body.*

Old woman   Oh, these long years! I was young when I got married. Twenty plus fifty . . .

She calculates on her fingers.

It's a lot. (*Pause.*) Come closer so I can see your face.

*The **Maid** takes a step toward the **Old woman**.*

Old woman   The house is dark.

Maid   It's better this way. We got tired of seeing each other's faces.

Old woman   Yes, it is much better.

*A ball of yarn falls from the **Maid**'s hand. She touches her face.*

Maid   I grew old, right? (*Pause.*)

Old woman   Twenty and fifty. It's too much . . . too much . . . of course it's too much. An eternity spent fighting ants, spider webs, and endless layers of dust.

*The **Old woman** moves toward the clothes rack but stumbles over the balls of yarn on the floor. The **Maid** clears the way for her.*

Old woman   But he suddenly died.

*A ball of wool falls from the **Maid**'s hand and a noise is heard coming from elsewhere in the house.*

Old woman   He had to achieve many things before he died. He had to wait a bit. He betrayed me with his death.

Maid   Who died, ma'am?

Old woman (*next to the General's uniform*)   My husband. The General. Look! He left me alone. (*Pause.*) A few seconds before his death, he tried to get up, he couldn't so he screamed with pain and regret, "I will die while the world is still lost in chaos."

Maid   Yes, ma'am, I know, you've already told me this.

Old woman   He had a passion for order and organization. He interfered with every simple thing. "This goes here . . . and that goes there . . . no, no, above . . . a little to the right." He was a great man.

Maid   We think everyone we love is great.

Old woman   But he left me alone. He left no child.

She strikes her crutches forcefully against the floor.

That hurt him.

Maid   It's really painful when we find out that we're lonely and nobody asks about us.

Old woman   Even when we used to walk in the street or at a party, he tried to match his steps with mine. Left, right . . . left, right, he used to say. (*Pause.*) Until one day I discovered that I had become like him.

Maid   Yes, ma'am. One day he tried to . . .

Old woman (*interrupting*)   He didn't like you very much. He always told me that. You didn't try to make him like you.

Maid   The problem was we couldn't understand each other.

Old woman   You deliberately created that misunderstanding; what's more, you weren't as obedient as you should have been. (*Pause.*) What do you want?

The **Maid** *takes an envelope from her pocket.*

Maid   The postman sends you his greetings and regards. He said you received this express letter today.

Old woman   Put it on the table, there.

She goes back to knitting. The **Maid** *puts the letter on the table.*

Maid   Do you need anything else, ma'am?

Old woman   I heard a noise in the house. There's always a noise in the house but I don't know what it is.

Maid   Who else other than she who makes the noise? It's your sister, ma'am. She had another fit. As always, she locked herself in her room, singing, crying, and hitting herself.

Old woman   Go and get her out of her room. (*Screaming.*) WHY DID YOU LEAVE HER ALONE?! I have told you many times to always stay with her! Watch her! What were you doing?

Maid   I was busy cooking and cleaning the dishes and then . . .

Old woman   Stop talking and go to her. Go! Her situation has been deteriorating lately, and we have to watch her.

Maid   Yes, ma'am.

She turns to leave.

Old woman   Come here! Give me that letter.

Maid   Express mail from your friend.

The **Old woman** *tries to stand on her crutches.*

Old woman (*yelling*)   Have you started opening my letters, too?! You want to know my secrets, right?

Maid (*anxiously*)   No, ma'am. Sorry. I never open your letters. The postman told me that.

Old woman   Hmm . . . the postman?! He tells you a lot. (*Sarcastically.*) And he's nice too, huh? Tell me what you talk to him about.

Maid   Nothing.

Old woman   Nothing? Strange! How is that possible?

She raises her crutches and yells.

You stand in front of the door waiting for anyone who passes by, or in front of the window for a long time waiting for the postman or the peddler, and still you tell me nothing!

Maid   We don't talk much. He just sends you his regards and asks about your health.

The noise becomes loud.

Old woman   Stop! Go to this crazy woman and get her to come out.

The **Maid** *exits.*

Old woman   Nobody left but the postman . . . she will bring scandal on us . . . I know her and her ways. (*Pause.*) She's becoming strange.

She opens the envelope and reads.

"My dear friend, warm greetings. I hope that your health is excellent now, and that you have recovered from your recent illness." (*She raises her head.*) Strange, how did she know I was sick? (*Pause.*) She wishes me death now. (*She changes her tone.*) No, I wasn't sick. But who told her about my sickness? It must be the maid. There is no one else. (*Reads.*) "I will visit you today." I wonder, what's the purpose behind her frequent visits? It's been only three weeks since her last visit, and now she's back. Why? Is it the house? I see greed in her malicious eyes . . . the way she looks at the walls, the floor, the rooms.

The **Crazy woman** *enters, sneaks behind the* **Old woman**, *and snatches the letter from her hands.*

Crazy woman   This letter is from him, isn't it? (*She laughs happily.*) I saw the postman through the window. (*She reads and dances.*) "I will come back, wait for me." He lit a candle before he left and he said he would come back before it burned out.

Old woman   Give it back to me.

Crazy woman   No, no . . . why?

Old woman (*gently*)   Darling, this is mine.

Crazy woman   No, it's mine, not yours. He said he would write to me.

She pulls many letters out of her clothing.

See! See! They are all from him.

Old woman   Don't be insane. I said that one is mine.

Crazy woman   Sister, why do you always imagine that all things belong only to you? As I remember, you were always like that. Even when we were children, you imagined our mother was only yours.

Old woman (*angrily*)   It's from my friend, telling me that she's visiting today. She'll bring you presents. She likes you.

Crazy woman   But she doesn't like you. (*She laughs. Pause.*) Why do you lie to me? You have been lying to me for years, but I always believe you, so much that I don't understand what's going on in this house.

Old woman (*yelling*)   I am not lying to you, and I don't want to hear about your hallucinations anymore!

Crazy woman (*yelling more loudly*)   And I want my husband, now!

She grabs the balls of wool, plays with them, and spins around the **Old woman**.

Crazy woman   I want my husband because your husband took him, but I don't know where. Since then he hasn't come back. Do you remember? He seduced him with medals and honor, with manhood and its difficult tasks. (*She laughs.*)

Old woman   Stop your nonsense and give me the letter!

She tries to get her but the **Crazy woman** *continues spinning around the* **Old woman**, *with the balls of wool.*

Crazy woman   Your husband came back with more medals and more manly honor than ever. I remember . . . but my husband has not come back. And you want to take his letters, too. Before he left, he said: (*In a man's voice.*) "I will return victorious." (*Pause. She stops spinning.*) I don't understand what happened. (*In a child's voice.*) What happened? Why hasn't he come back yet?

The **Old woman** *jabs at her with her crutches.*

Old woman   Stay away from me! You make me feel dizzy!

Crazy woman (*angrily*)   No, I won't stay away! (*Beseeching.*) Tell me sister, what happened?

Old woman   Listen darling, my child, my sweetheart . . . be a good girl and give me the letter.

Crazy woman   I won't give it to you until you tell me what happened. OK?

Old woman   Stop it! Stop it! You wear me out. Your husband died in the war and returned, honorably, in a coffin. You must remember. We buried him together. Must I remind you every single day? I'm so tired.

Crazy woman   There you go, the same old story. No, I won't believe you. I am not a child. I believe only him. (*She reads the letter.*) "I will come back. Don't believe anyone."

She dances and provokes the **Old woman**.

Old woman (*furiously*)   I can't tolerate you anymore.

She chases the **Crazy woman** *and trips her with her crutches.*

Old woman   You have been torturing me for years with your hallucinations and stupid madness. I've warned you not to speak about your husband. Listen, I will throw you out if you keep asking for him. Yes, I will throw you out in the street. Do you understand? Come back to your senses. Your husband wasn't the only one killed in the war. Many died before and after, and came home wrapped in flags. (*Yelling.*) Come back to your right mind. You moved in to help me, not to torture me.

The **Maid** *rushes in.*

Maid   What's wrong, ma'am?

Old woman   Nothing . . . mind your own business.

The **Crazy woman** *rises and approaches the* **Maid**.

Crazy woman   Who are you, dove? Since when have you been in this cage?

She looks at the **Old woman** *and back to the* **Maid**.

Crazy woman   Did they steal your beloved, too?

Old woman   Take her away from me. Don't leave her alone, and watch her. Do you understand?

Crazy woman (*imitating the* **Maid**'s *voice, bowing obsequiously*)   Yes, ma'am. Yes, I hear and obey, master.

The **Old woman** *exits.*

Crazy woman   What hypocrisy and malice! (*She laughs.*) Do you find it interesting?

Maid   Come with me, darling, come with me and I will tell you a secret.

Crazy woman   A secret? (*Sarcastically.*) There aren't any secrets in this house anymore. (*In a low voice.*) We are all a disgrace . . . I, you, and she.

Maid   Let's go to your room. You know I love you.

Crazy woman   But I don't love you. (*She laughs. Imperatively.*) What were you doing with the postman? Listen, don't deny it. I saw you through the window.

Maid   Nothing. He just gave me a letter for your sister.

Crazy woman   A letter? Liar!

She runs and hides behind the General's uniform and positions her head under the beret, pretending she is him.

You were planning with the postman to escape. I saw your hands pointing to faraway places. Listen, if you even think about escaping from this house, I will kill you.

The **Maid** *plays along.*

Maid   No, sir. I never think about escaping. Why would I think about escaping? I live here.

The **Crazy woman** *continues to speak as the General.*

Crazy woman   Don't deny it. It's obvious from your face and your every movement. I can read your mind, your hidden evil, all your hatred, every grudge.
I see all of that in your eyes. Look at me! This house owns you, and you should know it! (*Yelling.*) Do you understand?!

Maid   I understand, but don't yell.

The **Crazy woman** *drops the role.*

Crazy woman   Not like this! Not like this! Repeat what I say exactly as you used to do. (*Back to the role of the General.*) Come on, repeat what I said so I'm sure you understand.

Maid   This house owns me and if I escape you will find me and kill me.

Crazy woman   I inherited this house from my great-grandfather. He was a great fighter. All you have to do is keep it clean and put things in their right place.

Maid   Yes, I know.

Crazy woman   I'm like my great-grandfather—and what a great man he was! I will restore order to the world by force. I have my own vision as to how the law will prevail.

Maid   That's enough. If the madam sees us, she will kill us.

Crazy woman (*still in the role*)   Don't interrupt! I'm talking about what I hope to achieve, my goal in this worthless life.

Maid   Stop! Let's go to your room.

Crazy woman (*hysterically*)   No one should interrupt me. You should listen when I speak. Just listen! I am the only one who has the ability to restore order to this muddled world. Get out! Get out of my face, you ugly bitch!

The **Maid** *tries to hold her, but the* **Crazy woman** *hits her and tries to strangle her as she pins her to the floor.*

Crazy woman   You are trying to kill me. You have been planning to for years. You want to kill me, but I will kill you first.

The **Maid** *escapes and grabs one of the letters.*

Maid   The postman gave me this for you. He said I should give it to you. Yes, I forgot to tell you.

Crazy woman (*calming down*)   Why didn't you tell me, idiot?!

Maid (*confused*)   I forgot; I just remembered now. Let's go to your room.

Blackout.

Scene Two

The **Old woman** *is alone, talking to the General's uniform.*

Old woman   It's strange! What's going on? There must be someone who can reveal the secrets of the house. Yes, I'm sure about that, otherwise how did she know I was sick? (*Pause.*) No, I'm not sick at all. My body is still strong.

She strikes the floor with her crutch.

I'm strong and will never die. (*Pause.*) Why does she want to visit? To make fun of me? Maybe she's coming back to talk about the house again. She thinks that I'm dying and weak and will submit to her. Impossible!

The **Maid** *enters. The* **Old woman** *moves away from the uniform and addresses the* **Maid**.

Old woman   Listen, something is wrong with the house. I feel like its foundation is shaking.

Maid   What are you saying, ma'am? I don't think I've done anything wrong. I do my job perfectly.

Old woman (*yells*)   Do you think I'm old now and can't handle my affairs anymore?

Maid   I don't understand . . .

Old woman   As for me, I smell something fishy . . . her visit to us. I mean, her coming back that quickly is strange.

Maid   I don't know, ma'am. She is your friend.

Old woman (*trying to stand up, furious*)   Am I dying?! Tell me! Am I sick?!

Maid   No, you are in good health.

Old woman   OK. Was I sick?

Maid (*fearfully*)   Yes, your health was poor, but you've recovered completely.

Old woman   Listen, I'm not sick at all, and I've never been sick in my life. (*Pause.*) And I will never get sick. I will live another twenty-five years. This is what the doctor told me. Then I will be a hundred years old, maybe more.

Maid   Yes, you already told me that.

Old woman   Who told my friend I was sick? Who reveals the secrets of the house?

The **Maid** *looks confused.*

Old woman   Answer me, why are you silent?!

Maid   I told her.

Old woman   Keep going, I'm listening.

Maid   What should I say?

Old woman   Tell me when, why, and how you told her. Speak! I want to know everything.

Maid   When you were sick, she called. (*Pause.*) I think this is very normal.

Old woman   No, it's not normal at all. What else? Speak! Tell me when she called and what she wanted.

Maid   A few days ago. She didn't want anything. She asked about you and I told her you were sleeping.

Old woman   Why didn't you tell me?

Maid   You were sleeping, ma'am, and you weren't feeling well; that's why I didn't want to wake you.

Old woman   Enough lies! Tell me the truth.

Maid   I don't lie, ma'am. Stop abusing me! That's what happened. She asked me about your health and I told her you weren't feeling well. She also asked me not to wake you.

Old woman   I don't believe you.

Maid   Why do you always accuse and mistrust me?

Old woman   You have a guilty conscience, as if you did something you shouldn't have.

Maid   I don't deserve this interrogation.

Old woman   It's impossible for you to change. My husband tried hard to make you a member of this household but you rejected his attempts and kept to yourself. I also tried to raise you as my child but you refused to be part of the family. You haven't learned anything at all.

Maid   Maybe it's because of where I come from. I'm different from you.

Old woman   You were raised here. You were five years old when they brought you here, only a little child.

Maid   Ma'am, I'm only a maid. Please, I don't want to talk about this. It hurts me.

Old woman   You refused, all these years, to be one of us. Since you were a child you regarded us with doubt, suspicion, and hatred. You insisted on keeping apart from us.

Maid   It wasn't like that. I'm not your daughter, that's all.

Old woman   You didn't want to be. You deliberately isolated yourself.

Maid   Ma'am, you and your husband couldn't give birth, that's why you bought me. At first, you thought I was a boy. The man who sold me deceived you. I had nothing to do with that. I was a little child. He was your husband's friend, that's why you trusted him so much that you didn't even check.

She puts her hand over her crotch.

To know what was here. A few hours later, when you discovered that I was a girl, the General and you got mad. All you could do was pour your anger over me. You couldn't make me your child; you took revenge by turning me into your slave.

Old woman   Shut up!

Maid   You turned me into a domestic servant, doing everything from cleaning the toilet to polishing the shoes. You treated me no better than any object you had bought.

*The **Old woman** hits the **Maid** with her crutch and the **Maid** falls to the floor.*

Old woman   I told you to shut up, bitch! Whore! Filthy bitch!

Maid   These are the facts; I'll never forget them. I just don't belong to this house.

Old woman   And I won't let you leave!

Maid   I don't recall asking to leave. I don't want anything; I'm satisfied.

Old woman   You don't know what it means to be satisfied.

Maid   I was never treated as part of the family. I remember the first thing that happened when I entered the house. Your husband ordered me to bring him his boots. They were too heavy for me. When I dropped them, you both laughed at me. I was very young, but I remember as if it were yesterday.

Old woman   Shut up!

Maid   Your husband made up for his losses on the battlefield by vanquishing me. Me, a defenseless child! I was an easy target for the mighty General.

Old woman   If you keep up this nonsense, I will kill you. I will strangle you with my bare hands. Get out of my sight—now!

*The **Maid** doesn't move.*

Old woman   This house means everything to me. It's the only thing he left. I have been wandering through its rooms and hallways for fifty years. I feel as if I was born here. (*Talking to herself.*) Everything should stay in its place. This painting here, that chair over there. The General's uniform should be dusted. It should be cleaned three times a day. After his death, nothing was left but the house, which protects me, and warms me, and allows me to feel his presence. His passion was organizing things.

Maid   I was the one who had to carry out his passion. His orders came at me all the time, from all directions.

Old woman (*yells*)   Don't interrupt me! I'm talking about something else, about my friend and her interest in this house. (*Imitating her **Friend**.*) "I will build this place into a tower that touches the sky, shining with lights of every color." No. I'll kick her out if she brings it up. I know who she is beneath her mask of sympathy, kindness, and fake friendship. All she wants is to take over this place by any means necessary . . .

Maid   I don't know anything about that and it's none of my business. The house is your problem and you have both talked about it more than once . . ..

Old woman (*yelling*)   Get out of my sight! Go away!

She doesn't notice that her **Friend** *has entered, but the* **Maid** *sees her.*

Old woman   I don't want to see your face.

Friend (*with a smile*)   Good evening. I found the door cracked open. I pushed it a little and entered.

The **Maid** *exits.*

Friend   Do you see how easy it is? Imagine how easy it would be to enter a place you love where the door is wide open and there is no one to stop you. All you need to do is move your feet.

Old woman   You're wrong. The door stays closed, and no one can enter so easily.

Friend   Of course, darling. This house is like an old military fortress.

Old woman   There you go. You begin to understand the secret behind its strength.

Friend   And there lies its weakness, too, for every fortress has dozens of secret entryways. (*Wickedly.*) Also, old books tell us that fortresses always represent authority, muddled thinking, and chaos.

Old woman   What are you saying? I don't believe your sick ideas.

Friend   Also, I don't know why it's said that old houses are haunted.

Old woman   Ghosts are too scared to approach the walls of this house.

The **Friend** *notices that the* **Old woman** *is becoming anxious.*

Friend   There's no need to get upset, my friend. I was worried about you, and I'm very happy to see that you're in good health.

Old woman   Why are you worried? Let me assure you: I'm very healthy. I never get sick, that's what the doctor says. I'll live another 25 years, which means I'll die after I pass the 100-year mark.

Friend   This makes me very happy. (*She laughs.*) Now I'm assured that you're OK.

Old woman   It wasn't necessary to worry and come all the way to see me to make sure I'm OK.

Friend   Why would you say that? We're friends, aren't we? Old friends. We have known each other a long time, and it's my duty to visit you.

Old woman   What I mean is, you don't have to leave your business and your important projects to come see me, especially since it's been less than three weeks since your last visit.

Friend   Let me think. (*Pause.*) It's been twenty-six days, which is three weeks and five days. But it was a nice visit.

Old woman   Maybe for you it was.

Friend   A nice visit . . . we talked about many things and remembered the old days.

Old woman (*with clear hatred*)   Especially that party where you were hitting on my husband, even though he ignored you.

Friend No, darling, it wasn't like that. You're wrong. On that day, I had just returned from a trip. I'd heard that you had been married but I hadn't seen him. I didn't know he was your husband. I discovered him in a corner in his military uniform, with his cruel face, standing like a statue chiseled from granite. (*Calmly.*) He was staring at me . . . oh, what exciting times those were!

Old woman Then you told him about your dreams and ambitious projects . . . about buildings, markets, and casinos. When he asked you, "Have you achieved any of these dreams?" you stuttered and didn't know what to say. After a short while, you said, "I will achieve them in the future, yes, I will achieve them in the future."

Friend He was short and somewhat fat. I approached him, and without any introduction, he whispered to me, as if he was revealing a military secret, "The world suffers from chaos, real chaos." I didn't know what he meant. But after the glass fell from his hand and shattered into pieces, and I noticed his pale face and trembling hands, then I understood what he meant by chaos.

Pause.

Old woman (*with disgust*) You simply lusted after him like you do all men. You wanted to have him, even if only once.

Friend (*changing the subject*) It's a little dark in here. The lighting is depressing.

Old woman I like it; it helps me see clearly the present and the past.

*The **Friend** looks around.*

Friend I can transform this place into a paradise, and chase away the darkness with dazzling light. The property occupies a big lot and is located in the city center. We can build a large mall on the lower levels with apartments above . . . an elegant hotel would be perfect . . . don't forget the luxuriant gardens . . .

Old woman You've brought up the same old topic. I thought we were done with that.

Friend This property has enormous potential; we should at least talk about it.

Old woman Let's not. I'm not in the mood and you already know what I think.

Friend You won't have to lift a finger. I'll take care of everything. Just say yes.

Old woman (*shouting*) Listen to me: forget about it! I knew that the only reason you came was the house.

Friend (*seriously*) You have to think, darling . . . please.

Old woman I will never sell the house, and I won't turn it into anything, not even if you can transform it into paradise. Maybe after my death, but I will never die, I am strong. Can't you see that?

She strikes the ground with her crutch.

Look at me! I'm not a corpse waiting to be snatched up.

Friend You are strong, darling, really strong. And I don't want you to talk about death. I didn't intend to make you angry. All I'm saying is we can do something . . .

Old woman We shall not speak about this matter again.

Pause.

Friend   Listen, darling. It's the project of a lifetime. It requires a little bit of sacrifice. If you will only agree, I will turn this place . . .

Old woman (*shouting anxiously and hysterically*)   Listen! If you keep talking about it, I will kick you out. I don't have time for your miserable projects. I'm not dead yet for you to covet my house. I have been living here for fifty years. Fifty years I have been fighting dust. Do you understand me? Fifty years is a long time. And you want to destroy everything in seconds. The General inherited this house from his grandfather. He used to boast about it. "I inherited this fortress from my grandfather, the old warrior. He built it according to the old plans, solid enough to endure the old wars." I am still strong.

*The **Maid** enters. She looks at them and then begins to push the **Old woman**'s wheelchair offstage.*

Old woman   I'm still strong, and if you keep talking about your plans, I will kick you out . . . yes I will.

She strikes the ground with her crutch. She looks tired and her voice is quavering. She continues speaking as she is wheeled offstage.

Old woman   I am strong and I will live another twenty-five years. I will never die . . . I am . . .

*We can no longer hear her voice. Her **Friend** is left standing center stage. The lights gradually dim. Blackout.*

Scene Three

*The **Crazy woman** enters, pushing a large table center stage. Her body is covered with colorful tissues. Her letters and her husband's military uniform are on the table. She sits on the table and starts reading the letters.*

Crazy woman   Sweetheart, I am afraid that the moon will be hit by a stray bombshell and fall down in pieces. Bombs here fall like the leaves of trees in autumn.

She drops the letter and picks up another.

I am alone here, totally alone. I don't know what is going to happen. I'm afraid of darkness, of fire. I need you. I am still new to this war.

She drops the letter and picks up another.

Your damned brother-in-law deceived me. Oh, if you could only see how he behaves here! He behaves just like a god. He curses and beats anyone he wants when he's angry.

She picks up another letter.

We have nothing to do here but wait . . . and wait. I'm sick of it. I must do something. There's no sign that anything is going to happen. Nothing happens at all. That's why I must escape and come back to you. I'm here in hell because of your damned brother-in-law. He called me a coward. I had to prove him wrong. Then I found myself in this hell.

She now picks up a large piece of cardboard patterned to look like an oversized envelope.

Oh, what endless lies! Don't believe anyone, sweetheart. My corpse, which you insisted on washing, was not my corpse, nor was my coffin, which you saw wrapped in a colored flag, my coffin. Even my grave, the grave beside which you wept, didn't belong to me. Don't believe what anyone says, for I am not dead. I will come back to you.

She gathers the letters and spreads them on the table along with the uniform to form the effigy of a body at rest. Then she removes the tissues that cover her body and places them over the figure. She exits, repeating the following lines.

My corpse, which was torn to pieces, was not my corpse. My grave, over which you cried, was not my grave. Don't believe anyone. Wait for my coming. My corpse is not my corpse and my grave is not my grave.

Her voice gradually fades away. The **Maid** *and the* **Friend** *enter in confusion. The* **Friend** *sits on a chair near the table while the* **Maid** *clears the table.*

Friend (*worried*)   You are late.

Maid   I waited until I was sure she was sound asleep. Her anxiety is only getting worse.

Friend   We have to find a quick solution. The situation is deteriorating. If we don't act soon, we lose everything.

Maid   She hates you, so be careful.

Friend   I noticed, that's why we need to come up with a strong course of action.

Maid   What should we do?

She discovers the pile of papers left by the **Crazy woman**. *She searches the pile.*

Friend   What are you looking for? What's wrong with you?

Maid   I'm looking for the paper. The title of ownership that you requested during your last visit.

Friend   Don't waste your time. The old woman is too smart to leave it in that mess.

The **Maid** *sits in a chair facing the* **Friend**.

Maid   I have searched every corner of this house. In all the storage boxes, all the closets, and in the General's old papers. But I haven't found it. We have to look through these papers, since the crazy woman thinks every paper in the house is a letter sent to her. Also, she writes letters and deludes herself into thinking that they come from her dead husband. (*Pause.*) Come on, search with me. We don't have time to waste.

Friend   Listen . . . this is pointless. The old woman might have hid it in the basement or she might have put it in a plastic bag and buried it in the garden. We need another plan.

Maid   I'm tired. I can't bear this anymore.

Friend (*tensely*)   We have to think quietly. Haven't you heard her yelling? She was about to kick me out and everything was about to collapse.

Maid   It's because of your constant nagging. I already told you that it's impossible for her to accept your plan and simply sell you the house.

Friend   It's more difficult than I had imagined.

Maid   I can't stay here anymore. (*Pause.*) There are strange things happening. Horrifying things!

Friend   What?

Maid   The General's ghost lurks in every corner of the house. I don't see him, but I can feel him walking in the entryway at night. I hear his footsteps, and his voice gives orders to the dead who fill the house. Every night the old woman talks to him and begs him to stay, so much that I can't sleep for all the screaming.

Friend   That's terrifying. (*Pause.*) Be patient for a little while and everything will be alright.

Maid   And her crazy sister. Her fits have become dangerous. She can't control herself. She has tried to kill me more than once. She may succeed one of these days. I'm scared. We must do something.

Friend (*wickedly*)   Are you prepared to do anything? Anything at all?

Maid (*enthusiastically*)   Yes. Tell me what to do! Why procrastinate? We share the same goal. I want to escape from this dark fortress by any means. I want to run away to the farthest place in the world. The crone's orders are killing me. I have to wipe up her dirt and endure her trivial chatter all day long, day after day. Oh God, I hate this house. I'll do anything to escape.

The **Friend** *pretends to be touched by the* **Maid**'*s speech.*

Friend   Oh, darling. You are truly a great person. You are a saint to endure all that suffering. If you want me to save you, you must do everything I tell you to.

Maid   I told you, I'm ready to do anything.

Friend   Then our only plan is the direct and practical one.

Maid   What do you mean?

Friend   I've given it a lot of thought . . . none of the other plans work. The old woman is the main obstacle, right?

Maid   Yes, that's right.

Friend   So, we have to get rid . . .

The **Crazy woman** *enters. She is hysterical. She runs toward them, then stops and backs up a few steps. The* **Maid** *and the* **Friend** *are silent. The* **Crazy woman** *runs toward the* **Friend** *and puts her mouth close to her ear.*

Crazy woman   Finally, I have made my decision.

Friend (*smiling*)   What have you decided, darling?

Crazy woman   Everything needs to come to an end. Yes. (*Screaming.*) I never asked him to marry me. I didn't beg him. Believe me. I didn't cry on his chest. I didn't give him my virginity. All that mattered was what they told me . . . my older sister told me, "This is your knight in shining armor." So I threw myself at him. One day, he left and promised he would come back. He said—(*In a man's voice.*)—"Wait for me, I will come back." But he hasn't come back. (*To the* **Maid**.) Go and pack my things.

Maid   What are you saying?

Crazy woman   My things, you ugly, stupid woman!

She points at the tissues scattered around the table.

Collect them all.

The **Maid** *gathers them.*

Friend   What have you decided?

Crazy woman   Nothing . . . nothing.

She takes the tissues and starts to leave the house.

Maid   Where are you going? It's late at night.

Crazy woman   I will go to him. This is my final decision.

Friend   Who is he?

Crazy woman (*addressing the* **Maid**)   To my beloved. Since he hasn't come, I will go to him and find out what happened.

The **Crazy woman** *exits. The* **Maid** *tries to follow her but is stopped by the* **Friend**.

Friend   We don't have time to waste. We have to carry out the plan. We must act now.

Maid (*worried*)   I'm afraid that she'll get lost.

Friend   It's none of your business, let her get lost.

Maid (*fearfully*)   The old woman will kill me if she does anything crazy.

Friend   Listen, we need to start now.

Maid   Start what?

Friend   Carrying out the plan. We have to . . .

Maid   Wait!

She tries to remember what the **Friend** *said before.*

Maid   What did you say a little while ago? What were you thinking?

Friend   Get rid of the old woman, now.

Maid   Oh, my God! How?

Friend   What do you mean, how? You have to do it. You!

Noise is heard from inside.

Maid (*shocked*)   Me?! I have to think.

Friend   There isn't any time. Are you scared of her? It's so simple. A paralyzed woman who can't resist. All you have to do is . . .

The noise gets louder and closer. The **Crazy woman** *enters, pushing the* **Old woman** *in her wheelchair.*

Old woman   I will kill you, you crazy bitch! How dare you treat me like this?!

Crazy woman   This is my final decision.

Old woman   Stop it! Leave me alone!

The **Crazy woman** *pushes the wheelchair rapidly in circles. She speaks in a fit of madness.*

Crazy woman   No, I will never retreat from my decision.

Maid   What are you doing?

She approaches the **Crazy woman**.

Crazy woman   Stop! Don't come any closer! This is none of your business. Do you understand?

The **Maid** *tries to approach again, but the* **Friend** *stops her.*

Friend   Leave her.

As the **Old woman** *screams the following, her voice gradually becomes choked.*

Old woman   Do something! Stop her! I can't . . .

The **Crazy woman** *wraps strands of yarn around the* **Old woman**.

Crazy woman   He said he would come back, but he didn't. So, I will go to him.

She continues to wrap yarn around the **Old woman**'s *body and neck.*

Old woman (*screaming*)   STOP IT! I CAN'T BREATHE!

Crazy woman   It's very simple . . . if I go to him, I'll understand everything, right?

Old woman   I'm dying! Stop it! I'm . . .

The **Old woman** *dies, as the* **Crazy woman** *continues spinning around her body; finally, she stops.*

Crazy woman   Now . . .

She covers the body with tissues.

My corpse is not my corpse and my grave is not my grave and my coffin wrapped in flags is not my coffin.

Maid   She's dead.

She is crying, with fear in her voice.

She's really dead.

She touches the **Old woman**'s *body.*

Maid   Oh God! Her face is pale, her mouth is open, and her eyes are open.

Friend   She's dead. Enough!

Maid   What do we do now? Tell me.

Friend   Nothing to do. Everything is done. (*With relish.*) What we wanted has been achieved, and our hands are clean. We have not done anything that God can punish us for. You are free to go, it's that simple.

Maid (*in fear and confusion*)   Where?

Friend   To any place you like. Haven't you been dreaming of that?

Maid   But the place . . .

Friend   You don't want to go?

Maid   No . . . no . . . I don't know. Maybe after cleaning the house. Can't you see the mess is everywhere? I will clear the table and sort through these papers. Yes, what a dirty floor! I will clean it and polish it. Then I will go to the kitchen to . . .

The lights dim as the **Maid** *talks, the* **Crazy woman** *attends to the dead body, and the* **Friend** *regards the scene in a state of triumphant ecstasy.*

Introduction to *A Cradle*
Abdul-Kareem Al-Ameri

A Cradle was written at a time during which artists had to rely upon symbols, due to a repressive political environment, and closely observe the warning signs posted by authoritarian cultural institutions. However, this did not prevent me from entering the minefield with a boldness applauded by theatre critics. In fact, the play had a significant impact on the Iraqi theatre community, which still remembers it 15 years after its premiere.

A Cradle depicts the instability that threatened the Iraqi people, the volcano in which we lived during that dangerous period before 2003. The characters are from everyday life: the downtrodden woman who dreams of having a child; the carpenter who desires to build cradles instead of coffins; the soldier who returns from war without his legs and is abandoned by his wife; the madman who says what no one else dares to; and the teacher who sells cigarettes in the street. All of these characters suffer under intolerable conditions. They are rebellious and discontented and dream of a better future.

Perhaps it is the only play that has been produced in Iraq both during and after Saddam Hussein's tenure, in different locations. The first production took place in 2001 at al-Rashid Theatre in Baghdad, and the second in Basra, after Hussein's regime was overthrown in 2003 with the help of America and her allies. So, the play is not limited to a specific time, since daily life in Iraq has not changed significantly. Perhaps that is why it appealed to both audiences, even though no alterations were made to the script, directing style, or scenography.

A Cradle was first produced in 2001 at Al-Rashid Theatre, then, after the fall of the regime in 2003, at Behu Al-Idara Al-Mahliya Theatre, Basra.

A Cradle

Abdul-Kareem Al-Ameri

Characters

The carpenter
The son (Marwan)
The mother
The teacher
The madman
Saeed

A room in **The carpenter**'s *house. A coffin and a cradle.* **The son**, **The carpenter**, *and* **The mother** *are on stage.*

The son   Oh wood! Falling like snow![1] Hands cut you, somewhere in the world. As trees, you held within you the hush of the nighttime and the fluttering of the white wings of angels who descended to breathe life into an infant body.

He stands between the coffin and the cradle.

Oh wood! Be a coffin! Be firewood! Be death disguised in life! Oh wood!

He looks at a picture of his grandfather that hangs on the wall.

Enchanted by the language of the light, have you saddled the horse of lust and thrust the burden of the homeland upon its sons? My grandfather, oh you, the smell of gunpowder and the noble bravery of Fadha'![2] Oh you, the banner that waved the revolutionaries ever onward, drenched in waves of blood! The bread of the poor, the mother's tears wiped dry by the rocking of the cradle!

The mother *gently swings the cradle.*

The mother   From this cradle you will crawl, oh my son! You will grow up strong as a tree. I breastfeed you patience; patience that is tempered in the oven's fire. I breastfeed you chivalry so your eyes will guard this house. Oh my son! The land is your mother's *shila,* so protect that honor.[3]

The son   The honor of the land! We protected her honor and we fought on all her battlefields, buzzing in rage like bees in a hive, with time for neither sleep nor peace.

The mother *holds the cradle.*

The mother   From this cradle flowers spring.

The son   And thousands of troops advance, defying fire and embracing death with their steel fingers. I know that fire and that death.

The mother   Do you boast of fire and death?!

The son   Since the first nail rested in the teak plank until the last nightmare of the time of anger that spreads throughout God's land. Boasting . . . boasting about the wound that festers in my chest come good days and bad.

The mother   Oh the vileness of the bad days! Your bleeding filled the universe.

The son   We were not just defending the homeland; we were wrapping our souls around the canon's barrel so this cradle would stay safe.

The mother (*with determination*)   It is still safe! Keep it with you until he comes to fill the cradle with his cries and with joy.

The son   Oh, what a life! We enter with a heart-shattering wail and exit with the cry of one stabbed through the heart. What a life! It has never granted peace, not since Adam's fall from everlasting Heaven. (*He seizes the cradle.*) Tell me! What does tomorrow hide? We cling to life while death awaits. Each day leads to the next. We chase the days, which are coffins, not knowing that the dust of the passing years is as thick as the dust of war.

The carpenter   My son, I thought you left the war behind you. Why do you bring it up?

The son   Had it left no trace, I would not mention it.

The carpenter   Son, you hurt yourself and me.

The son   Have I forgotten Yasa or the burning in my chest?

The carpenter   Your cousin is no longer yours.[4]

The son   But she still is mine. I was infinitely delayed by death until I knew what love should be, when facing death.

The carpenter   She is a wife now.

The son (*sarcastically*)   Rather, say she is a maid serving her impotent master . . . I know Yasa . . . I know her. (*Holding the cradle.*) Were she mine, this cradle would bear our name. Did your brother not think I would survive?

The carpenter   My son, forget her! Forget Yasa!

The son (*in front of the coffin*)   Shall I bury my days in this coffin and imprison my heart in endless exile? Were this coffin meant to help me forget Yasa, I would forget her!

The carpenter (*to himself*)   I tried to stop it many times . . . Oh greed! What if Marwan had achieved his hopes and tasted love . . . (*To* **The son**.) Might I live longer to see your child?

The son   Might I live longer to witness another war?

The carpenter (*angrily*)   Another war!

The son   To settle what has been left unsettled between us . . . revenge on ourselves, revenge on the dust that has buried us up to the neck.

The carpenter   Is this your war?

The son   The war of millions of poor around the world; the war of those who sleep on the sidewalk of poverty and whose clay ovens sit empty and cold.

The carpenter (*blaming*)   Are you revolting against what you love and forgetting that it was you who protected this land?

The son   But I could not protect what brings me joy.

The carpenter   We have no control over fate.

The son   Is it fate that keeps one running away all his life, afraid of a shadow or a cry of despair? Is it fate that makes us open accounts in the bank of death? Ah! The entrance to hell has not yet been sealed!

The carpenter (*yelling*)   Are you insane?! These are just myths.

The son (*pointing to his grandfather's picture*)   Was this man a myth? Was that face, engraved in the annals of history, a myth? And the hooves of the revolutionaries' horses shaking the ground, a myth? Do we stoke the fire in yesterday's books to illuminate the falseness of our present reality?! Father, do we do that?

The carpenter   My son, we take pride in our heritage.

The son   But we are ignorant of ourselves, looking for another self in the refuse of the filthy past. We have become stray shells that don't know where to fall.

The carpenter   Should we give up the loaves from our clay oven?! Or the Berhi dates?! Or the call to prayer?! Should we, my son?!

The son   I can no longer distinguish between things; they are all the same. Even daylight does not help me see the way.

The carpenter (*holding a piece of wood*)   This will keep you from despair.

The son   My lungs are full of sawdust, and since this coffin I have started hammering nails in my head.

The madman *enters, hitting the ground with his stick.*

The madman   Blood . . . blood . . . blood! This is the first voice . . . The second will come. (*He rocks the cradle.*) Dulabi Abadan . . . Dulabi Abadan.[5] The *Eid* has gone, and a new one is coming.[6] Oh, the wheel of the crying child! Fly! Fly! Share your joy with all children. Fly, oh *Eid* swing! Shut your skyward-gaping mouth against the deadly missile! Oh, the wheel of *Eid*! How many *Eids* have gone and my child has not come back?! How many *Eids* have gone and Noor has not come home?! They talk about the moaning of her desk since she left it. The street asks me about her. Her clothes are still in the closet. Her *Eid* dress, red ribbons, and her toys spread her smile all around. (*Crying out.*) How has the safe house become a grave for all of its people?! Oh, wheel of *Eid*! (*He rocks the cradle.*) What joy of the cradle upon a child who is born to die!

The carpenter   All will die. We should know our destination, not to choose . . .

The son   They choose for us the ways of death.

The madman *lies down in the coffin.*

The madman   Oh death, this is my body! Let it die! No need for it anymore! No need for this wretched body! Take it! Take what you want and put out the fire in my chest! Take my soul but let my daughter come back home. (*Silence.*) Was I destined to carry the burden of the world?!

The carpenter   Ask for God's forgiveness.

The madman   I did, but Noor has not come back. What's the use of a roof that does not protect the people of the house?! (*Silence.*) The roof crushed them. The people walked over their dead bodies. I asked for God's forgiveness many times but who will forgive the hands that kill our children? (*He holds the cradle.*) Oh Noor! I am a madman. They say I am a madman. What madness is this when death is knocking at the door, crushing people, one after another, into bloody meat?! What madness is this?

The carpenter   He lost the house and his people.

The son   Can you see how love comes to be?

He looks at his grandfather's picture.

My grandfather, can you see? Can you see how this time is so cruel and bitter, kicking and tossing us like a snowball in summer?! The morning has changed and the night has changed, and even man has changed.

Saeed *enters in a wheelchair.*

Saeed   Who is there? Marwan?! I have not seen you in years!

The son   Saeed! Here I am, between the hammer and the anvil.

Saeed   I have not forgotten that you saved my life.

partial?

The son   I have not forgotten that you were singing in the trench. Are you still singing? I have not seen you on TV.

Saeed (*smiling*)   Do I look like a person on TV? People want moist white faces on TV, not my face, which is as dry as a parched willow tree.

The son   Your face shone in the trench at night.

Saeed   It has become dark . . . the *oud* keeps me company when I sing alone.[7]

The son   Alone?! What about your wife?

Saeed   She changed with time. She tired of me.

The son   You were happy with her. Why did she change?

Saeed   What could she do with a man who came back from the war without legs? What could she do with me? (*Silence.*) In the beginning she was kind and loving, taking me outside and sharing her thoughts with me. Days were passing slowly . . . very slowly until the heartbeat slowed down and she started to move away from me. Love was like salt dissolved as if in water by my disability, then I started spending my nights alone. I knew that failure had covered us with its black cloak. She has gone.

The son (*to himself*)   Ah! If she knew how much this man has sacrificed, she would not have left him.

The carpenter   This cradle has exhausted me, but the woman deserves the effort. You know, we have not heard a child's cry in years. This is the first child born after the beginning of sterility, and the first cradle made out of a coffin. Do you see this hand? If I don't have enough wood to make one, I will turn this hand into a hook to hold the cradle.

The son   Since my mother died of cancer, you have been faithful to her, to me, and to the wood.

The carpenter   I have not forgotten the moment the doctor told me about her cancer . . . she asked me to take care of you.

The son   They killed her . . . the uranium melted in her body like fire . . . We send our dead to where the *huris* and rivers of wine are . . . we send them to a point of no return.[8] No one told us about Heaven but we, the living, know for sure what Hell looks like.

The carpenter   If we are still alive.

The madman (*shouting*)   I don't know where she hid. People said she hid under the roof . . . the roof fell down while she was hiding under her cloak. Look at her! Look at her smile! How could a person with such a smile die?

He exits, running. **The teacher** *enters.*

The teacher (*tired*)   What a tax I am paying for my age! My feet are tired from wandering the streets. I used to oppose those who smoke, now I sell cigarettes to everyone. (*Silence.*)

The carpenter   Be patient! Goodness is still here . . .

The teacher   Everyone tells me to be patient, as I used to say. What is the use of patience if the dagger has already been plunged into my chest? Oh my years . . . every part of my body has been touched by fire.

The son   You are still great.

The teacher   One of my students was lazy and I used to rebuke him, hoping he would change, but instead he dropped out. Yesterday I saw him driving a luxurious car. He stopped and said, "Do you remember me? I am the lazy one!" He threw a coin in my face as if I were a dog. I became a dog. What use is an old dog?

The carpenter   You have built castles out of your knowledge.

The teacher   I am looking for someone who will dig me a grave.

The carpenter   It is enough that you have made men.

The teacher   Including the lazy one.

The carpenter   We don't deny your right but as for that ungrateful one, our homeland denies him his right.

The teacher   Has the homeland become Aladdin's lamp, granting every wish? Should he not judge between the good and bad son?

The carpenter   It is difficult.

The teacher   It is difficult to distinguish those who love sincerely from those who show off their love. What is difficult anyway? It is difficult when a student humiliates me because he fails to gain knowledge that brings nothing but poverty. It is difficult when I am lost in the bazaar hawking cigarettes that kill. It is difficult when I come back home to worry about the rent, my children's needs, and my debt.

Saeed   Who will give me his legs so I can follow her?

The son   Follow her?

Saeed   My heart left with her. This punishment tortures my soul to the core! I was not a coward . . . if I was, I would not have lost my legs. Loneliness and the wheelchair wound me.

The son   Don't worry. People know that you are a hero.

Saeed   Wheels for legs . . . living on a useless memory.

The son   You were like a wolf.

Saeed   What should I say: this hero was abandoned by his wife?

The son   Man's history is important, especially if his present does not help him. Do you remember those raids where we were carrying death on our shoulders and then kicking it with our boots that were ruined by salt?[9]

Saeed   Who can understand this? Does my wife understand it? She left a disabled man who cannot even wash his hands. Who will explain to her the pain at that moment?

The son   Oh, what a moment! Trapped in that ditch, not knowing whether we would live or die. Are you defeated by a woman, you wolf? I never thought I would see you weak.

Saeed   Losing his legs makes a man weak. Oh, what a punishment!

The madman *enters.*

The madman   Oh people of the earth, have you seen a white bird with white ribbons? (*Silence.*) Why?! Why was I born? To be tortured? Why?! Why?!Why?! (*Silence.*) Please God, bring her back to me in return for my prayers and the charity I have given in Your name. Please bring her to me, for I am your creation . . . your deputy on earth.[10] Please tell the roof to lift its weight from their bodies . . . let it be light . . . light roof! Command the fire to lose its heat and grant safety to the people of the house. Please tell Azrael to stop grasping at our souls.[11] Oh God, have mercy! (*Silence.*) Oh people of the earth, have you seen a white bird?!

The son   How much pain shall we endure?

The carpenter   Without pain, patience would not be great.

The son   How much patience do we need?

The carpenter   Let one eye protect you and the other gaze into the future. Hold your time in an iron fist and don't let it go. Do not waste.

The son   Never waste anything. Did we not waste enough of our lives on the battlefield? When shall this fire die out?

The carpenter   Look back to your people, to the shimmering of red swords. My son, those are your ancestors, the knights of war! (*He holds the cradle.*) We fight for this! Does it not deserve our blood?

The son   You have made a cradle from the remains of a coffin.

The carpenter   The same wood that carries this and that.

Saeed (*to himself*)   Where can I find the other half of my body? Where can I find new legs? Why are the legs dead while the head lives?! Oh legs, come back to me!

The carpenter   Oh, what glad tidings! This cradle will carry a child! The child is coming! A child who shines like a light in the darkness.

The son   I loved my cousin, and I loved my homeland. I have lost the first, will I lose the second?

The teacher   Nothing will be left if you lose that, too.

Saeed   I have chosen my way.

The son   You have nothing but patience.

Saeed   The way of no return.

The son   What a weakness is this! You struggled and fought, for what? And for whom?

Saeed   I did not have a choice.

The son   What would you say to the hero and the wolf inside you?

Saeed   Do not remind me again. I cannot stand it. The wolf is dead.

The son   If the wolf is dead, we all will die.

The madman   Close the doors! Do not look at the ceiling! Death comes from above. Watch out! Close all your windows and doors! Noor! Oh Noor! They told me that children come during the *Eid*. To whom shall I give the *Eid* gift! Who will take it from me? Oh, people of the earth! Who will take the *Eid* gift from me?! (*Silence.*) The missile has stolen her last childhood dream. The roof collapsed and the house turned into dust . . . the child's face and the mother's concealed dream crumbled into dust. (*Silence.*) Oh, the dust of the house! Why did you cover her beautiful braids?! Oh, the ceiling of the house! Did you want her to die, or did you collapse to kiss her?! They killed you, Noor! They spent millions of dollars to destroy my house and kill you! I do not cry for you, Noor, but I cry for my weakness. I could not stop the missile, and I could not lift the ceiling. Oh people of the earth, raise a toast to murder and shame!

The son   Has the child been born yet?

The carpenter   The nurse said the child will come, and I am afraid, praying to God. Oh God, save her from extreme pain . . . where can I find the palm tree to rescue her from the unbearable pain of labor? Shake toward you the trunk of the palm tree! Shake that trunk and fear will disappear![12] Our town is weary of infertility since the last child died, struck by a treacherous missile . . . we have not seen a child who can wipe the face of the night . . . Oh Maryam! The town eagerly awaits your child!

The teacher   What happy news for the town!

The son   The town has been fasting for a long time. Shall Maryam break that fasting?!

The carpenter (*to the cradle*)   Move, and fill the earth with joy!

The son   Damn those bats of the night![13] They cannot harm the cradle because it is here inside!

The madman   I was there. Nobody allowed me to enter the hospital to see Noor. Oh, a cage imprisons my dreams and prevents them from fleeing into my heart. I was there when they asked for the father of the child. No . . . not me! Not me! This burned face and dusty hair do not belong to Noor! (*Silence.*) Her face is like the full moon, her eyes like stars, and her hair is like the night. They told me to take the box and go, but where? Go to the grave! How could I bury my body?! How could I bury my heart?! What should I say when I see her smile while I cover her youthful body with dust?!

The carpenter   Another Noor will come and this cradle will carry many children that will fill the world! Oh, people of this town! The coming child will be safe within this cradle! Oh Maryam, daughter of the town! Oh, the cradle of joy! Move! Move! It is time for you to abandon your silence and laugh like a happy child!

The mother (*to the cradle*)   Oh my son! Heart of my heart! I have prepared the night to cover you and the day for you to shine. I have prepared my life to protect you. I have dedicated my love to you since your heart's first flutter. Oh my son, I have been waiting for you to grow up into a strong man who will protect me and my home.

The madman   Oh, what a shame, you bats of the night! The roof collapsed on them . . . The dust covered her . . . covered her with death!

The mother   Oh my son, they told me you came out of me like the light of the dawn, grasping onto your umbilical cord, hanging on, trying not to leave me. You opened your eyes and screamed, "Why?! Why?!"

The son   There . . . on the bank of the river. We saw him carrying the light in his hands. Oh river, have you irrigated the garden of his childhood? Have you quenched the infant's thirst? For the troops are surrounding the camp!

The carpenter   Have you seen the infant's tears? Have you ever seen a light die? (*Silence.*) Oh Maryam, your son died!

The mother   No, he did not, for his cradle is shining like the wings of an angel.

The son   The eyes have been stupefied . . . the sky has dissolved into smoke . . . torrents of flame have flooded . . . the paths of the lost . . . as if Doomsday has arrived!

Notes

1   In the sense that there is an overabundance of wood. The imagery of snow may also reference the white shroud wrapped around corpses before burial.
2   Fadha' was a popular female poet who lived in the late 18th and early 19th centuries in the rural area of Rumaitha, a district in the al-Muthana governorate in southern Iraq. She is commemorated for her bravery and beautiful vernacular poetry.
3   A *shila* is a scarf traditionally worn by an elderly woman who is a mother. It is a symbol of honor that requires protection.
4   It is considered acceptable and is common for cousins to marry in Arab culture.
5   "Dulabi Abadan" is a song local to Basra, dating to the pre-Saddam era (the 1960s and 1970s), sung during the *Eid* while pushing a child in a swing. *Dulabi* means "swing" and Abadan is a city in Iran situated close to Basra, inhabited mostly by Iranian Arabs. It was virtually abandoned during the Iran-Iraq war of 1980 through 1988. Special swings were built out of wood for the *Eid*, in the form of either a small Ferris wheel or that of a revolving disc on a pole from which seats were hung.
6   There are two *Eids*, or religious festivals, in the Muslim calendar. The *Eid al-Fitr* is the celebratory feast that occurs at the end of *Ramadan*, the month of fasting. The *Eid al-Adha* commemorates the willingness of Ibrahim (Abraham) to sacrifice his son Ismael (Ishmael) in submission to God.
7   The *oud* is a traditional Iraqi stringed instrument carved from a gourd and similar to a lute.
8   *Huris* are beautiful companions in Heaven.
9   A reference to the corrosive effect of salt in an arid environment and, by extension, the soldiers' perseverance under difficult circumstances.
10   The Sura of the Cow in the Quran states, ". . . your Lord said to the angels: 'I am placing on the earth one that shall rule as My deputy' (2:29), referring to humankind. From the translation by N. J. Dawood, Penguin Books (revised 2006).
11   Azrael is the angel of death.
12   In reference to Surat Maryam (Mary) in the Quran. Although the Islamic faith regards Jesus as a prophet rather than the divine Son of God, the Quran does grant Mary immaculate conception.
13   The phrase "bats of the night" refers to outlaws and murderers.

Introduction to *Ishtar in Baghdad*
Rasha Fadhil

Ishtar in Baghdad makes use of the cultural significance of Ishtar and Tammuz, mythological figures from Iraq's ancient past. This is not, however, a retelling of old stories; rather, I have conjured the two gods in response to the American occupation and its confusing aftermath.

I will never forget the horrible events that took place at Abu Ghraib and the violations committed by American soldiers there, which have left a black mark on the history of Iraq. Those soldiers tried to destroy the Iraqi detainees from the inside by submitting them to the severest physical and psychological degradation and, by extension, to desecrate Iraqi civilization itself, with its deep roots in the past. This painful incident inspired me to cry out, as loudly as I can, in opposition to those who invaded Iraq under the pretense of acting humanely, with the stated purpose of saving an oppressed people from a dictator.

The events at Abu Ghraib certainly motivated me to write this play, in which I try to come to terms with the magnitude of that violation against humanity. To do so, I have called up Ishtar and Tammuz to bear witness to what happened in Iraq, and to the archetypal Iraqi citizen, after the invasion; to bear witness to the transformation from one who used to be creative and productive, and who used to love and contribute to life, to one who is thwarted, frightened, and defeated. Ishtar and Tammuz witness the collapse of a present built on the edifice of history. This collapse penetrates the Iraqi psyche, shifting from the present into that deep, shared past.

Ishtar in Baghdad was written in 2004. It has yet to receive a professional production.

Ishtar in Baghdad

Rasha Fadhil

Characters

Ishtar
Tammuz
Female prisoners
Male prisoners
Americans (Officers and Soldiers)
Other minor characters

Act One

Scene One

A celestial balcony . . . beyond the reach of bullets and smoke . . . eternal melody of birdsong . . . unseen hands coax from strings angelic tones that fall like a cascade of tears . . . the balcony is infused with a white glow . . . the sudden flash of the rising sun brightens the scene to reveal a clear, blue sky. **Ishtar** *looks at the earth from her balcony and cries out in horror.*

Ishtar   The rising tide of blood engulfs the green earth!

Tammuz (*desperately*)   The lambs have died and the shepherds fled.

Ishtar   They are destroying my tower, the bridge between heaven and earth![1]

Tammuz   The umbilical cord is cut! The land you once made fertile cries out in thirst.

Ishtar (*pacing angrily*)   I will not abandon my land to the ravenous mouth of the desert.

Tammuz   The desert has swallowed everything.

Ishtar *studies the earth.*

Ishtar   Who are those strangers bristling with heavy arms? Their colors are foreign! Their words cannot be found in the dictionary of my people!

Tammuz   Those are the ones who scorched the earth and spilled the blood of your people across the valleys, laying a swelling carpet of anemones.[2]

Ishtar (*crying out in anger and sadness*)   The country that gave birth to civilization will never die! I will go down to bless them again . . . to charm them from death . . . to grace them with the plant of life.

Tammuz (*protesting*)   But the cup of your hand is smaller than their thirst!

Ishtar   There is the hand of Wadi al-Salam, whose water has not dried yet.[3]

Tammuz (*amazed*)   But look at Wadi al-Salam! There are many drowning people . . . children . . . women . . . toys . . . colorful balls . . . shoes . . . black cloaks floating over the waves . . . O what blackness!

Ishtar *buries her head in her hands, backs away in fear, and paces angrily around the stage.* **Tammuz** *chases her, then grabs her hands.*

Tammuz   You will not go down! They will hang your silver body in public squares to be spat upon and cloaked in buzzing flies.[4] Our time has passed. The land is no longer ours—it belongs to strangers.

Ishtar (*challenging him*)   But gods do not die. Even if they are killed, their immortality is rekindled.

Ishtar *approaches a passageway to the earth.* **Tammuz** *follows her.*

Tammuz   You will not go by yourself.

Ishtar (*stopping him*)   I want you to observe how greenness pushes back the tide of blood.

Tammuz   Rather, it is your hand that plants life.

Ishtar *regards him with gratitude. They walk together toward a cloud. It embraces them and they disappear from view to strains of music.*

Scene Two

The earth, with all its contradictions, turbulence, and energy. **Ishtar** *and* **Tammuz** *descend.*

Ishtar   Where are we in the land of Sumer?[5]

Tammuz   Perhaps we got the wrong address!

Ishtar *smells the soil.*

Ishtar   I know this scent.

The place is dark with ruins and thick with the stench of smoke. There is an explosion. They fall to the ground. Heavy smoke covers the stage. Cries for help, howling and screaming. **People** *run in horror: a crying* **Child** *carries a torn school bag; a* **Woman** *sobs over her baby.* **Men** *in torn clothes run and shout. A* **Man** *runs and cries hysterically while bleeding from his head and other parts of his body.*

Voices   Oh! Allah! Help Us! Where is the ambulance? The police? The world? My friend is bleeding!

The **People** *pay no attention to* **Ishtar** *she moves among them.*

Ishtar   How the weeds have choked your land!

Tammuz *holds* **Ishtar**'s *hand.*

Tammuz   Don't go far! This place is full of fire.

Ishtar *continues walking and wailing. She approaches a* **Child** *who is crying, as she holds her school bag and looks around in confusion.* **Ishtar** *takes the bag from her and wipes away her tears.*

Ishtar   Who tore your bag?

The **Child** *cries bitterly.* **Ishtar** *lifts the* **Child**'s *face in her hand and wipes her tears again.*

Ishtar   Tell me.

Child   I was on my way to school . . . my friends were with me . . . we were studying for the exam . . . and suddenly there was an explosion. (*She cries harder.*) We didn't go to take the exam . . . we'll fail . . . my bag was torn and I lost my books in the noise and the fire and the chaos.

Ishtar *embraces the* **Child.**

Ishtar   Where are your friends?

Child   I don't know . . . the smoke swallowed them.

Ishtar *leaves the* **Child,** *who is sobbing uncontrollably.*

Tammuz (*chasing* **Ishtar**)   Wait! Don't go further! I'm afraid the smoke will swallow you up.

Ishtar   This is my land! I won't allow my people to be burned . . . Let's find her friends.

Ishtar approaches the source of the flames. Ambulances and police sirens are heard . . . security forces surround the area. The sound of wailing over the dead. The wounded are carried off. The sound of shooting. *Ishtar* is separated from **Tammuz**.

Ishtar   Tammuz! Where are you?

She searches for him among the weeping people, who do not sense her presence.

Have you seen Tammuz? He was with me.

A wounded man   Don't worry. He was taken in for interrogation.

Ishtar (*crying out*)   What interrogation?! We're not criminals! He is your god! He is the one for whom you used to perform mourning rituals . . . dream and sing for his return . . . and offer him sacrifices and oblations.

The wounded man *regards* **Ishtar** *with pity.*

The wounded man   I beg forgiveness from Allah the Almighty! May Allah judge the doers! Those who were not physically wounded were driven mad!

Ishtar *grabs* **The wounded man**'s *shoulder.*

Ishtar   Where will I find Tammuz?

The wounded man   O woman! It's only June, Tammuz is yet to come.[6] What is the connection between the months of the year and the one you seek?

Ishtar (*angrily*)   I am Ishtar! Goddess of Heaven! Your goddess! Is this really the land of Sumer?!

The wounded man *gives her a strange look.*

The wounded man   Sumer?!

Ishtar *walks away from* **The wounded man**, *crying.*

Ishtar   You slipped from my hands. Where are you?

She bends her head to the ground, kneels down, and weeps to the earth.

Be merciful to him!

She searches for him among the crowd. A group of **Boys** *gathers to see the explosion. She approaches them.*

Have you seen Tammuz? He was standing beside me, a short while ago.

One of the **Boys** *turns to his friends, and they exclaim together:*

Boys   Tammuz?!

Ishtar *realizes how odd the name sounds, and asks again.*

Ishtar   Where in Sumer are we?

Boys (*in astonishment*)   Sumer?!

Ishtar (*angrily*)   Yes, Sumer! Don't you know what the word means? Don't you know your own history, from where you came?

The **Boy** *turns to his friends for an answer.*

Boy   In fact . . . Sumer? Yes, I remember. It's a cheap cigarette.[7]

Ishtar (*angrily*)   Cheap cigarette?!

Disappointed, she leaves them and continues to search for **Tammuz***. She scrambles amongst those who are running away from the explosion. She passes by a* **Woman** *selling household items on the pavement. Her indifference catches* **Ishtar**'s *attention.*

Ishtar   Why don't you run away like everyone else?

The **Woman** *is busy arranging her goods.*

Woman (*ironically*)   Because he is weak before those who wait for him. Every morning I sit here waiting for him but he escapes from me.

Ishtar *sits in front of her.*

Ishtar   Why do you wait for him?

The **Woman** *waves her hands to keep flies off of the desserts that are on display.*

Woman   For three years I've been making dessert for him, hoping he will desire it . . . maybe if he decides he wants it then I will make him take me with him as payment. But he hasn't come.

Ishtar   Who extinguished hope in you?

The **Woman** *speaks as if talking to herself as she continues to brush away the flies.*

Woman   If his bag had been burnt with him in the explosion, I wouldn't sacrifice my soul for him! But they brought it to me with the smell of his pencil, eraser, dictation, and his math notebooks, where they didn't teach him that two minus one equals zero.

She drops her resentful tone and raises her head toward **Ishtar***.*

Woman   I saw them handcuff your friend and put him in a truck. (*With irony.*) Don't worry, they're just going to teach him some exercises.

Ishtar*, horrified, shakes the* **Woman**'s *shoulder.*

Ishtar   Who took him? Where did they take him? Why did they take him?

Woman   Don't be scared! He won't die. They'll ride on his back for a little while, then they'll fasten a leash around his neck, a leash borrowed from their police dogs, to kill the time that passes so slowly. Perhaps they'll teach him the Lion of Babylon exercise.

Ishtar   What exercise?! What does the Lion of Babylon have to do with it?

Woman (*angrily*)   As if you were from a different planet! The Lion of Babylon exercise! The pictures were shown everywhere, exposing us in front of the whole world!

Ishtar (*begging*)   Where can I find these trainers? Show me where they went.

Woman (*surprised*)   You want to go to them willingly?! Aren't you scared? Leave him there. I promise you he won't die, even though death would be better for him. He'll be released after several months. He'll come out a hermit and an ascetic, but still, he'll be alive.

Ishtar   Where are they? How can I reach them? I must explain to them that there's been a misunderstanding. They can't do that to him.

The **Woman** *stands up and furiously grabs* **Ishtar**'s *shoulders.*

Woman   You are determined to go to them?! Aren't you worried about your body? They'll make you a dumping ground for their filth, and no one will be there to hear your screams.

Ishtar *ignores her warning and leaves. She disappears among the crowd under the* **Woman**'s *sympathetic gaze.*

Act Two

Scene One

An American **Officer** *and* **Soldiers** *interrogate* **Tammuz***. He watches them as they circle around him. His body shows signs of torture. The* **Officer** *speaks through a* **Translator***.*

Officer   What's your full name?

Tammuz   Tammuz.

Officer   Full name!

Tammuz (*with determination*)   Tammuz!

Officer   Where do you live?

Tammuz   In Heaven.

Officer (*sarcastically*)   Why did you come down to earth?

Tammuz   This is our land!

Officer (*laughing*)   Aren't you going to leave anything for us! Heaven, earth, and oil!

Tammuz   Look to your own birthplace!

Officer   What is your mission here?

Tammuz   To protect Ishtar on her way to immortality!

Officer (*maliciously*)   So, she's your mistress! Is she also a terrorist, a suicide bomber?!

Tammuz *bolts up to hit the* **Officer** *but the* **Soldiers** *seize and handcuff him. The* **Officer** *stands before* **Tammuz** *and spits in his face.*

Officer   You'll dance for me now!

Tammuz *spits in the* **Officer**'s *face. The* **Officer** *hits* **Tammuz** *hard, then he takes up a whistle that is hanging from his neck.*

Officer   When I whistle, you will bark like a dog!

He whistles. **Tammuz** *glares at him. The* **Officer** *takes up a stun baton and approaches* **Tammuz***, gesturing to the* **Soldiers** *to move away. He starts beating* **Tammuz** *with the stun baton and laughs. His laughter overlaps with* **Tammuz**'s *cries for help. Blackout.*

Scene Two

Ishtar *appears in rags, asking everyone in the street about* **Tammuz***. Some look at her sympathetically, others with indifference.* **People** *pass by quickly as if they are pursued by ghosts; some of them look at their watches and scurry in fear.* **Ishtar** *sits in a corner. The* **People** *disappear. Exhausted, she lies down and falls asleep. An American patrol passes by. Sounds of* **Soldiers** *running and talking.*

Soldier   They must have passed through this way.

Officer   They can't go far. Our patrols are everywhere. Tonight we'll capture them.

The **Soldier** *recognizes* **Ishtar** *and points to her in astonishment. They run toward her with their guns and cameras. One of them kicks her to wake her up.*

Soldier   Why are you here? Don't you know about the curfew?

Ishtar *can barely open her eyes; she looks at them in shock. The* **Officer** *looks her over with admiration.*

Officer   Are all terrorists as beautiful as you?

Ishtar *tries to step back.*

Ishtar   I was looking for Tammuz.

They handcuff her and drag her to their vehicle.

Ishtar (*crying out*)   Leave me alone! I am the Queen of the Earth! Your queen! I am Ishtar! Let me go!!!

The **Soldier** *yells at her and puts her in the vehicle. Blackout.*

Scene Three

A big room. Naked **Prisoners***.*

Officer (*addressing* **Tammuz**)   You will do as they do. Look at them, they've become professionals.

He whistles. The **Prisoners** *bark like dogs. The* **Officer** *roars with laughter. One of them refuses. The* **Officer** *approaches him and hits him with a stun baton.* **Tammuz** *screams.*

Officer   Put him in the dog cage so he can learn their language.

Tammuz *sits naked under a spotlight. Only his face is visible, bearing an expression of defeat.*

Officer   Do you want to join your friends in the dog cage?

He whistles but **Tammuz** *is unresponsive.*

Officer   Take him to the kennel.

Two **Soldiers** *drag him outside. The* **Officer** *takes a leash out of a bag. He points towards one of the* **Prisoners** *and orders him to kneel and wear it. The* **Prisoner** *kneels and puts it on without resistance. The* **Soldiers** *laugh. The* **Prisoner** *barks. The* **Soldiers** *laugh more loudly. The* **Officer** *commands two* **Prisoners** *to kneel while another two ride on their backs. The* **Prisoners** *refuse his order; provoked by his insults, they attack him. The* **Soldiers** *rush in and beat the* **Prisoners** *with stun batons and other, sharp weapons. They continue beating them until their cries for help and curses fade away. The* **Officer** *returns and stands over them.*

Officer   Two of you will kneel down and another two will ride on their backs. If you don't, we'll make your wives, sisters, and mothers kneel down.

The **Prisoners** *exchange defeated looks. One* **Prisoner** *bursts into tears and cries out in despair.*

Prisoner   Kill us! We have died since we came here; since you seized our bodies and made us horses that neigh over each other. Shoot us with a merciful bullet. Nothing can bring back what we've lost but a merciful death . . . Kill us! Kill us! Kill us!

The **Prisoners'** *shouts turn into a demonstration, which forces the* **Officer** *and* **Soldiers** *to retreat and slam the doors behind them.*

Scene Four

Ishtar, *unconscious, lies on the ground in a deep sleep. Two* **Soldiers** *enter. They turn on lights and direct them towards her face.* **Ishtar** *can hardly open her eyes. One of them kicks her in an attempt to wake her up, while the other admiringly touches her face and hair. Once she wakes up, she spits in his face and he slaps her harshly in return, knocking her to the floor.* **Ishtar** *cries. The* **Officer** *enters, carrying a stun baton.*

Officer   What have you been doing late at night?

Ishtar *is crying and speaks only with difficulty.*

Ishtar   I was looking for Tammuz, whom I delivered to his death.

Officer   What was your mission?

Ishtar   To renew the gift of life to my people, my country, my sons and daughters who were cut down by your iron weapons. I am the goddess of their fertility, joy, and growth . . . I am the goddess of heaven.

Officer (*sarcastically*)   Don't you worry about that . . . we'll definitely send you back to heaven.

Ishtar *examines their faces.*

Ishtar   You are those who shed the blood of my people and extinguish the flame of life in them.

The **Officer** *laughs.*

Officer   A paranoid terrorist!

Ishtar   When I turn into a woman to spit out your insidious reality, then I must be a terrorist. It's a horrible truth! Your faces are white but you're sinking into darkness.

The **Officer** *kicks her angrily and draws blood from her face.* **Ishtar** *wipes away the blood and looks up at him.*

Ishtar   I know this land. The history of every grain of its sand is in my blood. I almost hear its sands boiling with hatred and desire for revenge on you. Put your hand on its soil to feel the heat of its furious craving to swallow you.

Officer   Not before it swallows you.

He assails her with blows and insults. He pins her head to the ground; she is smiling.

Ishtar   I almost hear the whisper of her flames raging for you, since you have stepped onto the threshold of your death.

The **Officer** *strikes her repeatedly until he falls beside her; he pants and curses in a low voice. He collapses onto the floor crying and orders the* **Soldiers** *to drag her out and put her in a different room. Blackout.*

Act Three

Scene One

A room filled with **Women** *who try to hide their nakedness in the darkness; they weep silently in anguish. Suddenly the door is opened and* **Ishtar** *is thrown onto the floor before them. Her clothes are torn. Her sobs subside into a silent weeping. She lifts up her head and is confronted with the nakedness that surrounds her. She is terrified.*

Ishtar   What is this?

She steps back in shock.

Why are you naked?

None of them respond. A **Woman** *looks at* **Ishtar** *with pity, then nods her head and moves into another corner to lie down.*

Woman 1   It doesn't take long to discover why we are naked.

Woman 2   What miserable fate has brought you here to this pit? You are still young and beautiful. What a shame for your life to end when it has hardly begun!

Woman 1 *falls down and cries out.*

Woman 1   I'm sick. I'm going to throw up!

Woman 2   Go ahead and throw up! Perhaps you can vomit up your life and find relief. Perhaps your womb will be cleansed, then you'll be purified of their filth.

Woman 1 (*fearfully*)   What if they don't kill us?

Woman 2 (*calmly*)   We kill ourselves.

Woman 1   What if they release us?

Woman 2   Again, we'll kill ourselves.

Woman 1 (*crying*)   But suicide is *harram*.[8]

Woman 2   What about *zina*?[9]

Woman 1   We didn't commit adultery . . . We did not. They raped us! Bastards! Monsters!

She falls unconscious. **Ishtar** *runs to her and cradles her head in her arms, praying to the gods and to* **Tammuz** *for help.* **Woman 1** *regains consciousness and pushes her away.*

Woman 1   Leave me alone. I must die before they let me go.

Woman 2 (*quietly*)   Don't worry. I wrote a message on a tissue and sent it to my parents with Ahlam, who left in dishonor. I asked them to fire rockets and mortar shells on us as soon as possible.

Woman 1   Wonderful! Did you tell them what happened to us?

Woman 2   Stupid! Woman asks for death for only one reason. Now cheer up and get ready for the mortars and rockets, and maybe Allah will have mercy on us and launch a rocket on us of His own.

Ishtar   You desire death so much? You live on this hope?

Woman 1   You'd better share this hope with us.

The distant sound of explosions. **Women** *wake up. Shouts of joy . . . dancing . . . weeping, they kiss one another.*

The women   They are coming. We will join the martyrs in Heaven. We will judge our tormentors before Allah's throne. We will go from here and be free from shame and from the children of adultery who are feeding on our bowels. Welcome, death! Welcome, our beloved. You have been slow in sending your purifying light.

Cries of joy. Blackout.

Scene Two

A dark room. **Tammuz** *lies alone; his tortured body is bruised and bloody and he is unable to move. The door opens. Two* **Soldiers** *enter and drag* **Tammuz**, *who offers no resistance, to a chair. They prop him up and shine a light into his eyes.*

Officer   You still don't want to confess your true mission?

Tammuz *speaks only with difficulty.*

Tammuz   I already told you the truth.

Officer   What stupid truth?! Do you think I am crazy enough to believe that you descended from Heaven? You have no ID, no papers, no family, no address, no phone number, and worse than that, you're trying to convince me that you were looking for a goddess.

Tammuz   We didn't know that the Earth would reject us even though it was us who planted its soil with fertility and love. We didn't know that Wadi al-Salam had turned into a cemetery whose gate is open only for death and that you brought down the Ziggurat and cut the umbilical cord which connects the Earth with Heaven.

Officer   So you confess that you wanted to go to Heaven? Suicide bomber?

Tammuz   No!

The **Officer** *angrily commands his* **Soldiers**.

Officer   Take off his clothes.

The **Soldiers** *surround* **Tammuz** *and remove his clothes by force, indifferent to his cries and resistance. Chaotic music. The* **Soldiers** *hold him naked before the* **Officer**.

Officer   Put this rag on him!

The **Soldiers** *put a rag on him, which covers the lower half of his body.*

Officer   This one also.

The **Officer** *gives them a hood, which they put over* **Tammuz**'s *head.*

Officer   Let him stand and spread his arms.

They spread his arms. The **Officer** *and* **Soldiers** *laugh and snap photos from every side. Another* **Soldier** *enters and cuts off their laughter. He whispers in the ear of the* **Officer** *and leaves. The* **Officer** *stops laughing.*

48   Rasha Fadhil

Officer (*to* **Tammuz**) I have good news for you. It seems that we've found your friend who came down from heaven.

Tammuz *is silent.*

Officer You don't believe me?

He laughs.

You'll see.

Two **Soldiers** *enter dragging* **Ishtar** *by the hair; her face is bleeding and her clothes are torn. They throw her onto the floor. The* **Officer** *approaches her.*

Officer So, you're his heavenly friend. (*He laughs.*) He came here to protect you. Do you know this naked man who wears a hood on his head?

Ishtar (*horrified*) No!

Officer (*to the soldiers*) Take off the hood.

They take off the hood. **Tammuz**'s *face is wet with tears and blood.* **Ishtar** *cries out and attempts to rush to him but the* **Officer** *stops her.*

Officer Not so fast! You can't rejoin him until you confess the details of your operation.

Tammuz I told you this is not our land. We came to the wrong address.

Ishtar (*ignoring the* **Officer**) True, this is not our land. Our dynasty is overthrown, conquered by those who are armed with death. We must die with our people to be faithful to them and to our noble civilization, which will be reborn after our death. This is what the prophecies say . . . let us die, my beloved.

Officer (*shocked and furious*) Nonsense!

Ishtar (*to* **Tammuz**) Let us die that we may blossom once more.

Tammuz Let us die now to share with the plants and animals their return to the womb of the Earth, which perpetually creates life from death.

Officer (*angrily, to* **Tammuz**) Your beloved will be stripped completely naked if you don't confess! Crying won't help . . .

The sound of explosions close by. The **Americans** *are confused. They shout and run away. The voices of the* **Prisoners**, **men and women**, *rise up celebrating the attack . . . sounds of joy, howling, guns, and explosions shake the stage . . . the voices gradually fade away until there is total silence, except for the rumble of the rain.*

Notes

1 The Mesopotamians believed that ziggurats, which were temples in the shape of terraced pyramids, connected heaven and earth.
2 In the myth, anemones symbolize the blood of Ishtar's subjects.
3 Wadi al-Salam ("Valley of Peace") is one of the oldest and largest cemeteries in the world. It is located in Najaf and contains the graves of countless Muslim notables, most significantly that of Imam Ali, and is considered the holiest burial place among Shiites. According to Shiite belief, Noah built his ark at this location.

4   Ishtar possesses human features but her body is silver and radiates a silver light.
5   Sumer was an ancient Mesopotamian civilization.
6   In Arabic, Tammuz can also refer to the month of July.
7   Sumer is a tobacco company in Iraq.
8   Forbidden.
9   Adultery.

Introduction to *Summer Rain*
Abdel-Nabi Al-Zaidi

The Iraqi populace has withstood the unbearable, including war, starvation, and imprisonment. It has survived a series of dictatorships and is, to this day, besieged by corrupt and manipulative forces. It is disturbing to inhabit a society that is confronted daily by killings that are justified by bloody religious ideology. I believe that it is the playwright's responsibility to respond to Iraqi politics, which have resulted in an environment in which the human being is oppressed and stripped of his/her will.

Summer Rain addresses a question that is often posed on the Iraqi street: who is real and who is a clone? This question arose after the 2003 war, during which time a group of people came from outside the country and started boasting about their heroic resistance against the now-deposed dictatorial regime. Ultimately, they seized power dishonestly. Who is real and who is fake among those who have flooded the country with patriotic and religious slogans, and who have disguised themselves in new clothes and hidden behind religious discourse in order to promote their failing and bloody policies? We are confronted with a new face of power, one that represents something more dangerous than the clearly defined dictatorship did. In *Summer Rain*, I attempt to answer the above question by stripping the phony political scene to its essentials.

The play appears to address social concerns, taking place as it does in a house, and between a wife and her multiple husbands. At the symbolic level, however, it calls upon the nascent science of human cloning in order to broach the subject of post-dictatorship politics in Iraq. In this work, I attempt to expose the false heroic deeds and religious masks that are employed to validate actions that strip humans of their freedom. This has been a concern of mine, as expressed in my plays since the 1990s.

Summer Rain was first produced in 2011 in Basra, Nassirya, and Diwanyia, then, in 2012, it was produced in Baghdad, Jordan and Erbil.

Summer Rain

Abdel-Nabi Al-Zaidi

Characters

Woman, *about 45*
Man #1, *in his 50s*
Man #2, *in his 50s*
Man #3, *in his 50s*

A humble house. The audience can see the main door and two bedroom doors. A balcony faces the main street. There is nothing of note in the house except for a picture of a man hung in the middle of the wall, and a clock. The man in the picture is somewhat handsome. A **woman***, about 45, is combing her hair and looking into a small mirror that she holds in her hand. She goes to the balcony and then returns.*

Woman   It's time. My dearest, the head of the household, and its shining light, will come now. Aaahhh, he will come.

She looks at the picture.

I am a *woman*, your wife. Do you remember me? Oh my husband, how handsome you are! Oh, light of my eye! Oh you, the laughter of my child as I have always imagined his voice! I'll never say a word against you, as we have no time for blame and reproach. The important thing is that you will come and I will forgive you for your long absence. That's what's important. I washed all your clothes, all of them, darling! I've washed them so much that their colors have faded. Your face and its color must have changed, too. Your favorite food is cooking on the fire . . . on the fire . . . ooooh, woe on the fire, boiling since you left me, and I have been boiling with it up to this moment. How worried I am about you, wandering endlessly on the paths that lead away from our house. Do you know that every morning I wash and comb my hair for you? Your favorite hairstyle! Until one morning I noticed that it had turned white. Completely white!

She hits her head with her hand.

But I dyed it for you, darling! I blacked out the whiteness that covered it. For years I have been dyeing it for you. I will dye it and dye it and dye it until you come back. For years I have been wearing the perfume you love. Do you remember it? Our perfume! Ah, what a lovely smell! And for years, I have been hiding my head under my cloak and searching for you in the street, down alleyways and inside houses. I have been looking for you in a stranger's eyes. Looking and looking, from one street to the next and the next and the next and the next, from one house to another and from every alley into hell, hoping to see you or even your shadow. I talked to everyone who knew you, and even those who didn't. It was pointless! The song that you used to sing for me still rings in my ears. I remember it well. (*She sings.*) "Zighaira chinet wenta zighairoon, te 'arafna ebnathrat el'yoon."[1] Of course you remember. May I be struck blind! Will you come now? He will come home now! I don't know how to welcome him or what to wear for him. What will a woman, who has not seen her husband for 20 years, do when her husband comes to her? It will be paradise! All I have to welcome him home is the bouquet of my white hair, tears of joy trapped in sorrow, and the memory of warmth. Oh God, what will I do?! I feel shy and afraid; look at me, I'm trembling. I know I'll be tongue-tied, as usual. What will he say when he sees me like this, my life sucked out of me by these walls, left sleeping alone in a cold bed, in a cold room?

Oh, how I need to cry on his chest, to cry with all my heart. My tears will speak for me. (*Firmly.*) Come on, knock on the door! Knock on the door for your beloved! They told me that you would be coming this hour. (*Shouting.*) THIS WOMAN IS COMPLETELY READY TO WELCOME HER HUSBAND! Her angel until the last ray of sunshine at the last moment of the dawn. My soul! My life! Knock on the door! Knock!

The sound of knocking is heard. She becomes anxious and confused. She mumbles and sighs. Silence.

It's his knocking, I know it. Ah, he's finally here.

The sound of knocking resumes.

Coming!

She goes to the front door. She hesitates, then opens it. A man enters. He is in his 50s. He appears to be exhausted, weak, and confused. They hug each other. Silence. They burst into tears and weep for some time. Then they stop.

Man #1 (*sighing*)   Aaaahhhhh.

Woman (*sighing*)   Aaaahhhhh. How have you been, my love? You are my life, my whole life! I swear to God, I don't know what to ask you and what not to ask you. Oh God, what should I do? Forgive me, I'm worried, confused, no, no, I'm scared . . . no, no, I've been waiting for you. I was . . . I don't know what I was . . .

Man #1   I need you, not your words. You look exactly the same as the day I left.

Woman   As if I didn't know this face which I have been imagining, missing, crying over and longing for.

Man #1   A corpse has come back to celebrate his birthday, a corpse that was carried away by the trains. A train gives it to another, to another, to another, to another (*shouting*), another and another!

Woman (*she shouts with him, in anguish*)   Oh, my God! Hush, my darling!

She looks at the clock.

I carry the burden of a thousand wives.

She calms down.

You're late. You're a few minutes late. But never mind.

Man #1   A few minutes?! It seems that time in your heart has stopped.

Woman   Not in my heart only . . . never mind.

Man #1   Why are you looking at me so closely?

Woman   Aren't you examining me, too?

Man #1 (*looking around*)   Many things have changed here.

Woman   Many things? Everything.

She changes the subject.

How much I miss my husband!

Man #1   Your husband? He's standing right in front of you, in your sadness, with all his white hair.

Woman   My husband? Oh yes, you are my husband. I'm sorry.

Man #1   I don't remember living one second without you.

Woman   I don't remember living one second without my husband.

She changes the subject.

Are you hungry?

Man #1   Ahh, hungry for you.

He changes the subject.

Did you cry for me?

Woman   Rather, ask me if I ever stopped crying! I must now clean your face of dust, smoke, absence, and death. Oh, may the name of God protect your heart! Just a second.

She leaves and comes back with water. She washes his face.

Man #1   My eyes are burning!

Woman   Oh, God!

She washes his eyes.

Man #1   That's better.

Woman   All those who were absent came back like smoke. Alas!

Man #1   It seems that tears have fallen in love with your eyes.

Woman   Don't worry about my eyes. Your favorite food is boiling, boiling, ooohhhh God, boiling . . . oh, my love! I have put your tea on to simmer for many long years.

Man #1   I can't believe I'm here with you.

Woman   I believe that's all that matters.

Man #1   Is your love for me still the same as when I left?

Woman   Love?! What?! The important thing is that you're back.

Man #1   I need you to tell me that you love me.

Woman   Let me get used to your existence.

Man #1   You're shy toward your husband?

Woman   No, I'm shy toward you.

Man #1   Toward me? I am your husband. It's OK to feel shy. Has my appearance changed?

Woman   A lot. I told them to bring you back as a young man. Oh, God! What should I do? I emphasized that.

Man #1 (*laughs*)   Bring me back? How do they do that?

Woman   They can. They told me they would create an exact replica of my husband.

Man #1 (*laughs*)   Create a husband? Where?

Woman   In their factory.

Man #1   A doll?

Woman   A clone.

Man #1   What's the matter with you?

Woman   They create clones of missing husbands and send them to their wives. Come here, look through the window. Come on, don't be afraid!

She takes him and makes him look.

Do you see that man?

Man #1   I do. He's my friend. (*Calling out to him.*) Hey, my friend, can't you hear me?

Woman   He isn't real.

Man #1   He isn't?!

Woman   He's a clone. They made a clone and sent it to his wife. She's my neighbor. She was tired of her long, lonely nights, can you believe that? They've given birth to baby clones, but they're happy. Everyone in that house is a clone. (*Turning to him.*) Oh, how handsome you are!

Man #1   Where did my real friend go?

Woman   When real people leave us, they never come back, but maybe what's left of their limbs can be stitched together, as in the case of your friend.

Man #1   Limbs?! That means . . .

Woman   Were you dead?

Man #1   Dead? Can the dead stand on their own two feet like this?

Woman   I don't mean you, but my real husband, who was killed in the war.

Man #1   I didn't die at all. Please woman, I'm tired.

Woman   If you had been brought back as your younger self, you wouldn't feel tired. A big mistake!

Man #1   I feel as if I'm in an insane asylum.

Woman   I told them about my husband's personality and physical features, as they requested. I gave them a copy of your picture hanging there. I told them a lot about you. So they created a copy of my absent husband.

Man #1   I wish I could understand this madness. Try to say something that makes sense.

Woman   How can I make you understand? You'll never understand. Let me say this to you: women, nothing but women. These streets, houses, and narrow rooms were filled with women. Our lives consisted of only women. Men were gone, dead and buried. Women here, women there. Life almost stopped. Something had to be done to find men. They made them and then sent them to their mothers, wives, and loved ones in batches.

Man #1   But I'm your husband, your true beloved.

Woman   Nothing has changed in you, that's why you say that you're real. You are real, a real clone.

Man #1   No, I'm your real husband. What can I do to make you believe me?

Woman   Never mind.

She scrutinizes him.

Only a genius could create such an exact copy of my husband!

Man #1   I still don't understand!

Woman   I tried to put something on my face to restore its beauty for you, but it's dry, refusing every color. I wanted to restore my old hairstyle that you liked, and wear my pink dress, your gift to me on our honeymoon. Useless. It seems that the beautiful woman in me is gone, too.

Man #1   I want you as you are . . . no makeup, my sweetheart!

Woman   How impressive! They created in you a memory just like my husband's.

Man #1   I want your mind, heart, and soul as I left them on that last night.

Woman   And I want you just as you were before you left at the last minute, to re-experience our longing, our last embrace. Do you remember that?

Man #1   I have been living on the warmth of that moment for twenty years.

Woman   And my life has been melting away, like a burning candle.

Man #1   Oh my wife, let's complete what remains of our lives together. Let's reignite what's left of our marriage.

Woman   You deserve a cloned wife.

Man #1   Oh, be reasonable!

Woman   Today is the day they shipped you out of the factory. Please understand.

Man #1   I can't.

Woman   Why can't you accept your status as a cloned husband?

Man #1   Because I'm real.

Woman   I know it's difficult to accept, but that's the way it is.

Man #1   Everything about you is cold—your greeting, your hug, your forced eagerness to become reacquainted. You sleep in a bed of illusion.

Woman   It's not just that you were absent; you didn't exist before today. How did you become so eager to hold me? Where does your longing come from?

Man #1   How cruel you are! All this, and you say I don't exist.

Woman   How can I explain it to you?

Man #1   I can tell you all about the past twenty years.

Woman   I know you can, but what you have to say isn't what happened to my real husband.

Man #1   Oh, how I need to explode, scream, laugh, cry . . .

Woman   I'm happy that my husband isn't dead. He has to come back.

Man #1   You're happy that *I* didn't die.

Woman   I don't mean you.

Man #1   I'm about to lose my mind . . . don't expect me to be rational anymore! I told you, my wife, I'm tired.

Woman   Of what?

Man #1   Of a thousand nights, night after night after night . . .

Woman   You never lived them. It was my beloved husband who lived their pain and cruelty, filled with homesickness. Why can't you understand?

Man #1   So where was I, then?

Woman   You weren't born yet. I mean, you weren't made yet.

Man #1 (*laughing*)   Then when was I born, made?

Woman   Today is your birthday, remember it well. Please stop laughing.

He stops laughing.

Man #1   What about the whiteness that covers my head?

Woman   My husband, too, will come covered in whiteness.

Man #1   Your husband who is still alive?

Woman   After twenty years, I know that my husband is still alive. You don't know him as I do. He loves me madly.

Man #1   Please believe me! I'm trying to offer you what's left of me. Maybe I have left only a quarter of my life, of my heart and mind. I confess that I'm only a collection of parts, but I will give them all to you, to you, my sweetheart.

Woman   Oh, God! He sounds like him! He used to talk like that about our love . . . during those warm nights . . . you drag me back to those unforgettable nights.

Man #1   I used to doze off, but in your arms, oh my love!

Woman   I know . . . he couldn't sleep unless I was beside him.

Man #1   Please say "you," not "he." I used to eat food prepared by your hands only.

Woman   I know . . . he used to sing me his favorite song always . . .

Man #1   Wait! It's my song. I remember it well. (*He sings.*) "I was young and you were too, when our eyes first met . . . ."

Woman   Oh, God! The same voice! That last night, he knew it was our last.

Man #1   I cried in your lap until your dress was damp with tears. I cried like a child lost in the streets—words wouldn't form in my mouth so I let my tears express my sorrow.

Woman   It was a night full of tears!

He takes a bottle of perfume from his pocket.

Man #1   Look at this!

She takes it and smells it with ecstasy.

Woman   This is my perfume. Oh God! Do you remember what I said to you when I put this perfume in your pocket?

Man #1   "When you miss my scent, smell the perfume, you will see me standing in front of you, eager and filled with longing."

Woman   Where did you get it?

Man #1   From you, I swear I got from you.

Woman   Impossible! What's happening to me?! A dream! (*Talking to herself.*) My husband! He is my real husband! The perfume, the words, the song, his spirit, all the details! (*She shouts at him.*) You must be my husband! My husband! My real husband!

She weeps and embraces him passionately. He cries with her.

Man #1   Finally, your soul has recognized me.

She shouts the following out the window.

Woman   Listen, people! Please! You cowardly scientists! My beloved husband, my real husband, has come back. And my soul has returned with him. You manufacturers of deceit, my husband is the only thing that's real in your cloned world.

Man #1   When the night grows cold, I cover myself and inhale your perfume, and you come and lie down beside me. I feel the warmth of your breath. I lay my head on your chest to hear your heartbeat, which pulses the words, "I love you, I love you, I love you." (*Pause.*) But in the morning, you're gone. Then I weep.

Woman   Every night the wind carries the scent of this perfume out my window. So I go out and open the door, but I can't find you. I look in the road, but I don't see you.

Man #1   I don't need the perfume anymore; I need you.

Woman   At night I used to leave my bedroom door open. I would dream that I woke up to find you leaning over me, whispering in my ear, "Wake up, darling, I'm home." Wait!

She leaves and comes back dragging a large suitcase. She opens it. It is filled with black clothing.

Look at twenty years of blackness.

Man #1   Why all this?

Woman   It's for you!

Man #1   But I didn't die.

Woman   Those who can't come back home are dead. Those who abandon their wives to the house of sorrow and remembrance are dead.

Man #1   But I left the homeland in order to live.

Woman   And I died so you could live. There's no use discussing it—that conversation died many years ago. Let's live under a new roof.

Man #1   Let's live, darling. I thought you had lost your mind.

Woman (*laughing*)   And I thought you were a clone . . . imagine that.

Man #1 (*laughing*)   Me, too . . . I almost believed you . . . imagine.

Woman   I was wondering how I would deal with having a human machine for a husband . . . imagine.

Man #1   I was feeling my body. I thought . . .

Woman (*interrupting with a laugh*)   Imagine!

Man #1 (*laughing wholeheartedly*)   Imagine!

They laugh loudly. A knock at the door. They stop laughing.

Man #1   Someone is knocking at our door!

Woman   This knocking . . .

Man #1   Are you waiting for someone?

Woman (*sighing*)   Ah yes, I have been waiting for him.

Man #1 (*shouting*)   Who?!

Woman   A clone with whom I can share my life between these walls.

Man #1   More madness!

Woman   Don't worry, I'll tell him, "I don't need you. Go back to those who made you."

Man #1   Don't let him in! Send him away! We want to be alone.

The knocking becomes more urgent.

Woman   I'll deal with him. You go to our bedroom. Don't worry.

Man #1   I'll send him away myself!

Woman   Please don't. I don't want you to fight. Let me end this myself. Please go.

Man #1   I'll go, but get rid of him quickly.

He exits to the bedroom. The knocking becomes even more insistent.

Woman   Two husbands! What a joke! Too much for a wife who has been dreaming of seeing her husband's shadow cross her threshold. I used to talk to his picture, his clothes, and his chair. I used to set the table for both of us, and ask for both of us, "Did you like the food?" His food grew cold, every day. I used to make him tea.

The knocking gets louder.

OK! I'm coming! I'll open the door for you! Wait!

She opens the door. **Man #2** *enters. He is in his 50s. His head is covered in grey hair. They look at each other. He tries to embrace her, but she withdraws. He is astonished.*

Man #2   What . . . what's the matter with you?

Woman   Nothing, nothing . . .

He looks her up and down.

Man #2   My beloved wife! How can you welcome your absent husband with such coldness?!

Woman   There has been a mistake . . .

Man #2   Come on, embrace me, embrace your husband. Why are you pulling away from me?

Woman   Just wait a minute!

Man #2   Wait again?! You must be shocked by my return.

Woman   No, no, not at all. Oh God! You look just like him!

Man #2   Who are you talking about?

Woman   My husband.

Man #2   Nothing has changed in you either, except . . . except . . . nothing at all.

Woman   Nothing at all!

Man #2   Why won't you embrace me?

Woman   I don't know.

She scrutinizes him.

You, too! They didn't make you young.

Man #2   Just like you, the years have left me behind. My wife! I'm tired.

Woman   Stop! I've just heard exactly the same words, a few minutes ago.

Man #2   How beautiful you are! Let's take up where we left off. I'll do my best to reignite our passion.

Woman   His words!

Man #2   Everything about you is cold: your reception of me, your lack of enthusiasm, your feelings toward me! What's the matter with you?

Woman   His words! You weren't absent; you didn't exist at all. Where do these feelings come from, this longing and desire?

Man #2   What do you mean?

Woman   I mean you aren't my real husband.

Man #2   I'm not? Then what am I?

Woman   A clone of my real husband.

Man #2   I'm about to lose my mind . . . don't expect me to be rational anymore! I told you, my wife, I'm tired.

Woman   His words, his words! I swear these are his words!

Man #2   My words, my words!

Woman   Who are you?

Man #2   Your husband, your real husband!

Woman   How is that possible?! My real husband is now sitting in that room.

She points toward the room.

Man #2   Another man in my room?!

Woman   You are the other, and he is my real husband.

Man #2 (*laughing*)   How can I believe you and disbelieve this body that stands in front of you, with this soul flowing through it and this heart that beats with a longing for you? These eyes that have thirsted to see your eyes and these hands that have gone numb with praying to return to you. I am real in every detail. How can I believe you and, at the same time, deny my very existence?

Woman (*coldly*)   You can yell as much as you want. But I need you to calm down.

Man #2   Calm down, my wife?!

Woman   I'm a woman who can't remember she's a woman; a wife who can't forget she once slept in a warm bed, and a mother whose breast has dried up waiting for you to give her a baby, to bring spring back into this house.

Man #2   I want to be your husband and your spring . . .

Woman   It's difficult to find the right spot for you in my heart.

Man #2   That's not possible! You must be an imposter who looks like my wife.

Woman   Maybe . . .

Man #2   I have been waiting to see you for 20 years, waiting for this moment to embrace you, to feel your breath against my cheek. And now you stand before me like a tree in autumn.

Woman   Where did you get all of that love for me, you creature?! I thought you were only a machine, a copy of my husband.

Man #2   What an outrageous thing to say!

Woman   Then what shall I call you?

Man #2   Your husband. I swear by your eyes, I am your husband. In the cold night I always dream of you, remembering the smallest things . . . I dream of the aroma of the tea in our kitchen . . . the whispering of your voice.

Woman   You are too late, dear. You should go now.

Man #2   If I had known you would welcome me with such coldness, I never would have come back to you. If I had known I would mean nothing to my wife, whom I adore with all of my heart, I wouldn't be standing at your door.

Woman   I can't tolerate all this love from you. It all comes at once. (*She cries out.*) Love has dried up in my veins.

Man #2   I can't withstand your cruel words.

Woman   I asked those people to make a clone of my real, absent husband, and while I was waiting for you, my real husband came back, just a few minutes before you got here. What should I do?

Man #2   I don't understand.

Woman   Look at him through the keyhole, look!

Man #2   At who?

Woman   At my real husband!

Man #2   Your real husband?

He looks through the keyhole. He is shocked at what he sees.

What's this?!! He is me! What am I doing in that room? Am I here or there? Where am I?

Woman   Now that you've seen him, you may leave.

Man #2   I'm your real husband. The one in the room is the clone. He should leave now!

Woman   He's my real husband. I don't know you.

Man #2   Do I need to prove it?!

Woman   How can I believe you without proof?

Man #2 *takes a bottle of perfume from his pocket. It is identical to the one produced by* **Man #1**.

Man #2   Look at this!

The **Woman** *takes it and smells.*

Woman   Oh, my God! It's the same as mine!

Man #2   You put this bottle in my pocket during the last night we spent together.

Woman   I truly did that to my husband.

Man #2   At that time, didn't you say, "When you miss my scent, smell the perfume, you will see me standing in front of you, eager and filled with longing?"

Woman (*dazed*)   No, stop!

Man #2   When the night grows cold, I cover myself and inhale your perfume, and you come and lie down beside me. I feel the warmth of your breath. I lay my head on your chest to hear your heartbeat, which pulses the words, "I love you, I love you, I love you." (*Pause.*) But in the morning, you're gone. Then I weep.

Woman (*screaming*)   STOP! STOP!

Man #2   I don't need the perfume anymore; I need you.

The **Woman** *embraces* **Man #2**.

Woman   My beloved husband!

She pushes him away.

Get away from me! Who are you? My husband, for whom I've been waiting? Oh! Darling! Wait!

She exits and returns with a man's white suit.

Ask the suit how long I've been waiting for you!

She exits and returns with children's clothes.

Ask the clothes of the children who didn't and will never come, how often they were bathed in my tears! Ask!

She exits and returns with newspapers.

I studied every newspaper for news of your return. The house was filled with newspapers, but nothing about you. Not a single word.

She starts to exit.

Man #2   Please stop, don't go!

Woman   You came back too late, dear!

Man #2   You have to kick him out, now!

Woman   He wants me to send *you* away.

Man #2   You made a mistake when you welcomed him. (*Calling to* **Man #1**.) Hey you, get out of the room! Get out of my room! Get out!

Woman (*trying to calm him down*)   No, not like this. One of you should leave the house. But which? Which one of you?

Man #2   Get him out now! My wife, I'm tired! I will force him out!

Woman   No, not like this. Go into the second room. I have to think of a solution.

Man #2   I'll go into the second room but he shouldn't be here when I come out, or he'll be sorry.

He goes into the second room.

Woman   Who should leave? Who is the real husband? (*Calling out to them.*) You, my beloved husbands, speak the truth. Who is my real husband? (*Neither responds.*) What silence!

She peeps into the rooms through their keyholes, in turn.

Oh, how sweet! They are both lying down on the bed. One body in two rooms. Shall I the toss a coin to decide which is my real husband? What nonsense! (*She sings.*) "*Izghaira chint wanta izghairoon, taarafna eb nathrat aleyoon.*"[1]

Man #1 *comes out of his room.*

Man #1   Aha . . . have you sent him away? It's the least you can do.

Woman   I did not send him away!

Man #1   So he left without a fuss. I didn't expect that.

Woman   You are an exact replica of him.

Man #1   He is a copy of me.

Woman   You're identical down to the smallest detail.

Man #1   What's important is that he's left. You'll be my bride tonight.

Woman   He didn't leave. He's in the other room.

Man #1   In the other room! What's he doing in there?!

Woman   He's lying on the bed, accusing you of being the clone. He wants you to leave.

Man #1   And no doubt you yelled at him, saying, "Get out! He is my husband and my beloved. You must leave!"

Woman   No need to yell. Go and check yourself.

Man #1 *peers through the keyhole.*

Man #1   What's this! He is me! How could I be lying in that room and standing right here at the same time?

Woman   No more craziness. I'm already crazy enough.

Man #1   He has to go.

Woman   Maybe.

Man #1   I'm going to kill him if he doesn't leave right now!

Woman   Kill who? The husband or the copy?

Man #1   So, you still doubt me?

Woman   I'm skeptical about one of you.

Man #1   Who is your real husband?

Woman   One of you.

Man #1   Me or him?

Woman (*screaming*)   ONE OF YOU! ONE OF YOU! ONE OF YOU!

Man #1   It's me! I'm the real one! I am the real one!

Woman   You came with proof, so I believed you, but he came with the same proof. What do you want me to do? If I doubt him, I doubt you, too, and if I believe him, I believe you, too.

Man #1   I don't understand your babble. Just order him to leave my house. Obey your husband!

Woman   I would love to obey you if you were my real husband.

Man #1   Why do you insist in believing that I'm the clone?

Woman   Because something that's real can't survive in a fake world.

Man #1   I can't survive in such an arid environment.

Woman   As you see, we have no choice.

Man #1   I can't live without love.

Woman   Do you think that you're a living being?

Man #1   I'm trying to stay alive. The life I want is not like yours. It's a dream, it can't be grasped by the mind or felt by the heart.

Woman   Go and wash these ideas out of your head!

Man #1   I warn you and him, if you stay in my house . . .

He calls out to **Man #2**.

Hey you, cloned creature! Get out of my room! Leave my house now! Get out, you cloned monster! I will not allow you to stay anymore. You . . . you cloned abomination!

Woman   Please stop! I'll give him your message. We have to sit and talk. We have to uncover the truth.

Man #1   I'll confront him.

Woman   Not now! Let me do something for both of you. Please go to your room.

Man #1   I will go to my room, hoping to find at least one real thing that can remind me that I am still alive.

He goes to his room. The **Woman** *goes to the other room and knocks on the door.*

Woman   You, man! Can you come out? I want to speak with you.

Man #2 *opens the door and comes out.*

Man #2   What happened? You must have kicked him out.

Woman   He didn't leave and doesn't want to leave and I did not kick him out.

Man #2   Doesn't he feel ashamed, imposing on a woman who isn't his wife?

Woman   He might be my husband.

Man #2   Might be?

Woman   And you might be my husband.

Man #2   I love you.

Woman   Oh, what pain to be caught between two lovers!

Man #2   I'm the only one.

Woman   He loves me, too.

Man #2   And you, who do you love?

Woman   Why can't you understand? One of you should admit it and I will respect him a lot for doing that. He has to stand in front of me, courageously, and admit that he is the clone, then leave the house peacefully.

Man #2   What about the story of our love?

Woman   It's the same one.

Man #1 (*calling from the room*)   My wife, come here, please.

Woman   Wait a sec, I'll be back soon.

Man #2   You shouldn't go to him. Aren't you ashamed to do so in front of your husband?

Woman   Maybe he wants me for something important.

Man #2   I am the man of the house. Maybe my manliness has been absent for some time, but it came back with me.

Man #1   Wife! Where are you?

Woman   I'm coming.

She goes to **Man #1**. **Man #2** *show signs of fatigue and anxiety. He calls out to* **Man #1**.

Man #2   Hey you! Clone! Get out of my house, now! Go find yourself a cloned wife! Go and live in your cloned world, and stay away from us! (*Pause.*) I must find a weapon. He might be vicious. One of us must be eliminated by any means necessary.

He goes into the second room. The **Woman** *enters and looks through the keyhole of the second room.*

Woman   He's looking for something. What does he want to do?

Man #1 (*entering angrily*)   No one can kick me out of my own house! I'm the real one around here.

Man #1 *knocks angrily on the door of the room that contains* **Man #2**.

Man #1   I'm the real one.

He tries to open the door.

Open the door, clone! I'll kick you out by force! I'm still strong enough to clean up my own house! If you're really a man, come out and face me! I'll give you a beating and kick you out! (*To the* **Woman**.) Can't you see how brave I am?! I'll get something from the room to fight with.

He goes into his room. **Man #2** *comes out of his room holding a knife. He goes to the room that contains* **Man #1**. *He pounds on the door with the handle of the knife. He tries to open the door.*

You, clone! You're nothing! Get out of my house, now! Come on, face me if you dare! Where's your courage, clone!

He opens the door and enters the room. The **Woman** *enters the room as well. The audience can hear incomprehensible words, screaming, shouting, blows being exchanged, and objects being broken. Loud knocks on the front door are heard. The* **Woman** *comes out of the room with a look of horror on her face. She runs to the front door and opens it.* **Man #3** *enters. He is in his 50s. He looks exhausted.*

Man #3   Come here and embrace your husband.

He moves toward her.

Come here! Come here, my beloved wife!

The **Woman** *screams in horror.*

Woman   NO NO NO! My third husband! No, no, no! Another clone! Another and another and another and another . . .

Man #3 *takes a bottle of perfume out of his pocket and points to it.*

Man #3   This is our perfume . . . our special perfume.

Woman (*shouting*)   Another clone has stormed the house! Oh, dear God! GET OUT!

She goes to the other rooms.

GET OUT! ALL OF YOU! GET OUT OF MY HOUSE, NOW! My heart no longer needs you, clones! My soul no longer needs your words, memories, dreams, lies, and your misshapen faces. My heart holds no place for your love. Never! (*She talks to her heart.*) Oh, heart! Stop beating! Stop loving! Stop feeling hope and longing! Please stop! I must cleanse this heart of the dirt accumulated during its long vigil. I was waiting for the truth. Only the truth! I will be waiting for it here, alone, alone, alone! (*Shouting.*) It will come! Truth must come one day. As for you, all of you have to leave my house right now. Leave . . . leave . . . leave.

She opens the front door. The three men file out, disappointed. She slams the door shut.

Note

1   A line from a song by an Iraqi-Armenian, Christian, female singer named Seta Hagopian: "I was young and you were, too, when our eyes first met."

Introduction to *Romeo and Juliet in Baghdad*
Monadhil Daoud Albayati

When the Royal Shakespeare Company asked me to write something for the World Shakespeare Festival, the tragedy of *Romeo and Juliet* jumped before my eyes. So I read the text and then forgot it and started to write an Iraqi play inspired by the story of Romeo and Juliet. I found Shakespeare's text to be relevant to my Iraqi audience, which has been suffering from sectarian violence since the American invasion. It was a big adventure to struggle with a classical text, which is implanted in the memory of both the Iraqi and world reader. The process of writing took more than a year and a half. The adaptation should grow out of the Iraqi spirit, entangled as it is with deep internal problems. Since I believe that theatre should be for the people, I had to adapt the Iraqi and local collective memory to the tradition of Shakespearean tragedy.

I am the true heir of tragedy. Yes, I wrote while my clothes were drenched in blood which had not yet dried, because the struggles that terrified us continued. Our politicians led the country into horrible wars in which thousands of young people were victimized. Our grandmothers' stories were illuminated in my mind and the features of my text became consistent with the struggle of writing it. Sometimes I enjoy writing, and sometimes I suffer from a fever which makes my writing a fresh and hot act, with a full belief in what I am writing at the moment of inspiration, and I come back again to attack what I've already written. If a scene is well-constructed and my doubt cannot shake it, then I leave it as it is and continue what I started. As such, the text was finished and my friends read it, as I usually have them do after each project I write, and I listen to the opinions of friends whom I trust. Then I cast a team according to whom I found suitable for every role, and we rehearsed daily for more than five months, and we all enjoyed the rehearsal process, by which I mean actors, designers, and musicians, like a beehive buzzing with happiness.

Romeo and Juliet in Baghdad was commissioned by the World Shakespeare Festival held in conjunction with the London Olympics and premiered in 2012.

Romeo and Juliet in Baghdad

Monadhil Daoud Albayati

Characters

History professor
Juliet's father, brother to Romeo's father
Juliet's mother
Juliet
Tybalt, brother to Juliet
Nurse
Romeo's father, brother to Juliet's father
Romeo's mother
Romeo
Mercutio
Benvolio
Gregory
Officer
Paris
Men in ski masks
An American General
Two men with Tybalt
Father Thaer
A mute child

Scene One

The sound of gunfire and explosions. The scene conveys the atmosphere of a civil war. Young people run in all directions, carrying weapons. Cello music. The **History professor** *enters and addresses the audience.*

History professor   A long time would pass before we would comprehend the magnitude of what had happened. Alas, our homeland had become an arid wasteland, unable to support our ambition. (*To the characters onstage.*) Why are you smiling at the darkness? Turn away. I don't belong to you.

As the **History professor** *addresses the audience, the other characters gradually exit.*

History professor   I want to inhale the fragrance of palm trees, not the stench of war. I crave the lovers' night, the night of those deeply in love. I am the water of life. I am the legal heir of this country. Bear witness. I belong only here in Baghdad, and only to Romeo and Juliet.

Scene Two

The stage is imbued with an atmosphere of warmth. **Tybalt** *enters from the left, riding a bicycle.* **Gregory, Benvolio,** *and* **Mercutio** *enter from the right, also on bicycles.*

Tybalt   What are you looking at?

Mercutio   I'm free to do whatever I want.

Benvolio   Please, we don't need trouble.

Tybalt   Shut up.

Mercutio   He's just trying to act macho.

Tybalt   I am a man and I will break your head.

Benvolio   Mercutio, let's go.

Tybalt *and* **Mercutio** *grab each other by the collar.* **Juliet's father** *enters from the left.* **Romeo's father** *enters from the right, with* **Romeo's mother**. *The sound of gunfire. A large* **Police officer** *enters, on crutches. He addresses the young characters.*

Officer   What's wrong with you? This is your last warning. Get out of my sight. I don't want to see you here again.

They leave, quickly. **Juliet's father** *bows his head, as does* **Romeo's father***. The* **Officer** *looks at them accusingly.*

Officer   They act this way because of you. Your sons are fighting each other because you don't like each other. I would love to see them play together. Go to school together, hand in hand. Why? Why do you encourage your sons to be enemies? Do you like the sound of gunfire and the color of blood? Alas! Listen, this is your last warning. What times we live in, when a brother hates his own brother.

The **Officer** *exits. All others exit except for the two fathers.*

Both fathers   You!

Romeo's father   Even if the sky were to fall, I would not give it to you. Do you understand?

Juliet's father   Why? Why? Doesn't the bridge belong to me?

Romeo's father   But we built the boat, not you. You were a little boy and just sat there and watched us sweat. Your clothes were white and spotless while we sweated under the sun, working ourselves ragged. We built it plank by plank until our hands were bleeding, while you sat there, the son of the new bride.[1]

Juliet's father   True, because your mother was poor. She didn't care what you did. But my mother was young, beautiful, and strong. She said to me, "Don't go with your brothers." She slapped me in the face. Then she took me in her arms and hugged me and kissed me. She said, "Go with your father to learn from men and be my man."

Romeo's father   While we worked, you sat in his lap.

Juliet's father   Didn't you notice him giving orders while you guys scurried like rats? Didn't you see how he seized the helm and piloted the ship? I liked the bridge. I would put my hand on the wheel. He put his hand over mine and taught me. I loved the bridge and he loved me.

Romeo's father   Who secured the sails when the wind raged?

Juliet's father   And who gave the orders that guided you?

Romeo's father   My father.

Juliet's father   You learned from him. You learned from him, step-by-step.

Romeo's father   You stole from us, you deceived us.

Juliet's father   No. We were standing there together. Why did you go downstairs?

Romeo's father   My father was at the helm, and to obey the father is to obey God.

Juliet's father   And me, I didn't disobey him. My hands loved the wheel, look at them. They're shaking. Look at them, the life is draining out of them. Look at how they've withered. It's been nine years and the bridge belongs to me.

Romeo's father   You're dreaming. Your time is over.

Juliet's father   You wouldn't know. This isn't your job.

Romeo's father   We will learn.

Juliet's father   We're going to drown.

Romeo's father   I'm tired. All my life, you've been my boss. I want to stand on my own two feet.

Juliet's father   You can't do it, it's not your thing. You spend your life crying, you're sad when you eat, sad when you drink, sad when you sing, even sad when you pray, and you collapse in your bed every night, defeated. You want to command the ship while you're sad, it doesn't work that way.

Romeo's father   I've been suffocating all these years. I need to breathe. I want to be happy. Things have to change; I want to change.

Juliet's father You can't change who you are. You just can't. I'm the one who needs to change, not you. Don't worry, I'll give you your share.

Romeo's father I trusted you a long time ago and look where it got me. I don't want to make the same mistake twice.

Juliet's father Don't forget, I can demolish you completely.

Romeo's father I'll stop at nothing to destroy you.

Juliet's father I will cut you to pieces and throw your head to the dogs.

Romeo's father You've already done your worst, and here I stand in front of you.

Paris *appears, far upstage.* **Men in ski masks** *enter, one after another.*

Juliet's father I swear to God, I will burn your house to its foundation.

Romeo's father You're dreaming—the fire is out and the fuel is gone.

Juliet's father Never underestimate us.

Romeo's father You're going to strangers for help.

Juliet's father Just like you. An eye for an eye.

Romeo's father He who acts first must be punished.

Juliet's father I swear on my father's soul, you will regret it when the slaughter begins.

Romeo's father I swear on my father's soul, we will wipe you out.

Juliet's father We will scatter you to the ends of the earth.

Romeo's father We will destroy you.

Juliet's father I warned you, I did what I could, as God is my witness.

Romeo's father Thanks be to God.[2]

Juliet's father Thanks be to God, even for misfortune.[3]

Juliet's father *exits.* **Romeo's father** *stays behind. From afar, the sound of* **Romeo**'s *voice singing a traditional sailing song from Basra.*

Romeo *"Oh yamai yatheheb nahwahu alab . . . ."*[4]

Scene Three

Romeo *sings and dances in the rain.*

Romeo's father Are you crazy? Aren't you worried that you'll get sick? It's cold, my son.

Romeo Something's happened.

Romeo's father It's winter. Aren't you worried that you'll get sick?

Romeo From the rain?

Romeo's father Yes, it's cold out here.

Romeo   What about a person with a hot heart?

Romeo's father   The weather has nothing to do with the heart.

Romeo   I have fire in my heart, Dad. Fire. Put your hand here and you'll see. All the water in the world can't quench this fire. My heart will evaporate the water. Put your hand here and feel my heart. And if you don't believe me, feel the water. The water is hot. Your winter is not winter. Your winter is summer because you don't have a heart. And if the heart is dead you can't tell the difference between the seasons, and you won't understand pain. Go, Dad, go. My soul is in pain. Go, Dad. Go plan how to kill them.

Romeo's father   These are the words of a history professor. Right?

Romeo   And does the history professor speak falsely?

Romeo's father   Me, kill? How dare you? If someone overhears you, what will they say?

Romeo   They will say that, if a man can kill his son, it's easy for him to kill others. Go, Dad, go. You think it's too much for me to quench my heart with water?

Romeo's father   Oh, Romeo, all these years and your heart still hasn't felt the chill?

Romeo's mother *enters. She drags* **Romeo** *offstage and then reenters. The rain stops.*

Romeo's father   Rain, rain, wash away my problems.

Romeo's mother   Rain, don't listen to him.

Romeo's father   What do you mean?

Romeo's mother   I'm losing my son. I'm watching him wither away, day after day.

Romeo's father   You think it's my fault?

Romeo's mother   It's better to forgive than punish. Go, reconcile with your brother. All my life, I've never seen an older brother as scared as you are.

Romeo's father   I fear only God!

Romeo's mother   Stop yelling. We're tired of this problem. We're tired of crying. We want to move on. We want to live like others. We crave happiness. Look at your son.

Romeo's father   What about my son? What does he need that I haven't already provided?

Romeo's mother   Happiness. Your son wants to be happy. We're tired of crying. We are tired. We're going to explode. Do you understand me?

She exits.

Romeo's father   Oh, history professor. Where do you want to take us? Where? My family is using your words against me. Leave me alone with my problems.

Scene Four

Juliet's father *sits in a wheelchair, pushed by* **Paris**.

Juliet's father   Paris, the boat has run aground. I'm going crazy.

Paris (*quoting the Quran*)   Let's "cooperate in righteousness and piety."

Juliet's father   How?

Paris   My money is your money and your honor is my honor.

Juliet's father   Cooperate? How?

Paris (*referring to a* hadith, *or saying by or about Muhammad*)   Believers should stick together. Agree, my brother.

Juliet's father   Are we back to the same subject?

Paris (*referring to another* hadith)   Oh youth, if you are capable of getting married, then do so.

Juliet's father   It's not that easy.

Paris   The boat is stranded and with my money, it will move.

Juliet's father   Money isn't everything. Do you know who Juliet is?

Paris   Yes, I do. She is young and beautiful. I am *mujahid*, in the name of God.[5] She will be honored and you will defeat your enemies.

Juliet's father   Yes, I want to defeat them and free the boat and I see it moving in front of my eyes. It will be a day of celebration.

Paris   Let's celebrate tonight.

Juliet's father   Tonight?

Paris   Yes. So that they know who they're dealing with, those nonbelievers.

Juliet's father   Yes, but we haven't asked the girl yet.

Paris   When the boat sails in the right direction, your daughter will be happy and guided on the righteous path.

Juliet's father   The boat is the boat. The girl isn't that important.

Paris *is happy at this response.*

Paris   Let's celebrate tonight.

Juliet's father (*as if in a dream*)   We will defeat them.

Paris   So we have a deal?

Juliet's father   But you already have three wives, and here in Iraq we don't like polygamists.

Paris   Don't you like the Prophet's *Sunna*?[6]

Juliet's father   Who says I don't? I seek forgiveness from God.

Paris (*he quotes from the Quran*)   "Marry the women of your choice, two or three or four."

Juliet's father   True, but . . .

Paris   I'm going, but the boat will be yours.

Juliet's father   How?

Paris   I came here to save the people of the two rivers from the filth of those others, which means I am a project in martyrdom.[7] Life, for you and for me, is in Paradise with the *houraeen*,[8] by the side of the Prophet.

Juliet's father   Tonight is a good night to celebrate by reciting the name of God.

Paris   *Dhikr*? Don't be ridiculous.

Juliet's father (*quoting the Quran*)   "For without doubt, in the remembrance of God do hearts find satisfaction."

Paris   *Dhikr*? We are *mujahidin*.[9]

Juliet's father (*he repeats this several times*)   I will defeat them.

Paris   What matters is that we have an agreement.

Juliet's father (*he repeats this several times*)   The boat, the boat will come back to me.

Paris *exits, happy. The voice of the* **History** *professor can be heard from offstage.*

History professor   Shame on you. You sell your daughter cheap. Why? Why do you do that? Did Paris buy you? Did he buy you?

Juliet's father   No, I bought him. Nobody can buy me. I bought the boat.

The wheelchair disappears. The scene becomes nightmarish.

Scene Five

Benvolio *and* **Romeo** *enter from a drainpipe.* **Benvolio** *is talking on his cell phone with* **Mercutio***.*

Benvolio   Mercutio, where are you?

Mercutio   I'm in Basra.

Benvolio   Wait, someone's calling me. (*To someone else on the phone.*) Yes. How? Oh, really? Of course I'll tell him. (*To Mercutio.*) Mercutio, I have good news for you.

Mercutio *sneaks up behind him.*

Mercutio   What's the news? I can't wait to hear the news.

Benvolio *turns around and sees* **Mercutio***. They laugh.*

Benvolio   And you told me you were in Basra?

Mercutio   What's the news?

Benvolio (*whispering into his ear*)   What are you going to do, Abu Samara?[10]

Mercutio   What I have to say will change everything.

Romeo   What's the matter with you?

Mercutio   The news I have is priceless.

Benvolio   This is the opportunity of a lifetime.

Romeo   The opportunity of a lifetime?

Mercutio   A meeting with your beloved.

Romeo   How?

Benvolio   Her father is hosting *dhikr*.

Romeo *jumps up and down for joy.*

Romeo   Really? When?

Mercutio   Sit down. Tonight.

Romeo *thinks.*

Benvolio   Isn't that great news?

Romeo *is silent.*

Benvolio   Why don't you say something?

Mercutio   Of course, he's a lover, dreaming of seeing her.

Romeo *weeps.*

Romeo   I haven't seen her in nine years.

Benvolio   And today you will see her. It's your chance.

Romeo   I won't go.

Benvolio and Mercutio   Why not?

Romeo   What do you mean, why not? Have you forgotten the war that has lasted for nine years? Nine years stolen from my life? Nine years of hatred and resentment. Nine years of darkness. Nine years of death. Suppose I say yes? How will I enter the enemy's house?

Mercutio   Her father is hosting *dhikr*.

Romeo   But—

Mercutio   Oh, Romeo, are you scared?

Romeo   Don't be a jerk.

Mercutio   Am I a jerk?

Benvolio   This is your chance.

Silence.

Romeo   Yesterday I dreamt.

Mercutio   Like me.

Benvolio   I dreamt, too.

Romeo   You dreamt? What did you see?

Benvolio   No, I slept.

Mercutio *laughs.*

Romeo (*to* **Mercutio**)   Speak, what did you see in your dream?

Mercutio   A beetle was sitting on her doorstep, all dressed up and made up with red lipstick and kohl, waiting.[11] The radish peddler passed by, hawking his produce. "Radishes, radishes, get your fresh radishes!" He saw her and asked, "Oh beetle, beetle, all dressed up, with your red lipstick and your kohl, what are you waiting for?" She answered, "I'm weaving a carpet for my future husband." He proposed to her, "Will you marry me?" She asked, "If I marry you and one day you get mad at me, what will you use to hit me with?" He answered, "The bulb of the radish." She exclaimed, "Ouch! I cannot tolerate even the lightest flick from the skin of an onion." So he left.

Benvolio   Let's say that the lettuce peddler came next and cried out, "Lettuce! Lettuce!"

Mercutio   How do you know?

Benvolio   This is just a dream—do you think your father owns it?

Mercutio *laughs.*

Romeo (*to* **Mercutio**)   Continue.

Mercutio   "Oh beetle, beetle, all dressed up, with your red lipstick and your kohl, what are you waiting for?" She answered, "I'm weaving a carpet for my future husband." He proposed to her, "Will you marry me?" She asked, "If I marry you and one day you get mad at me, what will you use to hit me with?"

Benvolio   He answered, "Lettuce, of course."

Romeo   "Ouch! I cannot tolerate even the lightest flick from the skin of an onion."

Mercutio   And then along came a rat. He saw her and said, "Oh beetle, beetle, all dressed up, with your red lipstick and your kohl, what are you waiting for?"

Benvolio   "I'm weaving a carpet for the man who deserves me."

Romeo   "Will you take me?"

Mercutio   "If I marry you and one day you get mad at me, what will you use to hit me with?"

Benvolio   "I will caress your body with my tail."

Mercutio   She was happy and married him. But at night, the beetle was hungry. The rat looked for food. He found a jar of date syrup. He tried to reach the syrup with his hand, but couldn't. So then he stuck in his leg, and then his head, and then he fell in.

All   Dead!

Mercutio   Our friend, the beetle, went looking for the rat. She couldn't find him. Then she looked inside the jar and found him dead. She went crazy. She screamed and cried. "Why did you die, my beloved, why? If the jar had been filled to the top with date syrup, he wouldn't have died. Why?" She continued crying and weaving, crying and weaving. "Oh father, I don't want the radish peddler. He's stupid and married and wants to hit me. I don't want him. I don't want the lettuce peddler. He was married three times and wants to humiliate me. I don't want the onion peddler. The rat was lovely and he was poor, like me. Yes, I got hungry. Did I think that once I got married I would stop being hungry? All my life I've been hungry and looking for a man. Where are the men, where are they? Do you know how many beetles don't have husbands? Do you know how many young women are in prison, without their men? *Allahu akhbar*,[12] war after war after war, where are they? Where are you, men? Where are you? They spend their entire lives at war and as soon as we say goodbye to our neighbors, we start to fight them. Haven't you had enough of these wars? We've been starving for date syrup." She shook out the carpet, on which she used to sleep with the rat, and flew away to visit Ali Baba and the Forty Thieves. She asked Ali Baba, "What's wrong with you? You used to steal from the rich to give to the poor. What happened to you? We are hungry. We want date syrup." He replied, "My left hand was taken from me. How can I steal now?" She flew away on the carpet to the street of Abu Nuas.[13] There she saw Scheherazade laughing and talking to herself. She asked her, "What's wrong, Scheherazade?" Scheherazade laughed and said, "Oh, I found out that Shahryar is a phony." The beetle felt happy and started to tell the young women, "The oppressor has died, so don't be afraid, go out." She started to visit them one by one and comfort them and said to them, "Be patient. Romeo is coming with a jar of date syrup."

Romeo   I feel like something's going to happen.

Mercutio   So you're a liar and you don't love her.

Silence. **Romeo** *looks at* **Mercutio**, *then at* **Benvolio**, *then he weeps and looks at* **Juliet**'s *house, from which the sound of drums can be heard.*

Scene Six

Juliet's *family is preparing for* dhikr. *Men with* tars *are playing in a circle.*[14] **Romeo** *dances in the middle.* **Juliet** *dances on the balcony, swirling like a dervish.* **Tybalt** *recognizes* **Romeo** *and becomes angry.* **Paris** *approaches* **Tybalt** *and whispers in his ear.*

Paris   What are those unbelievers doing in our house?

Tybalt   It's Romeo. Is this possible? Where did he get such courage? Okay, so you come here on your own two feet to meet your death.

Juliet's father   What's wrong? There's evil in your eyes.

Tybalt   Evil is a small word.

Juliet's father   You've lost your mind.

Tybalt   Of course I have. Because Romeo challenges us in our own house.

Juliet's father   You have lost your mind. This is our house, which means that he is our guest. Since when do we betray our guests? You've been raised here. I will cut off your hand if you so much as touch Romeo.

Tybalt   I can't—

Juliet's father   Yes, you can and you must. I'm the head of this household. After I'm dead, do whatever you want.

The drumming becomes louder as the dhikr *party gets underway. Everyone is dancing, including* **Romeo**, *in the middle of the circle.* **Juliet** *dances in sync with* **Romeo** *from the upper level of the house. After the dancing finishes, everyone exits except for* **Romeo**, *who remains center stage.* **Romeo** *turns toward* **Juliet**.

Romeo   Please, come outside for just one minute. Just one second. Just one second will heal the wounds of many years. Nine years, Juliet. I just want to see you and then I will go, I swear.

Juliet *appears at the balcony, talking to herself without seeing* **Romeo**.

Juliet   Is it possible that Romeo was here? No, no, they will slaughter him. Yes, they will slaughter him. We have real men, men who would kill anyone who dared to even look at their girls. But my heart is telling me that Romeo was here. I smelled his fragrance. And my heart never lies.

Juliet *disappears.*

Romeo   Oh mother, oh mother![15] O people, this is Juliet speaking as if she were the *eid*.[16] God has never created anything as beautiful as her. Not every girl is a girl. Oh, I'm going to die! Oh mother! Oh father!

He begins to dance. **Juliet** *enters, watching him in disbelief.*

Juliet   My heart told me that you are here! I swear.

Romeo   Nine years, my Juliet, nine years.

Juliet *(looking up toward the sky)*   God, nine years. Nine years and you haven't had enough mercy on us to make it right.

The sound of a song from afar: "We hope that God will now have mercy on us and heal us." The singer continues to repeat this lyric under **Juliet***'s dialogue, which follows.*

Juliet *(continues)*   Nine years, isn't that enough? Nine years of vengeance and killing? Nine years, God, I praise your name. Here is Romeo, please give him to me.

She weeps copiously. **Romeo** *starts to go. She holds him back.*

Romeo   If the sight of me makes you cry, then I will leave.

She continues to hold him back.

Juliet   I'm worried about you. They will kill you. Many young people are gone already. Like flowers. They did nothing. They didn't deserve to die.

Romeo   A lot of them. Massacres. A lot of bloodshed. And everyone is responsible. Everyone is involved in this bloodshed. I will not excuse anyone. Everyone is responsible.

Juliet *looks at him innocently.*

Romeo   What's the matter with you?

Juliet   Everyone, Romeo?

Romeo   Yes, everyone.

Juliet   Everyone?

Romeo *catches on to what she is insinuating.*

Romeo   But there's no blood on my hands.

Juliet   How could that be?

Romeo   Because the dead cannot kill.

Juliet   Dead?

Romeo   Of course. Do you believe I'm alive?

Juliet   God forbid.

Romeo   I am dead, my Juliet. I mean, I was dead but now I'm alive.

Juliet   I love you. I love you. I would die for you.

Romeo   I would die for you. I love you.

Nurse (*from offstage*)   Juliet!

Juliet   I can't bear it, Romeo. I'm going to explode.

Romeo   What can we do, Juliet?

Juliet   Tomorrow.

Nurse (*from offstage*)   Juliet!

Romeo   What about tomorrow? Tell me.

Juliet   We are going to get married, and whatever happens, happens.

Romeo   Married?

Juliet   Yes, we will get married. We don't have any choice.

Romeo   What about your brother and your family?

Juliet   Do you love me or not?

From offstage, sounds of celebration.

Juliet   We have to get married, my beloved.

Romeo   We have to?

Juliet   Now, my beloved, go away before they see you.

Romeo *starts to go, but she holds him back again.*

Juliet   Do you love me?

Romeo *looks up toward the sky.*

Romeo   We pray that God will now have mercy on us and heal us.

Romeo *wipes away* **Juliet**'*s tears.*

Romeo   Tomorrow.

Juliet   I don't know what's going to happen.

Romeo   How will we know where to meet?

Juliet   I'll send the nurse with instructions.

They exit.

Scene Seven

Romeo's father *and* **Romeo's mother** *enter.* **Romeo's father** *drags an* IV *stand with a transfusion bag. An* **American General** *stands beside him, giving him blood.*

Romeo's father   Oh, *eid*, stay longer, wash away my worries and cleanse my soul.[17]

Romeo's mother   We are suffocating. We are drowning in blood.

Romeo's father   What do you want from me?

Romeo's mother   In all my days, I've never asked you for anything, or your brother. Leave Romeo alone.

Romeo's father   He's my son, too. How can I leave him alone? He's my only son. He is the son of my heart.

Romeo's mother   You don't have a heart.

Romeo's father   I don't have a heart?

Romeo's mother   That's right. You don't have a heart. As I've told you many times, when you took the helm it killed your heart.

Romeo's father   How can you talk like this? What about the stranger?

Romeo's mother   Enough. Your time is up.

Romeo's father   Look at the price I've paid. What was mine was taken from me.

Romeo's mother   All your life you've been whining. Learn from your son.

Romeo's father   Me, learn from my son? It should be the other way around.

From offstage, the voice of the **History professor**.

History professor   Don't teach your son your ways, because he was born into a different world.

Romeo's mother   Romeo wants to be happy. Let him be happy and be happy with him.

Romeo's father   Be happy with him? How? How?

They exit.

Scene Eight

Romeo *and the* **History professor** *enter.*

History professor   What's wrong with you, Romeo? Do you want to say something?

Romeo   I'm going to die.

History professor   I thought you had something new to say.

Romeo   No, but this time it's serious.

History professor   It's always serious.

Romeo   I saw her yesterday.

History professor   Where?

Romeo   In their house.

History professor   Why, Romeo? Why did you go there? Do you want to get your family in trouble? Do you want to bring on a new massacre?

Romeo *weeps.*

History professor   You cry and people die.

Romeo   Yesterday they had a *dhikr* party, so I went with my friends and when everyone left, I couldn't leave.

History professor   Yes?

Romeo   I saw her.

History professor   Yes, continue. Tell me what happened.

Romeo   She still loves me.

History professor   Yes?

Romeo   And I love her, too.

History professor   Just tell me what happened after that.

Romeo   We decided to come to you.

History professor   To me? What for?

Romeo   We have nobody but you.

History professor   How can I help you?

Romeo   You will marry us.

History professor   And you will put both of your families in danger. That's brave, Romeo. However, nobody will listen unless you do something like this. When are you going to get married?

Romeo   Tomorrow.

History professor   Let's do it, and may God bless us all.

Scene Nine

Juliet's father, Juliet's mother, Juliet, Paris, *and the* **Nurse** *enter.* **Juliet, Juliet's mother**, *and the* **Nurse** *listen to the conversation between* **Juliet's father** *and* **Paris**.

Paris   Let's do it, with God's blessing.

Juliet's father   What's the rush? We agreed on Thursday.

Paris   The sooner the better. Thursday is on the morrow.

Juliet's father   "On the morrow?"

Paris   Yes, on the morrow. Have you changed your mind?

Juliet's father   Have I changed my mind? That's it then, "on the morrow." But Juliet—

Paris   Since when are women allowed an opinion?

Juliet's father   Don't worry about it. Juliet's my daughter and will do as I say.

Paris   So then, the wedding will be tomorrow.

Juliet's father (*to himself*)   So he is capable of talking like a normal person.

Juliet   No.

Juliet's father   What did you say?

Juliet   I don't want him.

Juliet's father   Why not?

Juliet   Dad, I—

Juliet's father   You what?

Juliet   I want—

Juliet's father   What do you want?

Juliet   I want . . .

She is afraid to continue.

Juliet's father   You're cutting a hole in my heart.[18] How can you say no?

Juliet   Because I—

Juliet's father (*a little angry*)   Listen, you. Don't think that just because I've spoiled you all your life, you can have whatever you want. You can't make me break my word. I swear to God.

Juliet's father grabs **Juliet** *by the hair.*

Juliet's father   This head—

Juliet   I know, you'll cut it off. You are my father, and the crown on my head.[19] But do not break my heart.

Juliet's father *starts to calm down.*

Juliet   But how can you give me away so easily? No, father, no. Do you want me to feel defeated and degraded? What did I do to you, father, to make you want to humiliate me like this? Why do you want to get rid of me? Why?

Juliet's father   Humiliate you? Get rid of you? Daughter, I want you to be happy, I want what is best for you. I want to secure your future before I die.

Juliet   You didn't ask for my opinion; you just gave your word to this stranger. As if I don't exist.

Juliet's father   What am I going to do now? I'm asking you.

Juliet   But I didn't say no.

Juliet's father   What did you say a little while ago? You shocked me. You're driving me crazy.

Juliet   I'm not against marriage.

Juliet's father   Okay, continue.

Juliet   I want to get married, but not to Paris. He doesn't smell good.

Juliet's father   What do you mean?

Juliet   It just doesn't feel right. I just don't like him.

He grabs her hair again.

Juliet's father   Do you have another man that I don't know about?

Juliet   Everyone knows who I want.

Juliet's father *lets go of her hair, in shock.*

Juliet's father   After nine years you haven't forgotten? It's my fault, I didn't let your brother kill him. I'm an idiot and Tybalt is smarter than me.

*The **Nurse** steps forward.*

Nurse   Please, don't hurt her. She's young and made a mistake. We're asking for your forgiveness, and you'll get everything you want.

Juliet's father   Tomorrow's her wedding, and if she doesn't agree—I swear to God, I will call for Paris now and you will get married right now.

Juliet   No, father, please, I agree.

Juliet's father *retreats out of* **Juliet***'s sight.* **Juliet** *cries, then stops and wipes away her tears.*

Nurse   What are you going to do?

Juliet   I will do what my father wants me to do.

Overhearing this, **Juliet's father** *smiles and disappears.*

Juliet's mother   Yes, daughter, your father is intent on evil, and you hold the solution in your hands.

Juliet   Don't be afraid.

All exit.

Scene Ten

Romeo, **Mercutio**, *and* **Benvolio** *are on stage. The* **Nurse** *enters in a rush. She stumbles over her cloak and falls down.*

Mercutio   What an idiot!

Nurse   You are the idiot. You're a useless piece of crap. You are shameful. Don't you have any sisters? Haven't you ever seen a woman as beautiful as I am?

Mercutio   You're beautiful?

Nurse   I am beautiful, I just need to work out a little.

Benvolio   She's right.

Nurse   Shut up, you moron. Are you mocking me?

Mercutio   No, he's mocking me.

The men laugh amongst themselves.

Nurse   Laugh. Tomorrow I will start on a diet and exercise and my waist will become beautiful and tiny so that I can wear a party dress. And I'll go to Paris to buy the most gorgeous perfumes and I will invite the English ambassador, even though the English are misers—they won't help me unless I meet their demands.

All the men   What demands?

Nurse   That I become an extremist. Anyone who wants to go to London, he must be an extremist because the British love extremists and one could become famous after that. And then the American ambassador will send for you and I'll become an important person and they will give me fat contracts with many security guards—Blackwater security guards. Then they'll break the heads of anybody who tries to laugh at me. Laugh! The Iranians and Saudis are begging me, and it's up to me to accept or decline. I'll do the opposite and marry the rat.

Mercutio   Why, my darling?

Nurse   Oh, I don't want to marry the onion seller.

Romeo and Benvolio   How did she know?

Nurse   It's a dream. It doesn't belong only to you.

Mercutio   We've been scandalized. Let's run away.

Nurse   The most important one is you, Romeo.

All of them turn to **Romeo**.

Nurse   Look at how handsome you are. Juliet deserves to fall in love with you, because you're so handsome.

Romeo   So you are—

Nurse   Yes, I am the one sent by Juliet to tell you that she wants to come to you. What should I say to her?

Romeo   *Allahu al-atheem*—God is great—

Nurse   Terrific! We have a deal.

Mercutio   Just wait—let him finish.

Nurse   Don't interrupt, you jerk. Haven't you ever seen a woman as beautiful as I am?

Romeo   Please, Mercutio, leave her alone.

Nurse (*referring to herself*)   Please, leave her alone.

Romeo   This evening?

Nurse   This evening. It's the best time. You must hurry because Paris is engaged to her, and he is rich but ugly.

Romeo   What are you saying?

Nurse   She said, I don't want him.

Romeo   And what's going on now?

Nurse   This evening, she will go to the salon to get her hair done for the wedding.

Romeo   What will she be doing at the salon?

Nurse   It seems that you don't know how to think anymore.

Romeo   What do you mean?

Nurse   Going to the salon is a trick.

Romeo   Trick? What are you talking about?

Nurse   How else would she meet up with you? This is an excuse, sir.

Romeo   Which salon?

Nurse   What salon are you talking about?

All except Romeo   It's a trick to see you!

Nurse   Yes, but where should she meet you?

Romeo   At Sheikh Zubare.[20] I love you.

Romeo *puts his hand in his pocket to take out money.*

Nurse   No no no no, don't pay me.

Mercutio   Don't be shy.

Nurse   Not now, maybe after I've been on the diet. Oh, all right, give me the money. Bye. This evening.

Scene Eleven

Juliet *waits on her balcony. She is worried. The* **Nurse** *slowly crosses the stage toward her.*

Juliet (*to herself*)   Where did she go? Come, come back now. I'm going crazy. Where has she been? I hope she wasn't in an accident. Nothing will happen to her, God willing. Why is she late now? Please come back.

The **Nurse** *reaches her, out of breath.* **Juliet** *is overjoyed to see her.*

Juliet   Tell me, have you seen him?

The **Nurse** *doesn't respond as she continues to catch her breath.*

Juliet   What did he say to you? What did you say to him? I know you're tired but I've been waiting. Speak! Don't cut a hole in my heart.

Nurse   I'm tired. I ran all the way there and back.

Juliet   You're right, my darling. What did he say to you?

Nurse   You are selfish. You only think about yourself.

Juliet   What's the matter with you? Are you upset?

Nurse   Yes.

Juliet   If you have bad news, say it after you catch your breath, if you have good news, say it quickly.

Nurse   I want water. My lips are parched from running. I can't speak.

Juliet *runs to bring water. She waits for the* **Nurse** *to drink.*

Juliet   Have you seen him? What did you talk about?

Nurse   You haven't found any other man besides him? Why do you like him? I know he's handsome and fit and he loves you but what are we going to do with Paris?

Juliet   Enough torturing me. Paris, who? Don't remind me of his name. Paris is worthless compared to even just the name of Romeo.

Nurse   You're yelling at me? Is that how you reward me after I raised you up and deprived myself of marriage.

Juliet   Does that mean that I'm not getting married?

Nurse   Says who?

Juliet   It seems that you didn't find him.

Nurse   Where did I go then?

Juliet   Speak!

Nurse   He is waiting for you, darling, this evening.

Juliet   I love you.

Nurse   No no no no no no, it's on me this time, don't joke around.

Juliet *laughs.* **Tybalt** *enters suddenly.*

Tybalt   What are you talking about?

Silence.

Why don't you say something?

Nurse   There's nothing to say.

Tybalt   Nobody asked you, stupid.

Nurse   I'll shut up, darling, I'll shut up.

Tybalt (*to* **Juliet**)   I hear that you've upset my father.

Nurse   No one would dare to upset your father.

Tybalt (*to the* **Nurse**)   Shut up! (*To* **Juliet**.) Why did you upset him, Juliet?

Nurse   Who said that? Poor Juliet.

Tybalt   You again? I told you to shut up. I'm going to cut your head off if you don't shut up.

Nurse   Oh, mother. I will not speak anymore.

Tybalt *grabs* **Juliet** *by the hair.*

Tybalt   Whether you like it or not, you're going to marry Paris. He is *mujahid.* He has shown us the right path. He only wants what's best for us. Can you imagine anyone sacrificing his soul and expecting nothing in return? This is Paris. Do you know who Paris is now? Do you understand why I love him? I will kill you.

Nurse   She's going to marry him, darling. She has agreed to marry him.

Tybalt   Shut up or I will kill her.

Juliet *cries.*

Juliet   What you want to happen will happen.

Tybalt   Why are you crying?

Juliet   I have nobody but you, and you are doing this to me.

Tybalt   I don't know what's wrong with me, Juliet. I don't know. Extremism has blinded my eyes. We've stopped working. My dad's old now and they are persistent. One day I wanted to kill one of them, and he wouldn't let me. He stood in my way and rebuked me.

Juliet   Don't be angry. You know I would do anything for you.

He embraces her.

Tybalt   Yes, I am very angry. I hope I haven't made you upset.

Juliet   Has there ever been a sister who was upset over something her only brother did?

Tybalt   Don't be upset, please.

Tybalt *cries and exits.*

Scene Twelve

Mercutio *and* **Benvolio** *enter.*

Mercutio *fires his gun into the air, and this frightens* **Benvolio**.

Benvolio   Why did you do that?

Mercutio   Why do you tremble like a little girl? This isn't a soccer game. Go home. We need a better player. (*Sarcastically.*) Messi.[21]

Benvolio   Now you're joking about soccer, Mercutio? You're laughing at me by calling me Messi? Yes, I want to be like Messi. Messi is good. He makes his audience happy. Messi scores goals and I want my family to be like him. Happy. I want to score goals but not against you, not against anyone else. I want a nice soccer field, a green field where there aren't any weapons like your guns. Do you understand now why I like Messi and I want to be like him?

Mercutio   I swear to God, I didn't mean to upset you. I'm upset. I want to be happy. I want to have fun because I'm going to die sooner or later. And who knows what will happen tomorrow? I want life. I want to dance. I want to be happy. Oh people, I want to be happy. Is it wrong for someone to be happy?

Romeo *enters.*

Romeo   We have the right to be happy. Guys, I have news. But you can't tell anyone.

Mercutio   If it's good news, I will listen.

Benvolio   We are all ears.

Romeo   I'm going to get married.

Silence.

Romeo   Why don't you say something? Don't you want me to be happy?

Mercutio   Who is she?

Benvolio   Yes, who is this woman that you're going to marry?

Romeo   There is only Juliet.

Mercutio and **Benvolio** *lift* **Romeo** *on their shoulders. They sing a traditional Iraqi wedding song, sung during the ceremony while escorting the groom to join the bride.*

All (*singing*)   "He is the groom and his friends escort him to his bride with joy and happiness."

Romeo   Guys, this is a secret. Keep it between us.

Mercutio   We're not going anywhere, just celebrating here.

Romeo   Celebrating what? I'm telling you it's a secret. I don't want her family to know.

Benvolio   How will you get married, then?

Mercutio   By Bluetooth?

Benvolio   No, but maybe by Facebook.

Romeo   Guys, stop joking about it.

Mercutio and Benvolio   Are you serious?

Mercutio   I told you guys that something important would happen today.

Romeo   Yes, but I don't want anyone to know.

Benvolio   At the Professor's place, nobody can come and we can—

Mercutio   Celebrate and dance until morning.

Romeo   But I'm afraid—

Benvolio   Guys, we want to celebrate.

Mercutio and Benvolio   As if it were a dream.

Juliet, *the* **Nurse**, *and the* **History professor** *enter.*

History professor   No, it's not a dream, it's real. Romeo's marriage to Juliet is real and that's what I've been dreaming about for a long time.

They quickly prepare, and then the celebration, with music and dancing, begins. **Juliet's father** *enters, suddenly. Silence.* **Juliet** *shivers in fear.*

Juliet's father   Your father set this up and then he hid his head.

Romeo   My father has nothing to do with this.

Juliet's father   Shut up. Stand up when you talk to your master.

Romeo *stands up while* **Juliet** *bows her head.*

Juliet's father   If your father were a man, he would understand tradition and propriety and he would have come to me to ask for her hand.

Romeo's father *enters.*

Romeo's father   I am a man and more than a man.

Juliet's father   If you're a man, why did you violate tradition and propriety?

Romeo's father   It's not me who violated them. As God is my witness, I'm opposed to this marriage.

Juliet's father   Then who married them?

History professor   I married them.

All stand.

Juliet's father   You?

History professor   Yes, me.

Juliet's father   Why, Professor, why? You, who know better? Is this how we're going to raise our children? With the adults setting the example by violating tradition and propriety?

History professor   If tradition and propriety keep two people who love each other apart, then we don't need them. If the traditions that you adhere to encourage resentment and hatred, we will oppose them and teach our children to forget about them.

Romeo's father   But our *sharia* and our religion say that this is *haram*—

History professor   Enough. All you can talk about is religion and religion has nothing to do with what you claim it does. It's been years. Haven't you had enough of killing? Haven't you had enough of animosity? Your clothes are stained with blood. The ground is angry at you. You've been fighting each other for years. When are you going to have had enough? When are you going to have had enough? When are you going to stop and consider the future? Life is going forward and you are going backward. In this country happiness has been forbidden for many years. I've never heard of people that love anger and sadness as much as you do. Enough.

Silence.

Juliet's father (*to the* **History professor**)   I don't have a problem with you. I know who I need to talk to.

Romeo's father   To me. You want to talk to me. I agree to everything you say. I said thank you for everything you gave me. And when they ask me why, I say, "He's my brother. And one day he will realize that and he will treat me fairly." But you haven't done that.

Juliet's father   You never complained.

Romeo's father   Where was I going to complain? To you, about you?

Juliet's father   That's not true. You always worked with me, you and your sons.

Romeo's father   Worked for you. Did you ever ask yourself why we work for you? This is our father's boat.

Juliet's father   You received your share.

Romeo's father   What do you mean, my share? You call it my share when my sons go sailing for three months diving for pearls, and bring them back to your hands? Have you seen any of our women wearing even one pearl? Have you seen any of our women wearing even a ring with a pearl? Pearls are for you but our women are only good for carrying them.

Our women have nothing but dreams. They dream that we will come back safe. And when we return, it's just like *eid* for them.[22] That's why the boat doesn't work anymore.

Juliet's father   Keep dreaming, it's better for you.

Juliet's father *takes* **Juliet** *by the hand and leads her offstage.* **Romeo's father** *exits, sadly.*

Romeo   I am unlucky. My beloved has left.

History professor   On the contrary, she has not left. I wish that what happened today had happened a long time ago.

Romeo   What do you mean?

History professor   They opened up to each other.

Romeo   But the result is, I lost.

History professor   They will lose, not you. Don't worry, I will come up with a solution.

The **History professor** *and* **Romeo** *leave.*

Benvolio (*to* **Mercutio**)   Let's go.

Tybalt *enters in a rage, with* **two other men.**

Tybalt   Romeo? Where art thou, coward? Come out! You're hiding like a frightened woman. Come out.

Mercutio   What do you want?

Tybalt   I want one of your men, just one man, if you have a man among you.

Mercutio   If you want to die, come on.

Tybalt   I want Romeo.

Romeo *enters.*

Tybalt   You pretend to be a man, you coward?

Romeo   Thank you.

Mercutio   Romeo?

Romeo   Don't interfere, Mercutio.

Tybalt   Don't interfere, I will take my revenge on this disgraceful person.

Mercutio   Disgraceful? He calls you a disgrace and you say nothing?

Romeo   You know full well that I'm not a disgrace. Tybalt, go home.

Tybalt   Are you afraid of me?

Mercutio   Shut up, you dog. Who do you think you are, to accuse Romeo of being afraid of you?

Tybalt *points his gun at* **Romeo.** **Mercutio** *stands in front of* **Romeo.** **Tybalt** *shoots* **Mercutio,** *who falls to the ground.* **Tybalt** *runs away.* **Romeo** *bends down to help*

Mercutio *stand up.*

Mercutio (*as he tries to stand up*)   Don't worry, it's just a flesh wound.

Romeo   You need a doctor—it's serious.

Mercutio *realizes that the wound is fatal.*

Mercutio   I'm going to die.

Music.

Mercutio   Beetle, beetle, sitting and waiting . . .

Benvolio   The radish peddler comes to her.

Romeo   He's going to die because of me. And my brother-in-law killed him.

Mercutio *dies.*

Benvolio   Mercutio is dead.

Romeo   Juliet, you made a coward out of me. Because of you, I became a coward. Mercutio sacrificed himself. Why this torture, why?

Tybalt *enters suddenly, pointing his gun at* **Romeo**. *The* **Nurse** *enters and watches from a distance.*

Tybalt   I will put you out of your misery.

Tybalt *shoots.* **Romeo** *sinks to his knees.* **Romeo** *points his gun at* **Tybalt**. *He shoots and* **Tybalt** *falls.* **Romeo** *is shocked.*

Benvolio   Run away, Romeo! He's dead. We have avenged Mercutio.

Romeo   Avenged?

Benvolio   Revenge for Mercutio. What's the matter with you? Have you forgotten?

Romeo (*still shocked*)   Mercutio? But I am not—

Benvolio   You must run away, my brother.

Romeo   Where should I go? Where?

Benvolio   You killed him. Do you understand that? Now your life is in danger.

Romeo   This means I have become a criminal. Have you heard, Juliet? I have become a criminal.

Benvolio   You must go to Shaikh Subair. He has a solution.

Romeo   What solution? What am I going to do with my life? What am I going to do with a solution? Juliet has left.

Romeo *exits and* **Juliet's father** *enters, shouting.*

Juliet's father   My son. My son, I will avenge you ten times over. An eye for an eye.

Benvolio   He who acts first must be punished.

The sound of a police car's siren. The **Officer** *enters, on a crutch.*

Officer   What am I going to do with you? Haven't you drunk enough blood?

Juliet's father   My son, officer, was killed by Romeo. I demand justice.

Benvolio   But your son killed Mercutio.

Juliet's father   What? When? Where is Mercutio? I don't see his body.

Officer   Benvolio, if you lie to me you will be punished.

Benvolio   Officer, Tybalt started it—he wanted to kill Romeo but Mercutio sacrificed himself to protect Romeo. He's the one who started it.

Juliet's father   I want revenge for my son, Officer.

Officer   We don't use words like that around here. What do you mean, revenge? Here, we follow the law.

Juliet's father   Will the law return my son's life to me, Officer?

Officer   Law is justice, and Romeo must be punished.

Juliet's father   An eye for an eye, and a tooth for a tooth.

Benvolio   Whoever started it should be punished.

Officer   I swear by God the Greatest, I will throw all of you in jail, and Romeo will not escape from the fist of justice. If not today, I will arrest him tomorrow. I will dig even under the ground or ascend to the seventh heaven to bring him back to justice.

All exit to sad music.

Scene Thirteen

The **Nurse**, *crying and wailing, enters and approaches* **Juliet.**

Nurse (*wailing*)   Oh, Romeo! Oh, what an exemplary young man! How and why, why so much killing? When will it stop?

Juliet   Is Romeo dead?

Nurse   Oh God!

Juliet   Did he commit suicide?

Nurse   Oh God, life is turned upside down. Look, it's not going to end, your father is coming, screaming revenge, revenge. Screaming, "My son is gone. My dear son is gone." Oh, oh, Tybalt, what a beautiful young man.

Juliet   Did Tybalt kill Romeo? That's what I was afraid of. Oh, Tybalt, why did you do it?

Nurse   He was sinking in his blood. I saw him with my own eyes, which will be eaten by ants.

Juliet   Why, Tybalt, why? Oh, what bad luck, what bad luck I have.

Nurse   Romeo did it and ran away. He has no fear of God.

Juliet   You're driving me crazy. Who's dead? Tybalt or Romeo? Who killed whom?

Nurse   Romeo killed Tybalt and ran away.

Juliet (*lamenting her brother*)   Oh, brother, oh, brother, the crown on my head. My beloved killed my brother. Oh Romeo, why? I thought you were loyal, with a pure heart. Why, Romeo? He who loves is not capable of killing, Romeo. I turned against my people and believed in you and sacrificed my family for you. And I said, this is my destiny.

Nurse   What an unfortunate destiny. We can't trust them. God willing, you will be hit by a stray bullet, Romeo, and we will be rid of you.

Juliet   How can you pray for that? We're talking about my husband. May your tongue be cut out, God willing.

Nurse   He killed your brother.

Juliet   Shall I cut my heart in two? What should I do? One is my brother and the other is my beloved. He is my husband and my only love. Where will I go? Of course, he will be executed. There will be no punishment less than this.

Juliet's father's *voice can be heard from far away.*

Juliet's father   An eye for an eye and a tooth for a tooth!

Sad music. All exit.

Scene Fourteen

Romeo *and the* **History professor** *enter.*

Romeo   What am I going to do, professor? Please, advise me. I don't have anybody but you.

History professor   You must hide until we come up with a solution.

Romeo   I swear to God I wasn't—

History professor   It's not important now, you have to disappear.

Romeo   And I won't be able to see Juliet? Do you think they will execute me? Does this mean that I will die without seeing her? It's okay, let me die, but I need to see her first. Please.

History professor   Let's come up with a solution, Romeo. Don't be childish. Be strong. Let me think.

Romeo   What's the use? They certainly told her that I killed her brother. She will hate me.

History professor   Father Thaer—

Romeo   What about him? What does he have to do with my problems?

History professor   The best place for you is with Father Thaer.

Romeo   In his house?

History professor   No, in the church. The best place is Sayyeda al-Najat Church. Nobody knows about it, not even the government. We have to go, and now.

Romeo   What about Juliet?

History professor   Later. Let's go.

They exit.

Scene Fifteen

Sad music. **Juliet's father** *and* **Paris** *enter, followed by* **Juliet***. Both are crying. The* **Nurse** *is on the balcony talking on her cell phone.*

Juliet's father   Oh my son, my back is broken.

Nurse (*into her phone*)   Where?

Paris   Sadness is *haram.*

Nurse (*into her phone*)   In the church?

Juliet   My brother, my beloved.

Paris   Crying is *haram.*

Juliet's father   I want to see him. I miss him.

Paris   Visiting graves is *haram.* Romeo must die.

The **Nurse** *beckons* **Juliet***, and they both exit.*

Juliet's father   Where is Romeo? It's as if he were a piece of salt that dissolved away to nothing. Where could he have gone?

Romeo's mother *enters.*

Romeo's mother   May what was taken from his life be added to yours.[23]

Juliet's father   What are you doing here? Get out now!

Romeo's mother   It's shameful to kick out a guest.

Juliet's father   A guest? Now, you know how to speak, don't you?

Romeo's mother   It's okay. All your life you're used to bossing people around. How would you know how to listen?

Juliet's father   And who do you think you are that I should listen to you?

Romeo's mother   How long are you going to continue to be a snob? Enough of this. Don't you see that the person standing in front of you is your sister-in-law? Which means that I am your sister.

Juliet's father   No, you are not my sister.

Romeo's mother   Have you forgotten the food and the salt?[24]

Juliet's father   What food are you talking about? All of your life, you've eaten from my generosity.

Romeo's mother   Your generosity? I will not respond to that and I will not repeat what your brother has already said.

Juliet's father   Get out.

Romeo's mother   You can't look me in the eye. You know why? Thirty years you have been eating from these hands.

Juliet's father   Me, eat from your hand? How can that be when your husband works for me?

Romeo's mother   Don't fool yourself. You've been eating from my plate for thirty years.

Juliet's father   Me?

Romeo's mother   Yes, you. The servant used to come to me and say, "Ma'am, Juliet likes your cooking." And I would say, "Here you go, to your health." Juliet is my daughter. It's a lie—you like my cooking, not Juliet. Sometimes you would pretend that you were looking for Juliet, but you'd pass through the garden and look at the palm tree while I was watching you from the kitchen, and I pretended not to see you.

Juliet's father   That's a lie.

Romeo's mother   No, it's the truth. How many palaces have you built, but your soul is still planted in that house, like the palm tree that you always come to visit.

Juliet's father   How do you know?

Romeo's mother   I saw it with my own eyes, when your father, God bless his soul, planted it on your birthday. He was so happy when you were born. He said, "He's the same age as the palm tree. They will grow up together."

Juliet's father   You are a liar. Get out.

Romeo's mother   Coward.

Juliet's father   Don't drive me crazy—and I don't want them to say that I hit a woman.

Romeo's mother   You want to hit me? Hit your sister?

Paris   He will hit you and break your head, disbeliever.

Romeo's mother   Who is this? Why, brother, why?

Juliet's father (*to* **Paris**)   It's none of your business. Don't interfere.

Paris (*to* **Juliet's father**)   You say this to me on account of this disbeliever?

Juliet's father (*to* **Paris**)   You are the disbeliever. You are the lowest of the low. Get out or I will kill you.

Paris   What about Juliet, father?

Juliet's father   Don't speak her name or I will cut out your tongue.

Paris   What about the boat, father?

Juliet's father   Get out! Damn you and damn the boat! Look, this is my sister-in-law! Just one of her sandals is more honorable than you are. This is my sister, get out.

Paris *runs away.*

Juliet's father   Why didn't I kill him? What's he doing among us? What did those people do to us?

Juliet's father *runs out, chasing* **Paris**. **Romeo's mother** *follows him. The sound of shooting.*

Scene Sixteen

Father Thaer *is in the church with* **Romeo**. **Romeo** *talks to a* **mute child**, *and then into his cell phone.*

Romeo (*into his cell phone*)   Yes, my beloved, I'm in the church.

He turns to **Father Thaer**.

Father Thaer   Why did you do that? Why did you tell her?

Romeo   She has to know where I am. It's been forty days.

Father Thaer   You should have told me.

Romeo   I couldn't help but tell her, Father.

Father Thaer   This is not the way a man behaves.

Romeo   Thank you, Father.

Romeo *starts to exit.*

Father Thaer   Where are you going?

Romeo   It seems that I have burdened you. You want to get rid of me.

Father Thaer   This is not my house, my son, this is God's house. I'm concerned about you. I am responsible for you. The Professor put you under my protection. What will I say to him if something happens to you?

Romeo   What's going to happen to me? Is Juliet going to tell him my whereabouts?

Father Thaer   Yes.

Romeo   It's impossible. This is my Juliet and I know her.

Father Thaer   I told you that you're stupid.

Romeo   Father, I can't take it anymore. Juliet has to know where I am.

Father Thaer   So she can come and you can see her, right?

Romeo   Is it *haram* for me to see my wife? It has been forty days, my father.

Father Thaer   You're only going to see her dead body. Right? Not only her, but you, too. You'll be dead. In the church. What am I going to say to my God, Romeo? Why do you do things without telling me? Your life is in danger. And her family is looking everywhere for you. And when she goes out, they will follow her and they will know where you are.

Romeo   Father, what did I do?

Father Thaer   You told her to come here, didn't you?

Romeo   Yes.

Father Thaer   Okay, you have to leave now.

Romeo   Where can I go?

Father Thaer   They must not know that you are leaving the church. (*To the* **mute child**.) Quickly, take him to the basement of the church. Quickly.

Romeo *leaves with the* **child** *and a* **woman** *enters wearing a* niqab, *or veil, covering her face.*

The woman   *Salaamu aleikum.*

Father Thaer   *Wa aleukum as-salaam.*

The woman   Where is Romeo?

Father Thaer   Romeo? Which Romeo?

The woman *uncovers herself, revealing that she is the* **Nurse.**

Nurse   What do you mean? Where is he?

Father Thaer   Who?

Nurse   Swear by Muhammad, and I will believe that you don't know.

Father Thaer   Daughter.

Nurse (*laughing*)   Look at how stupid I am! Father, please forgive me. I'm as stupid as a child. I forgot that you're a Christian. Sorry, Father. Romeo called me and asked me to tell Juliet to come to the church. Yes, Father, they have been looking for him for forty days. If they catch him they will cut him to pieces. He killed their son. Good for you, Romeo. Nobody knows that you are here. Where is he, Father? Juliet is going to marry Paris tomorrow. What are we going to do? We are only women, Father. Please advise us.

Father Thaer   Can you please stop talking for a minute?

Father Thaer *thinks.*

Nurse   Yes, I will stop talking. If there is a solution, I will stop talking. They will slaughter her if they catch her out.

Father Thaer   Stop talking.

Nurse   I've stopped, father.

Father Thaer   Not a word.

He puts his hand over her mouth.

One more word and I will kick you out.

Another woman *wearing a* niqab *enters, then reveals herself as* **Juliet**.

Nurse   I swear to God I'm not married yet.

Father Thaer   Disaster! What brought you here?

Juliet   I can't take it anymore.

Father Thaer   Go out before they see you, both of you.

Juliet   Where is Romeo?

Father Thaer   Later. Later. How did you find us? Get out, now.

Juliet   Please, Father, where is Romeo?

Father Thaer   This is a disaster. Come with me, let's close the doors. Surely, Juliet's family is coming.

Father Thaer *and the* **Nurse** *exit.* **Juliet** *is left alone, frightened upon hearing the sound of heavy gunfire.*

Juliet   What's going on? What's happening? Oh, mother. Romeo, where are you, Romeo?

The sound of shooting.

I'm afraid my family has come. Yes, this must be my father. They're going to kill each other. What did I do? This is impossible. No, no, this might be the despicable Paris.

The sound of shooting. Blackout.

Juliet   Romeo!

She cries.

Romeo, come and get me out of here. I'm going to die, Romeo. Come and embrace me, Romeo. Come, I want to smell you. I'm going to die.

She lifts her head up toward heaven.

Juliet   When are you going to heal our relationship? I don't want to die. I want Romeo. (*Hysterically.*) I want Romeo. I want my beloved. Bring him to me now.

She looks at the cross.

Where's my beloved? Where is he? Answer me, where is he?

She looks up toward heaven.

I want my beloved, I want Romeo.

A huge explosion. She falls to the ground. **Romeo** *enters.*

Romeo   Why didn't you wait for me, even for a second at least? Just one second? You who blew up the church—I've been waiting for you all my life. Why, why, why? You followed us to the church—where am I going to go?

He looks at her, for only a second.

Romeo   Why, Juliet? Why did you leave me? You can't do that. We live together, we die together. Speak to me. Answer me. It's not up to you to stop talking. You die alone and you leave me alone. Why? What will I do in this life after you've left?

Romeo *looks at her more closely. He looks up to the heavens.*

Romeo   Has a woman as beautiful as this ever died? This beloved died. Look at her cheeks—they haven't withered yet. True, her eyes are closed because she is asleep and doesn't want to see me. She doesn't want to see anyone. She's upset. Upset at everyone. We are no good. What are we? We are killing each other. We are killing our brothers. She got fed up with that. She got fed up with us. Not just one or two years—killing and killing. "Good man, you killed him! Brave man, you killed all of them!" Killing and killing!

Juliet *moves.* **Romeo** *is shocked.*

Romeo   She's alive! She's not dead! Thank you, God. My beloved, my Juliet!

Juliet   What happened? Where was the explosion?

Romeo   Huh?

She examines his face closely.

Juliet   I love you.

Romeo   Did you see God? Did you see him? You must have seen him.

Romeo *looks up at the heavens.*

Romeo   Finally, You took mercy on us. You heard our suffering. God loves me. He sent you back to me. He loves me and loves you.

Paris *enters, wearing a belt of explosives.*

Juliet   I would die for you, my beloved. Where have you been?

Romeo   Huh?

Juliet   I love you. I love you as much as an orange.

Romeo   I love you as much as a tangerine.

Juliet   I love you as much as the sky.

Romeo   I love you as much as the sun.

Juliet   I love you as much as Baghdad.

Romeo   I love you as much as Basra.

Paris *approaches them and blows himself up. The two families enter. They find* **Juliet**'s *scarf with that of* **Romeo**. *The* **History professor** *hands them to the families. The two brothers shake hands and exit. The end.*

Notes

1   A reference to an Arabic saying in which the son of a new bride represents one who is spoiled and stands by while others work.
2   "*Alhumdulillah*," a common Arabic expression.
3   Another expression, "*Alethi la yuhmad ala makrouh siwah*."
4   "Dancing and singing, oh water . . . ." This song belongs to a genre known as *kheshaba*, the name of which is related to the word *kheshba*, which means literally "piece of wood," but figuratively refers to the local type of drum common to the genre.
5   A *mujahid* is one engaged in *jihad*. *Mujahidin* is the plural.
6   The *Sunna* refers to collective knowledge about Muhammad's life and words.

7   Paris refers to the people who live between the Tigris and Euphrates using the elevated word *Rafidain*, rather than referring to the region as Iraq. This is consistent with his conspicuous religiosity.

8   The *houraeen* are virgins who, it is believed, will be companions of the righteous in the afterlife.

9   *Dhikr* refers to the practice of chanting a name of God in order to induce a state of ecstasy. The playwright depicts Paris as a *mujahid* who believes only in action and, specifically, violence, rather than traditional Islamic practices.

10   A term used to refer to dark-skinned Iraqis.

11   Mercutio relates a version of a traditional story from Mosul about *khamfasana*, a beetle. In one telling, it concludes after the death of the rat, with the moral, "Don't marry a rat."

12   God is the greatest.

13   A street in Baghdad that was at the center of an entertainment district, with many restaurants and nightclubs.

14   *Tars* are flat, round drums.

15   In this instance, an expression of amazement and happiness. "Oh, father" and "oh, mother" are used by Iraqis as exclamations of happiness or dismay.

16   As if she were beautiful, shiny, bright.

17   *Eid* is used here as a term of endearment toward his wife.

18   A colloquial expression of impatience.

19   The colloquialism "you are the crown on my head" expresses an obligation to respect the person being addressed.

20   A made-up name that is a near homonym to "Shakespeare."

21   Lionel Messi, one of the most highly acclaimed soccer players of all time.

22   The *eid* is a Muslim holiday.

23   An Iraqi expression of condolence.

24   This comment is a reference to an Iraqi saying that asserts that if one has shared food with someone else, one becomes part of that person's family.

Introduction to *Me, Torture, and Your Love*
Awatif Naeem

Perhaps the stage, with all its components, is the most expansive place for madness and revelation, and perhaps it is the only space in the whole world within which the artist can rave, go mad, and take on any challenge; within which the artist can devise codes and puzzles to assault or shock the spectator, arouse his or her emotions, or provoke questions without being stopped or interrogated by anyone, since the event occurs on stage, not in reality.

In a country whose long-smoldering fire has been reignited, and in which confusion reigns, everything is jumbled, and death roams freely and delights those who desire to wreak havoc upon this earthly paradise. It is necessary to dance around the issues through the medium of theatre to allow for revelation, disputation, and madness. Because I am a woman who is in love with Iraq and the gorgeous, complex tapestry of its cultural heritage, I wrote *Me, Torture, and Your Love* to present, through the play, a discourse that situates the homeland as the essential location of loved ones, of memories, images, feelings, and visions. The homeland cannot be sold because we are the homeland: it is defined by neither bricks nor borders. The homeland is us, the people who live in it; we who feed it, elevate it, and bestow upon it beauty and glory from the pride of our souls and the beating of our hearts.

Simply, the homeland is us, we who are human, who gather on one land which starts and ends with us. Hence the wise tramp says, "Take the money but save the homeland!" because he is aware that without this homeland that he adores, for which he tolerates deprivation, and in which he is satisfied with scant food and meager sleep, he will be lost and he will lose his fortitude.

Me, Torture, and Your Love attempts to awaken the patriotic spirit in people everywhere and more specifically in Iraq, where the occupation, imposed by America and its submissive allies, has deliberately divided the Iraqi people and has weakened the country and pillaged its wealth. My aim is to restore that bond through the medium of the free theatre space; the play is an invitation to save our homeland and our heritage.

Me, Torture, and Your Love was first produced in 2012 at the National Theatre in Baghdad.

Me, Torture, and Your Love

Awatif Naeem

Characters

The first, *elegant*
The second, *a tramp*

Lights up. In the center, a bridge on a river. On the right, a bench. The sound of waves.
There are frequent flashes of lightning followed by thunder. The lighting gives an
impression of foggy weather. With a flash of lightning, **The first** *enters, carrying a black*
umbrella in one hand and a black suitcase in the other. He looks confused. He wanders
around the stage, then stops near the bench. He is anxious. He listens to the flowing water.
He lifts up his head and sits on the bench. He puts his umbrella aside, opens his suitcase,
and grabs some papers. He looks at the papers; sadness appears on his face. He angrily
puts the papers back into the suitcase, opens a small notebook, and tries to write
something.

First flash of lightning

The first   When you receive my letter, I will be . . .

He returns the pen and notebook to the suitcase. He looks concerned.

Who cares whether I was or I will be . . . nobody will ask nor care . . .

He looks up.

If it rains . . . I need the rain . . . perhaps it will wash out all the sadness that has covered
me, surrounded me, and has been tossing me here and there. Let me finish what I came for.
I will not look back. I don't want to weaken . . . . Any look back will open me up to
vengeful glares and *schadenfreude* jeers. If it rains. I will not hide from the raindrops
because I am already drowning in intoxication. Let it thunder! Let your ironic water fall
around me. It's a catastrophe. Losses are pouring down on me . . . falling into loss. No
protection from the madness of the market. Let me finish what I came here for. It is but a
fearful step, shivering and falling into nothingness. After that you will be left with all that
you read, knew, and memorized about the Judgment Day and its calculations. Strange! Why
won't figures and calculations leave me alone? Well, the time has come. Let me get rid of
my shoes.

He unties the laces then stops.

Funny! Does it make any difference if I wear shoes or not? It's not an invitation to a
business deal, after which glasses are raised up and zeros tacked on to large sums of money.
Rather, it is a dispossession of everything tied up, rolled around, or buttoned up. It is a
dispossession to nakedness. It is like a child slapped on the ass as he leaves his mother's
womb.

He tries to turn but stops.

No . . . no, don't turn back . . . do what you want to do. Don't be weak! What led
you to this but your weakness for shiny things? Move! You who are weak and indecisive!

He gets ready, breathing deeply and walking toward the wall of the bridge. **The second,** *a*
tramp wearing ragged clothes, storms onto the stage, wobbling as if he is running away
from someone.

Second flash of lightning

The second   Oh, sons of . . . uncertain origin! You will see—I will return you to where
you belong, to the bottom of . . .

The first *hesitates, then stops. He looks at* **The second,** *who is agitated and mumbling to*
himself.

The second   Oh . . . eeeh! Oh, my poor body groans! Oh, my poor ass! I will not sleep on my back tonight. Those bastards! Bloated and well-dressed! They hit me. What did I do to them? Before I could finish saying, "Oh almsgivers . . ." they started beating me. That's enough! If you don't want to give, don't do so. You will not be granted even a meter in Heaven. May you accumulate money until it bursts into flame and scorches you. Is it my fault that numbers have manipulated you? Oh, you slaves of money! You who possess capital! You rise up and stuff yourself like pigs while we waste away and vanish. Leave us alone! Let us breathe before you bottle the air and sell it to the people.

He turns and looks at **The first**, *who is standing on the wall of the bridge, ready to jump.* **The second** *screams.*

The second   Oh, man! You!

The first *stops and turns to him.*

The second   What are you doing, man?

The first   As you see: me, the bridge, and the water.

The second   I know, but what are you planning to do?

The first   I plan whatever I want . . .

The second   Get down.

The first   Why?

The second   They will think that you're stealing the bridge and connecting the two sides . . . here and there.

The first   What are you talking about?

The second   Here and there.

The first   What do they think?

The second   You're stealing the bridge, they will think . . .

The first   Stealing the bridge! Are you crazy?! What would I do with it?

The second   You take it, own it, capture it, and control it.

The first   Since you're so smart, tell me, what's the use of doing that?!

The second   There are many uses . . . for example, you attract attention: reporters flock to you, taping and broadcasting, making a mountain out of a molehill. You will create chaos in a country where everything is chaotic. You will impede communication and calls will flood in pleading for the rights of the bridge; you will obstruct the people and kill their dreams.

The first   All that because I want to jump off the bridge?!

The second   You want to jump?

The first   What do you think I'm going to do?

The second   Only an idiot would jump in such cold weather.

The first   It doesn't matter . . . I embrace coldness.

The second   But why choose coldness when you can be warm?

The first   Because I chose coldness as my companion.

The second   Oh . . . so you are like me, you have nowhere to go.

The first   No, I am not like you.

The second   So why are you here and not at home where it's warm, and there's food, and maybe a beautiful woman to take care of you?

The first   I have nothing but empty hands and lies that don't cover my nakedness.

The second   So, you are like me.

The first   Enough talking—leave me alone!

The second   OK, as you like. Take the bridge, take the river, take the sea and the ocean, and take everything you want while . . .

The first   Leave me alone! I am not in the mood to talk with you.

The second   But you are in the mood to jump into the freezing water.

The first   None of your business.

The first *gets ready to jump.* **The second** *screams.*

Third flash of lightning

The second   Stop!

The first (*angrily*)   You are so annoying!

The second (*angrily*)   Am I annoying?! You are a coward!

The first   Yes, you are annoying, you talk too much, and you are nosy! Leave me alone!

The second   I will not leave you alone. My humane duty requires that I stop your bad deed!

The first   Damn your humane duty! Who do you think you are? Mother Teresa? You don't understand anything!

The second   No, I do understand. Don't be fooled by this small head. I understand everything. You want to take your life, which I will not let happen.

The first   It's none of your business! Who do you think you are?

The second   Your life is a gift from God. You cannot dispose of it without shame or fear of the Giver!

The first   You've ruined everything! I cannot stay. I cannot go back. I cannot resist in the coming days. Let me make it quick and end my existence.

The second   This is wrong! It is the act of a coward and weakling. You're better than that.

The first   Please go away. What I am going through now is bigger than your small, miserable world.

The second   My small, miserable world?! OK. Go ahead and jump! Let's get rid of another bloated, boastful one. Go ahead!

The first   Are you mad at me? Can't you see? My situation is so terrible that I can't even talk properly.

The second (*thinking*)   Sit down.

The first   What?

The second   Sit with me. Let's talk. You may find something useful in my small, miserable world.

The first *sits beside* **The second**.

The first   Useful?

The second   Yes, useful; or do you want to strip me of anything useful?!

The first   Believe me, nothing is useful, only a miracle could save me but it is no longer the time of miracles.

The second   A human being is a miracle. I read that when I . . . I don't remember when or where.

The first   If a human being is a miracle, how do you account for your miserable life?

The second   You're insulting me again. What's wrong with my life?

The first   Don't you know?

The second   I am comfortable like this . . . free . . . no restraints . . . no commitments . . . No thoughts . . . no concerns. All I need is my daily food and then I sleep anywhere I want: on the sidewalk, in a tree, on a bench. I dream as I wish. I become an emperor when I want, because this land and sky and all they have to offer are mine. But I can give up everything without trembling and whenever I want, because sometimes what you possess fills you with sadness and anxiety, and I am a man who doesn't like to be worried. So, let me be king for an hour and a tramp for the rest of the hours.

The first   Oh, what a ridiculous fool! The king of something you don't have!

The second   Of what I dream to have. I am free to dream, choose, and reject. What do you have?

The first   I used to have wealth that put me at the top. People bowed when I passed by. I used to have stocks, bonds, deeds, and trusts—I could command the sky to rain money.

The second   What a greedy person! And you want to jump?

The first   What's the use? Suddenly it's all gone. Stocks and bonds plummeted and my real estate fell into ruin. Everything I had struggled to own was gone. The crisis shook the capitals and blew the Trumpet and poverty resurrected like a sword.

The second   Nothing left?

The first   Nothing at all, not even a straw. Nothing but concessions and settlements. What hurts me more is that, while I grieve my loss, nobody lends me a hand. Everybody has left me since there is no more honey on my table.

The second   But you forget the best thing you still have.

The first   What could be better than money that grants power and stature?!

The second   You still have your youth and health.

The first   What's the use of them without money?

The second They bring money. You are still young. Work on what you want to regain. Look around you. The stars are shining even though the clouds try to cover them. And the air is cold and clammy, brushing your cheek like a beloved's kiss, a beloved who waits for your warmth. What you lost yesterday can be regained tomorrow, with patience and persistence. Your youth and health are now your capital and wealth.

The first Words . . . just words . . . no more than words.

The second I think they are nice words. I repeat these words to myself. Don't you know that words can work magic? Sometimes a few words can raise you up to touch the sky and sometimes they drop you to the ground.

The first This is what they did to me: they dragged me down to hell!

The second What did you lose?

The first (*angrily*) Everything I owned! Do you understand?! All I had! I have nothing to live on . . . disappeared, vanished, gone.

Fourth flash of lightning

The second In spite of that you are still breathing, standing on your feet, and your heart is beating. The real loss is when you lose your ability to live.

The first The core of my life was my wealth, which I gambled away.

The second The core of your life is life itself. Look at me. I have nothing, but I am happy. Many kind people like you open their wallets . . . working here . . . running there . . . some water to moisten my lips and a few bites to appease my hunger, and the whole world is mine. I sleep here and there, wandering in God's vast land, with no fear nor baggage, where there is water, and smiling faces, and hands that never stop giving. Do you know who gives most?

The first Who?

The second Who do you think?

The first The rich.

The second Rather, the poor. They give most. They share their food and their sorrows with one another. Have you ever met anyone better than them? They open their doors and share with you their soup and bread as well as their tears and laughter. They get mad and scream at each other; they bare their teeth and raise their fists, but they soften like children when they hear a cry of pain and then they tend to peace. These poor are possessed by the fear of God and love for their homeland.

The first Who are you?

The second A man who wants you to live your life.

The first Who are you?

The second And wants you to live it as you wish.

The first Suppose I lose my life—what would happen?

The second Nothing. People are people. No one will cry for you or even give you a second thought, not even those who knew you. You will lose your dreams if you lose your life.

The first *looks attentively at* **The second**. **The first** *paces.*

The first   You're right.

The second   Say it again.

The first   You are right. Why should I lose what I have due to things beyond my control?

The second   What you need has come back to you now.

The first   What is that?

The second   Clear-sightedness . . . To look into yourself, beneath the surface.

The first   Into myself?! Myself! I who accumulated all that wealth, all of that real estate and capital. I who made money breed and give birth to more money. I am capable of starting again. I will take the first step, followed by other steps, and then it will rain money. Speaking of rain, I like it only when I can take shelter. Let's sit on the bench and chat while it's raining.

The second   Can we eat something, while chatting in the rain?

The first   Like what?

The second   A piece of bread, a slice of cheese; I like leftovers.

The first   Leftovers?

The second   What's wrong with that? Especially when they're fresh.

The first   I always clean my plate.

The second   What a ravenous eater you must be! Don't you think about people like me when you eat? No need to wipe the whole plate clean or to eat the whole sandwich. Leave little bits. Overindulgence is not good.

The first   I do have some sweets. Here.

He takes some sweets out of his pocket and gives them to **The second**, *who devours them.*

The second   Oh, what a slanderer! You eat such sweets and you want to commit suicide?!

The first   Loss has ruined my palate with colocynth bitterness.[1]

The second (*eating*)   Oh, goodness! Goodness!

The first   But everything will change starting from this moment. No place for fear, sorrow, or hesitation. By dawn I will start my day with the first step. I will not give up.

The second   I like you and your sweets.

The first (*enthusiastically*)   I will fight whoever tries to stop me. Why should I care about global warming, the ice melting at the North and South Poles, submerged continents, hurricanes devastating the earth, countries ravaged, kings toppled, and cities demolished? Why should I worry about a rogue meteor that sets the world ablaze? Why should I care about tanks churning under green meadows and bullets piercing the human heart? Why should I care about the oil sucked out of the ground? Why should I care about our heritage pulled up by the roots, our culture driven into the desert like a horse without a rider? Why should I care about palm trees smashed into the dirt, their dates scattered across the black asphalt to be trampled under the boots of foreign invaders? Why should I care about the return of oppression to those who desire it?

The second (*choking*)   Wait a second! Wait a second! Your emotions are getting the best of you.

The first   On the contrary, I am getting ready for the first step.

The second   You mean getting ready to give up your belongingness.

The first   First and foremost, I belong to myself.

The second   Your first step is to tear out your heart and abandon your soul.

The first   How else can I take the first step confidently and without hesitation?

The second   You don't care about global warming, the melting of the polar ice or the rise of new empires that will enslave us?

The first   I don't care. What I care about is getting what I want.

The second   Is global warming real? Or the hole of oza?

The first   The ozone hole, moron!

The second   So what if I'm stupid, can someone stitch it? The hole!

The first   Do you think it's a piece of cloth to be stitched by an Indian, or a Bengali, or a Filipino?! It's the space that surrounds us.

The second   Haven't they climbed to the moon with their dogs and cats? Can't they hold it and stitch it? Bring it together?

The first   You make me laugh. Stitch what?! I told you it's a vast gap . . . vast!

The second   How come they can't stitch a hole in space but they can storm into people's houses?! So tell me what you mean by "oppression and those who desire it?" Has the time of slavery and human trafficking returned?

The first   No.

The second   Thank God.

The first   We have evolved. We do it wholesale. Now homelands are sold, and many are willing; and, democracy and human rights are used as lures to control and subjugate.

The second   Did you say being sold? Homelands are being sold?!

The first   Are you surprised?

The second   I might have been lost in my loneliness; I might have been preoccupied with things around me; I might have been satisfied with what barely keeps me alive and with a warm place like a corner in a mosque or a bench in a park or under an old wall; I might have felt the hands that offer me bread and a bowl of soup . . . believing that winter will pass, no matter how cold, and that summer will come with its dates . . . and these thoughts made my day easy.

The second, *looking miserable, sits beside* **The first**.

The first   What's wrong? Where's your smile? What happened?

The second   I don't know.

The first   Are you afraid?

The second   I feel lonely. Tell me, how does the homeland feel when besieged by terror?

The first   I hadn't thought of that.

The second   Does the homeland give up on us? Does the homeland turn her face from us? I have no family nor wealth inherited from a mother or a father, nothing, but I am so rich that I can live and let live.

The first   You have nothing but these rags that cover your body.

The second   I have boundless wealth . . . an inheritance that cannot be seen but can be felt.

The first   What are you talking about?

The second   I am talking about memories and emotions . . . about friends, loved ones, places.

The first   I don't understand anymore.

The second   Because you are indulging yourself in severing your roots and cutting off your feelings.

The first   It's the first step.

The second   I am talking about the real step . . . the real inheritance . . . the everlasting wealth.

The first   What's that?

The second   The homeland.

The first   Money is the homeland.

The second   Take the money but keep the homeland!

The second *walks toward the wall of the bridge.* **The first** *follows him.*

The first   What's wrong with you?

The second   What do you want?

The first   A few moments ago you were convincing me to live my life.

The second   And you made me give up mine.

He runs and climbs the wall of the bridge.

The first   Stop! Where are you going?

The second   To your place on the bridge.

The first   Why?

The second   To jump.

The first   In such cold weather?

The second   What's the difference? A cold heart is crueler than the coldest day.

The first   Stop!

The second   Let me go!

The first   I won't let you go!

The second   Why not?

The first   Because you pulled me in.

The second   Me?

The first   Yes, you! When you redeemed my life. I won't let you lose yours!

The second   What do I lose?

The first   You will lose everything. Have you forgotten? "Your life is a reward from God, you ingrate!" Come on! I'm not that bad, and people are not that cruel. Come on, get down!

The second   Give me back the essence of my life!

The first   You are rich beyond anyone who claims to be so.

The second   Who? Me?

The first   Yes. Come here.

The first *holds out his hands and brings* **The second** *down.*

The first   Come here, my friend. You're rich, yes you are, because your beloved lives within you, in your mind.

The second   In my mind?

The first   In your soul.

The second   In my soul?

The first   In your heart.

The second   In my heart? My homeland lives in my heart.

The first   Throughout all of you.

The second   Here.

He points to the ground.

Here, in your soil, in your mud.

The first   Here?

He points to the ground.

Here?

Folkloric music. They hold each other's hands and dance. Rain falls.

Note

1   In Arabic culture, the colocynth (*al-ḥandhal*) represents the bitterness of life in contrast to honey, which signifies its sweetness.

Introduction to *A Strange Bird on our Roof*
Abdul Razaq Al-Rubai

As I wrote this play, I was preoccupied with a question about the relationship between victim and victimizer: is it possible to build a bridge between the two based upon a shared humanity? Both are feeling, thinking human beings, even though they may find themselves coping with different circumstances and encounter each other within a hostile environment. Is it possible for a human connection to develop despite these obstacles?

In this play, the relationship between the mother and the soldier is in flux: at first, she expresses her anger and discontent, characterizing him as a desert rodent. But when she calms down, her maternal instincts lead her to contemplate the suffering that the soldier's mother must be undergoing as she waits for her son's return. Despite their cultural and political differences, the mother and the soldier discover a shared humanity.

Or, the victimizer might change places with the victim as at the end, when the American soldier, despite the power vested in him, is unable to elicit an emotional response from Rasha, the Iraqi daughter. Rasha resists his overture just as her brother Ziyad opposes the American occupation.

In writing the play, I was inspired by an incident that occurred in 2006. The Iraqi writer Rasha Fadhil was living in one of the high conflict zones in Tikrit, and at that time there was an escalation of the insurgency against American forces. One day she told me about a family there. The Americans created a surveillance point on the roof of their house in order to ambush one of the sons, who was involved in the insurgency, and to put psychological pressure on the family. I imagined what might happen if, in this situation, an American soldier were to fall in love with an Iraqi woman.

In the play, the relationship between the soldier and the woman is fraught, governed by anxiety and distrust rather than higher human values. The Iraqi woman views the soldier as an invader and usurper, an opinion which he attempts to change as he reveals his humanity. However, since a human being is the product of his/her environment and circumstance, she is unable to alter her perception of him. Their differences keep them apart as they hold fast to their opinions instead of finding common ground. Hence, each goes his/her separate way, secure in his/her beliefs. The intransigence they exhibit, and ultimately their lack of compassion for one another, demonstrates the human qualities that allow for the destruction of civilizations. As the protagonist states, "Dialogue is impossible between the branch and the bullet."

A Strange Bird on our Roof has not yet been produced.

A Strange Bird on our Roof

Abdul Razaq Al-Rubai

Characters

The mother, *70s*
Rasha, *her daughter, 30*
Um Haider, *their neighbor*
An American Soldier
An American Sergeant
Additional American Soldiers
Three young, male, Iraqi insurgents
A Newscaster

Scene One

The stage is divided into lower and upper parts. The lower part occupies two-thirds of the stage, while the remaining third is occupied by the upper part, which represents a roof with a birdcage.[1] *Scattered feathers. Lights up on* **American Soldiers** *rummaging through the house. Some of them climb up to the roof as they search. They open the birdcage door and release the doves that are inside, which fly away. They stomp on bags of bird seed and the birds' nests. They exit, leaving behind one* **Soldier**. *Lights up on the lower part of the set. An old woman and her daughter enter in confusion.*

The mother   Are they gone?

Rasha   No, they left one on the roof.

The mother   Why did they leave him? What do they want from us? What do they want?! They wrecked the house and the garden. They didn't find anything, but still they insist that we tell them where Ziyad is, as if he were a slip of paper folded and hidden in a crack in the wall.

Rasha   Ziyad is just one of their targets. They have many others.

The mother   But is it our fault? Look how they rummaged through our things, which we've kept tidy for all these years.

Rasha   We will straighten things out, but who will sort through the memories scrambled in our heads? Who will mend our hearts, torn where their blades have entered?

The mother   They dug up the garden and cut down the flowers. Bastards!

Rasha   Quiet! He might hear you.

The mother   So what! He should understand that he is occupying our roof and that his prayers are false.

Rasha   Everything in this war is false, especially this man on our roof. He came from the end of the world seeking only to profit from our misfortune.

The mother   May Allah damn him and his greed!

Rasha   Money, Mom . . . its glitter blinds the eyes of the greedy.

The mother   Maybe he's just fulfilling a mandatory military service.

Rasha   There isn't any mandatory service in his country. He's here for money.

The mother   Why doesn't he work at home where he can earn *halal* money, and where his kind of prayer is accepted?[2]

Rasha   There's unemployment in his country.

The mother   And he came here to become a hero.

Rasha   Heroism is not a uniform for sale. It's a crown congealed from the blood of all, placed on the head of the deserving.

The mother   If I go upstairs and choke that jerboa nesting on our rooftop, will I be a heroine?[3]

Rasha   He will shoot you dead in cold blood.

The mother   Of course he will, he is an occupier, and of course, his prayers aren't answered . . . and his good deeds fly away like Ziyad's birds, to where, I don't know.

Rasha   But they will definitely come back, and so will Ziyad.

The mother   Ziyad won't come back as long as that jerboa is roosting on our rooftop.

Rasha   He'll get tired and bored and leave, but we need to deal with him realistically. He's imposed on us.

The mother   The killers and *kafirs* imposed him on us.[4]

Rasha   Rather, Ziyad did when he ran away, and now we are paying the price for his heroic ambitions.

The mother   Do you want your brother to hand himself over to the killers?

Rasha   Why start the fight if he wasn't up to it? Why run away? Only cowards run.

The mother   He knows they won't lay a finger on us.

Rasha   They already did.

The mother   What do you mean? Did they approach you?

Rasha   No, but they entered in the middle of the night with no respect for the inviolability and privacy of our home . . . violation of the sacred.

The mother   And you think the land, the occupied land, is sacred?

Rasha   No . . . no. Everything is defiled under the boots of the invaders.

The mother   Then our lives have no value. We should go up and strangle that jerboa and seize the crown of heroism.

Rasha   They won't let us take the crown. If we approach him, they will incinerate us in a blaze of fire.

The mother   Is he well-armed?

Rasha   Yes he is, and he has munitions.

The mother   What if they explode?

Rasha   We'll die. The Americans won't waste a soldier for two flies, an old woman and a spinster.

The mother   You're wrong! If I didn't matter, he wouldn't be here watching my every move.

Rasha   I told you, we aren't the target, Ziyad is. He abandoned us.

The mother   If running away saves one's life, then it's an achievement. Our gracious Prophet fled Mecca and the persecution of the Quraysh.[5]

Rasha   He didn't run; he obeyed the order of the Creator. Back then, people had morals. That's why the Quraysh didn't harm his family. Things are different now.

The mother   Is he going to stay a long time?

Rasha   As long as it takes to capture Ziyad.

The mother   Where is he going to use the toilet?

Rasha   My friend Maysa told me that once they had a military squad over their rooftop, too, and the Humvee used to come twice, in the morning and in the evening, so that the soldiers could discharge their waste in bags and receive canned food.

The mother   Disgusting! I'm going to throw up. How does he perform ablution?

Rasha   In wartime one doesn't need water to perform ablution; one purifies with fear.

The mother   They wash with dirt?

Rasha   No. We wash with fear to pray, but for them fear ruins the prayers of war. That's why they don't pray at all.

The mother   I seek refuge in God! Even if they pray, their prayers aren't answered.

Rasha   The war has no prayer because of the bloodshed, and blood is impure.

The mother   For years we fight and pray.

Rasha   The blood of martyrdom is pure and cleanses the earth.

The mother   We will seek martyrdom as long as the war rages on.

Rasha   It seems that war will never end, as long as the black gold flows below.

The mother   No, it will continue as long as we live.

Rasha   Many have been martyred before us, and the war goes on.

The mother   If we all attack that jerboa up there, with his urine bag, the war will end.

She moves to grab a stick in order to attack the **Soldier***.*

Rasha   Mother, calm down. Fear summons bullets and buys death.

The mother   At least I will make this soldier wet himself before he pulls the trigger.

Rasha   Please mother, calm down, for Ziyad's sake.

The mother   Ziyad! Where is he? He's gone and won't be back as long as that soldier is on our roof.

Rasha   Everything comes to an end. Do you think the soldier will outlast the summer heat?

The mother   How can he stay through summer? How will we sleep on the roof while he pees in his plastic bag?

Rasha   He'll leave eventually, but we must expect the worst.

The mother   The worst is that we tolerate this life. We can't climb our roof to hang the laundry while that jerboa is counting the stars in our nighttime sky. I'm going to teach him a lesson.

She prepares to attack the **Soldier***.*

Rasha   Please mother, forget about him and let's think about our future lives.

The mother   What future? What life?! After all this humiliation, do you call breathing in and out a life?

A vehicle stops and the voices of ***Soldiers*** *speaking in English are heard.*

Rasha   Listen . . . there's a Humvee at the door.

The mother   What do they want? I won't allow anyone to enter the house. This is a respected house, not a Khan Jighan.[6]

Rasha   Wait . . . their friend is here.

The mother   Is he Juha's nail?! The American Juha![7]

Rasha   Wait, Mother, and calm down. They haven't left the Humvee. Look, the soldier is lowering his bag in a basket.

The mother   His diaper bag?

Rasha   Don't make me throw up.

The mother   He moves his bowels and we throw up; is there an end to this farce?

Rasha   Everything has an end, whether happy or sad, straight or crooked, quick or slow, but what matters is the end.

The mother   When will we see the end of these jerboas?

Rasha   When we catch the beginning of the thread. Our problem is that we don't know how to start. We're stumbling, that's why they're here.

The mother   Is he done lowering his poo bag?

Rasha   Done. Now he's receiving the canned food and water bottles, in the same basket.

The mother   The same basket?

Rasha   War doesn't distinguish between what goes in and what comes out.

The mother   But we do.

Rasha   That's because we're the losers. We don't have anything to worry about. They're the winners and they guard their booty, including us.

The mother   Are you saying that the jerboa is guarding us?

Rasha   No, he guards his masters' victory over us. We're a threat to him.

The mother   But we're just an old woman and a spinster.

She cries.

Rasha   No, Mother. Don't cry. Stay strong in their eyes.

The mother   We are strong. Our tears prove our strength—they show that we're human.

Rasha   The killer rejoices in the victim's tears.

She repeats this line and cries until she falls to the ground.

The mother   Stand up, idiot! Stay strong in their eyes. Stand up!

Rasha   Why don't we leave?

The mother   Over my dead body.

Rasha   But mother, our life is in danger. The soldier might die.

The mother   To hell with him.

Rasha   You don't understand the danger we're in.

The mother   Do you want me to beat him so they have to cart his body away in the basket?

Rasha   You should know that our life depends on his.

The mother   What do you mean? Is he our guardian now?

Rasha   Listen to me. We are responsible for his safety.

The mother   How so?

Rasha   If he gets hurt, the Americans will burn down the house.

The mother   They already tore it apart.

Rasha   But we are still alive and breathing . . .

The mother   Breathing humiliation and disgrace.

Rasha   The entire country breathes the same air.

The mother   Do you want to leave our country?

Rasha   That's the answer. Ziyad ran away and our house is violated. Nothing is left but to turn our back on our country.

The mother   Life turns its back on those who turn away from their country.

Rasha   The world left us here, hanging between life and death, breathing fear and alienation with that jerboa.

The mother   For the jerboa, staying home is the hardest thing.

Rasha   But he is a jerbooooaaa!

The mother   A jerboa with a machine gun, bullets, and a poo bag.

Rasha *laughs and hugs her mother.*

Scene Two

Three young men *wearing ski masks are walking down a dark street.*

First   Is everything ready?

Second   Everything's ready.

Third   We planted a bomb on the road which delivers supplies to the soldier in Ziyad's house.

First   But the Humvee's late.

Second   Sooner or later it will come and take the hit.

Third   Let's wait. It will probably come before long. The *mujahid* has to have patience.[8]

First   I'm out of patience.

Second   It seems the Humvee has changed its route.

First   It's just running late. Why worry? The bomb will explode sooner or later anyway.

Third   It might kill civilians.

First   We win either way. The important thing is to keep the Americans from getting comfortable, and turn the people against them.

Second   The Americans sit on the people's chest while they suffer.

First   Then the people are better off dead.

Third   Let them die, but not by our hand. I'm not a murderer.

First   We aren't murderers! We are *mujahidin*![9]

Third   We're becoming killers!

Second   Stop bickering! I see a civilian car approaching.

First (*to the* **Third**)   How dare you say that, coward!

Third   We'll see who's the coward.

First   Coward!

Third   Shut up, murderer!

They fight. An explosion is heard. Blackout.

Scene Three

The mother *is listening to the news.*

Newscaster   Minutes before the American patrol arrival, a roadside bomb blew up a car and killed a family of five; meanwhile, the insurgents escaped.

Rasha   So that was the explosion we heard yesterday.

The mother   I knew it was for the American patrol.

Rasha   Americans are careful, that's why they survive these attacks while civilians die.

The mother   "And no soul knows in what land it shall die." Allah the Mighty has spoken the truth.

Rasha   Our land has become fertile soil for the seeds of death.

The mother   Seeds have already grown into large trees.

Rasha   Our land suffocates under a jungle of death.

The sound of a gun being dismantled is heard.

The mother   What's happening up there?

Rasha   It seems the soldier is cleaning his gun.

The mother   Let him clean himself first.

Rasha   They don't even give him enough water to satisfy his thirst.

The mother   Is he still a boy?

Rasha   I haven't looked closely at his face.

The mother   If he is a boy, why did his mother let him travel so far?

Rasha   As I said, for him it's just a job.

A voice from outside: "Um Ziyad . . . Um Ziyad."

The mother   Who is it? Um Haider? Is that you?

Um Haider (*confused and in haste*)   Hello, Um Ziyad.

The mother   Welcome, Um Haider. How are you? Please come in. Sorry for the mess. Everything has been a mess here since the black night the Americans searched the house.

Um Haider   Everything is a mess in this country.

The mother   Sit down and catch your breath. Rasha, prepare the tea for Um Haider.

Um Haider   No, thanks. I'm in a rush. I will drink tea with you on a happy occasion, *inshallah.*[10]

The mother (*to herself*)   Are there any happy occasions left? (*To* **Um Haider**.) What's the matter? Is everything all right?

Um Haider   We need Ms. Rasha's help.

The mother   Help? What kind of help? Do you want her to teach Haider English? She and I are at your service.

Um Haider   Thank you. Haider is doing well in English class, thanks to Rasha's help. But I came here about another matter.

The mother   Another matter? What's that?

Um Haider   I wouldn't ask for help, but it's for all of us.

The mother   Does the entire town need her? Please tell us what you want.

Um Haider   I don't know what to say. The Red Crescent came here with aid, and once the people saw the food rations, they broke into the Red Crescent building. The police couldn't control the chaos so they called the Americans and now we can't speak with them in English, so we need Rasha to . . .

Rasha (*furiously*)   I told you a thousand times: don't tell them I speak English. I don't want to mediate between killer and victim.

Um Haider   The situation is out of control. People will kill each other. There isn't any translator. Please . . .

The mother   We can't refuse your request for help, but you know the situation out there, and you know that Rasha doesn't want the Americans to know that she speaks English because they will want her to help them with everything.

Um Haider   But the people here know that she's an English teacher.

The mother   They know that she's a teacher who does her job at the school only and comes back home in one piece. You know what it means to get close to the Americans.

They're like the asphalt paver, with its scorching flames and poisonous stench. They don't smell nice, those cowards with guns. Their weapons stink of blood.

Um Haider   I know this, but we need her and we will protect her.

Rasha   I don't need protection from anyone. It's a matter of principle.

Um Haider   We all know your position, but necessity makes its own rules, as they say. I said what I came for and will leave it for both of you to decide. Now please excuse me.

The mother   Please wait.

She takes **Rasha** *aside.*

The mother   Rasha, what should I say? I'm embarrassed.

Rasha   Mother, you know what people think when they see a female translator.

The mother   But they are asking for your help.

Rasha   I'm not at their service.

The mother   We all need to serve the people. Go and help, but don't stay late. Finish your task and come back right away.

Um Haider   I'm very late. I must go back to help as best I can.

The mother   Um Haider, wait. We can't say no. Rasha will go with you but make sure she doesn't stay out late. The situation isn't safe. (*To* **Rasha**.) Finish quickly and hurry back. Watch out for car bombs and suicide vests.

Rasha   Don't worry, mother. I'll be careful and avoid traffic. Allah is the Protector.

The mother   Come back soon, my daughter. Don't stay long . . . (*To herself.*) Don't be like your brother. His friend came to see him that night. He said to me, "I'll be back in half an hour." Hour after hour and day after day have passed, but still no Ziyad. I feel his absence night and day. I wonder, where is he now? My heart says he is safe in a time without safety. Perhaps he left the country. No, no, my son wouldn't do that. My son hates to be away from home . . . my son . . .

She cries and sings a lullaby, "Dililol yalwalad yabni Dililol."[11]

What happened to your birds? Did they return to their cage? Or maybe they left because they can't stand the strange bird who roosts beside them. Maybe they returned, hungry and thirsty. How can my heart allow Ziyad's birds to die of thirst, starvation, loss, and homesickness? This isn't right. I must go up to check on them. What if the soldier on our roof doesn't allow me? He can't stop me. He is in my house. I am the owner of the house . . . I am the owner of the birds. But how can I go up? I haven't climbed upstairs in years. But I must do it, for Ziyad's birds. I must do it.

She moves with difficulty toward the stairs and mumbles to herself.

I must know . . . are the hearts of American mothers made of stone? How can this be? I must know. I will know . . . I will definitely know. Oh . . . I am tired.

The **Soldier** *detects the movement downstairs. He assumes a firing stance, pointing his gun in the direction of the movement.*

Soldier   STOP!

The mother *is terrified. Upon seeing her frightened face, the* **Soldier** *puts down his gun. Seeing the horror in her eyes, he tries to calm her down but she is still afraid. He apologetically kisses her hands. He sees her tears; he hugs her and cries. There is a long silence.*

The mother   Do you want to kill me? Why? Was that what they taught you in the army, to draw a target around a mother's heart? Don't you have a mother? A mother who misses you? (*To herself.*) Why am I talking to him? I don't understand his language, he doesn't understand mine. If he could understand me, I would ask him: how can their mothers stand being away from their sons? One of the poets said, "Wars break out, not on the battlefield, but in the hearts of mothers." Open my heart with your gun and you will find it shot through and through, blasted by war. I lost a son in the first Gulf War. He was handsome like you. He came back wrapped in a flag, while the national anthem played . . . a medal pinned to his chest . . . (*She laughs.*) What good is a medal, or valor?! I listen for his laughter, that used to ring through the house, but there is only silence. Then I lost my second son in the second Gulf War. He was martyred during an American raid. His body was ripped apart by a bomb from your country. And Ziyad has left us. When the Americans came, he said, "This is occupation," then he grabbed his gun and left. We have not heard from him since. Now you want to kill me. Kill me, my son. Kill me and earn a medal to give to your mother, who waits for you as I wait for Ziyad. You are young and handsome. How your mother must miss you!

The **Soldier** *takes off his helmet and goggles and cries silently.*

Soldier   I'm sorry.

A dove lands near the helmet. The **mother** *feeds it. The whole flock lands on the roof. She and the* **Soldier** *feed the birds. Then the* **Soldier** *empties his water bottle into a bowl and gives it to them. The* **mother** *smiles.*

The mother   Oh birds! You no longer have a refuge. Your nests are filled with weapons and so you must roost in helmets. I have to go downstairs but how can an old woman like me do so? I will try.

She gets up with difficulty. She looks downstairs but can't move. The **Soldier** *tries to help her, but she refuses. She moves, stumbles, and almost falls, but the* **Soldier** *holds her up and gently helps her down the stairs. When the* **Soldier** *sees the mess left by him and his fellow* **Soldiers** *downstairs, he looks at her, embarrassed and apologetic. The* **mother** *squeezes his hand in acceptance of his apology.*

The mother   Don't worry. We'll straighten up. Thank you. Thank you, my son.

The **Soldier** *smiles. He starts to go upstairs but she stops him.*

The mother   Wait—wash your face and wipe your tears. Wash up and take some cold water from the fridge.

She mimes to convey her meaning.

We're sorry the water isn't very cold. We haven't had electricity for six hours and the generator is out of gas. We couldn't wait in the long line for gas; as you can see, we're only two women.

The **Soldier** *refuses to take the water but she insists. He drinks. When he is about to leave,* **Rasha** *enters and is shocked at what she sees.*

Rasha   What's going on? What are you doing? Why is he here?

The mother   I went up to the roof to check on Ziyad's birds but I couldn't climb down on my own, so he helped me.

Rasha   We should give him a medal now, shouldn't we?

The mother   He's a human being, he has a mother who cries blood for his absence.

The **Soldier** *puts on his goggles and holds up his gun.*

Soldier   I'm sorry for coming into your house without permission. I'm here to protect you.

Rasha   Leave us alone—we can protect ourselves. We didn't ask for your help.

Soldier   But your leaders did.

Rasha   But your leaders think about one thing only: how can they steal our oil? How can they take everything from us? So we stumble on in poverty and ignorance.

Soldier   It seems that dialogue between us is impossible.

He wants to leave.

The mother   Wait a minute. I'm going to make tea, and you talk with him in his language. Then ask him to leave us quietly later. We're lonely women and Ziyad is gone.

Rasha   Dialogue is impossible between the branch and the bullet.

Soldier   I'm not a bullet; I'm a wall. This gun protects both you and me.

Rasha   We know how to protect ourselves. We might have been friends, but the gun . . .

The **Soldier** *sets his gun aside.*

Soldier   But I mean you no harm. See . . . I'm talking to you, and I'm not afraid.

Rasha   I belong to the land that you destroy. Your fellow Americans are pointing their guns at thousands of Iraqis, and they are my family and friends, my brothers and sisters.

Soldier   We've come here to spread democracy and liberate you from a dictatorship.

Rasha   You exploited a historical circumstance, so you came to save us with your tanks. Why have you stayed? Why have you allowed chaos to engulf our country, a country ravaged by war and sanctions, and lost in darkness?

Soldier   Please let me . . .

Rasha   If you had read a little bit of history, you would have known that your journey was a waste of time. You can't offer anything that you don't have. You, for example, are here only for your salary. Do you call this liberation?

Soldier   I'm bound to fulfill my duty.

Rasha   Is that all you care about? Following orders with no regard for human decency? Are you a puppet at the mercy of your government?

Um Haider *suddenly enters carrying a box of meat. She is shocked and confused to discover the* **Soldier** *and* **Rasha** *talking. The* **Soldier** *looks at the box with suspicion, but he excuses himself and goes upstairs.*

Um Haider   Sorry, Ms. Rasha. I just wanted to thank you on behalf of everyone, and give you this box of food.

Rasha   Thank you, Um Haider. I could have taken as many boxes as I wanted, but there are other people who are more in need than I.

Um Haider   Come on, take it. It's from the Red Crescent, not Bush's pocket.

Rasha (*sharply*)   I told you, there are people who need it more than I do.

Um Haider   But . . .?

Rasha   We don't want it!

Um Haider   Maybe your guest needs it. Or does he eat only pork?

Rasha   We don't have a guest. That soldier isn't our guest; he's been forced on us. He was helping my mother while I was away. Take the box and consider it a gift from me to you.

Um Haider *is surprised at* **Rasha**'s *firmness.*

Um Haider   Thank you. Give my regards to your mother. (*Nastily.*) Goodbye. (*She leaves.*)

Rasha   What a nosy woman! We'll keep eating each other's meat until Doomsday. That's why Allah has inflicted all these troubles on us.

The mother (*entering*)   I made you Iraqi tea . . . tea with cardamom. (*Surprised.*) Where's the soldier?

Rasha (*furiously*)   Say, rather, where is the jerboa?

The mother   What's the matter with you? Did something happen to you while you were away? What happened?

Rasha   Um Haider came just now with my share of the food aid, but when she saw the soldier she started in with insinuations—but I put her in her place.

The mother   Perhaps she wanted to reward you.

Rasha   I don't want anyone to reward me. I went to fulfill my social obligation, but only because you asked me to.

The mother   Rasha, you're upset. Did something bad happen to you?

Rasha   Everything nauseates and disgusts me.

The mother   Speak up! What happened to you?

Rasha   When I got there, people pushed and shoved as if there was a famine—famine in the land of oil.

The mother   We should forget about that black plague!

Rasha   Should we forget about our dream for a decent life, or even just fresh water?

The mother   The water is contaminated, the soil parched.

Rasha   Our souls are parched and barren—it's terrifying.

The mother   Not as terrifying as the rumble of American tanks.

Rasha   True. When I saw the Americans at the aid center, I was scared. Their hard faces frightened me, but once they saw we needed them, they seemed to relax a little. Then, a soldier greeted me kindly and asked me about the distribution plan. The Americans started to distribute the aid in an organized way, kicking out anyone who tried to cut in line.

The mother   All that's excellent. What upset you?

Rasha   Mother, let me finish. One of my students climbed the wall and greeted me, saying, "How are you, Ms. Rasha?" I was happy but also scared.

The mother   Why?

Rasha   When the American soldier saw the boy, he hit his hands with the butt of his rifle and the boy fell down behind the wall. I got angry and insulted him, and yelled at him wildly. He was black, his goggles were black, too, everything about him was black. I said to him, and to all his fellow soldiers, "You are monsters. Even animals are kinder than you. How could you hit a child like that?" They fell silent.

The mother   Well done, my daughter!

Rasha   I said to them, "I know why you hit him, because you are afraid, even of children."

The mother   What did he say to you? Tell me!

Rasha   He took off his goggles and brought his Colonel to apologize. They apologized sincerely. The strange thing was that when they took off their helmets, they looked like normal human beings capable of sorrow, and rational conversation. One of them started talking to me about how much he misses his family and how he got stuck here.

The mother   I know they are stuck.

Rasha   But they have the power to choose. Their people can protest and overthrow their government. Why do they blindly obey their leaders?

The mother   Now the tea is getting cold. Let's invite the soldier to tea with cardamom and cookies.

Rasha   But . . .

The mother   No buts. I made the tea for him and he will have it. It's from the new tea ration.[12]

Scene Four

The **Three men** *in ski masks stand on a dark corner.*

First   It's wrong for the American soldier to have free run of the house.

Second   True, he does whatever he wants as if he's in his father's house. We must stop this farce.

Third   Wait. We should think of a way to get him to leave.

First   What can we do? The soldier is very vigilant, and the Americans are constantly patrolling around the house. There's no way we can get to him.

Second   Let's knock the house down on top of him.

Third   What about the mother and daughter?

First   To Hell with them, they'll get what they deserve.

Third   But it's the house of our friend, Ziyad.

Second   And the wife of Lut, who did not believe and thus deserved Hell.[13]

First   And the son of Noah, whose father did not save him from the Deluge.[14]

Third   Rasha has served the whole town, and taught its children.

Second   But she ran to translate for the Americans.

Third   She did it because the people asked for her help.

First   What about the soldier, whom she talks to every day, and provides with bread and fresh water? He doesn't need his canned food anymore and tosses it to the children outside.

Second   They say he has grown fat and no longer takes a dump in plastic bags.

First   Why should he, as long as Rasha's bathroom is wide open to him?

Third   Brothers! Remember Allah!

Second   There is no God but Allah!

First   Our eyes are wide open and can see everything happening upstairs and downstairs.

Third   We have to think clearly. The soldier is here for Ziyad. We have to be logical.

Second   And do you want Ziyad to surrender, just like Rasha?

Third   If Ziyad had thought about what would happen to his mother and sister, he wouldn't have done what he did.

First   Why do you blame Ziyad and defend Rasha?

Third   I don't blame or defend, I only analyze.

First   Let's deal with this soon. It's up to us to sever the rotten limb from the body.

Blackout.

Scene Five

Ziyad's house. **The mother** *enters from the garden, holding a paper.*

The mother   Rasha . . . Rashawi. Did you drop this paper?

Rasha *reads the paper with astonishment.*

Rasha   Where did you get it?

The mother   I found it in the garden. Is it important?

Rasha   Disaster! Disaster!

The mother   Disaster?! What's the matter?! Is it from Ziyad? Something happened to him? Speak!

Rasha, *frustrated, sits down.*

Rasha   No, it's from Ziyad's friends.

The mother   Do they send news about him?

Rasha *drinks a glass of water, then speaks with difficulty.*

Rasha   It's a threatening letter.

The mother   A threatening letter! To whom?!

Rasha   To us.

The mother   To us! Why?

Rasha   Ziyad's friends think that the American soldier defiles the house. They warn us not to stay in the house because they are going to blow it up.

The mother   Blow it up?! Blow up my house! Impossible! As if they were firing a canon to kill a fly on a sleeping man's nose.

Rasha   Mother, they want his head no matter what it takes, even if they have to blow up ten houses.

The mother   Let them have his head! But what did we do? Where will we live?

Rasha   If we leave the house, the Americans will suspect us even more. Then they will remove their soldier and they will blow it up.

The mother   They will blow it up!

Rasha   We have to do something . . .

The mother   Speak quietly to the soldier, hopefully he can convince his superiors to withdraw from the house.

Rasha   Do you think they'll listen to him?

The mother   Just try, since we are all in danger, including him. Peaceful solutions are always effective, as they say in the media.

Rasha   Words, words, but in the end war settles the score.

The mother   Try for the sake of our house and home.

Rasha   OK. I'll speak to him.

The mother   What if you can't convince him?

Rasha   I'll show him the paper.

She goes upstairs. The lights are dim upstairs; downstairs, a spotlight illuminates
The mother.

The mother   What a disaster! With the American comes only sorrow. A disaster! Houses are like virgins; profaned if occupied by a stranger. Ziyad has left us, two lonely women. What are we going to do if they blow up the house? Where will we go? Our lives are here. My deceased husband and I built it with our hands, brick by brick. Everything in it is tied to a memory and echoes in the soul. How and where will we live? Perhaps it's not a serious threat. This is Ziyad's house and therefore belongs to his friends, too. How can they blow up their own house? Well, why wouldn't they? They will do it. That's why the American soldier should leave . . . he must leave, so our lives can go back to normal. He and his weapons and his friends must leave. This is the only solution.

Rasha *comes back downstairs, angry.*

Rasha   He wants to speak to his superiors about it.

The mother   When will he do that?

Rasha   I left him talking to them on the phone. He's sympathetic with us and doesn't want us to get hurt because of him. But he is just a soldier who must follow orders. He is a small cog in a big machine. We'll wait for a little while. Why is he here, anyway? They know for sure that Ziyad is gone. He might have even left the country, and we aren't a threat to their homeland security, not to the world. Rest assured. In a few minutes, the best solution for all of us will become clear. I don't think they mean us any harm.

The mother   Who?

Rasha   Either party.

The mother   We are unarmed and apolitical. Why don't they leave us alone?

Rasha   Mother, we are no longer free. Everyone is guilty and must be punished.

The mother   What's the crime?

Rasha   Being Iraqi. It's a serious crime, without a doubt. There are witnesses.

The mother   How could it be a crime to belong to a country?

Rasha   Belonging to a country like ours is an unforgivable crime. Mother, listen! An American patrol is coming for the soldier. It is coming to put an end to our torture. It is coming with our salvation.

A group of **Soldiers** *surrounds the house. A* **Sergeant** *enters the house. The American* **Soldier** *comes downstairs.* **Rasha** *and her* **mother** *disappear.*

Sergeant   I extend the Major's appreciation for your exemplary discipline and vigilance.

Soldier   Thank you, sir.

Sergeant   First, we're here to protect you.

Soldier   Thank you, sir.

Sergeant   And to ambush the terrorists that we want to eradicate, for the sake of America and the world. So, we'll withdraw from the house and wire it with explosives. When the terrorists come, they will be terminated. Any questions?

Soldier   What about the mother and daughter?

Sergeant   They'll be taken care of.

Soldier   Where will they live?

Sergeant   They'll be provided with a tent and supplies.

Soldier   A tent?

Sergeant   Don't any ask too many questions, soldier. A good soldier needs a hard heart, sometimes. The greater good calls for action. If we hesitate, soldiers die. For us, it's a matter of life and death—either kill or be killed. Duty requires us to strike proactively and decisively, not to loiter on rooftops, feeding the birds!

He laughs.

Soldier   I'm sorry, sir. What are my orders now, sir?

Sergeant   We want you to ask the mother and daughter to leave.

Soldier   Yes, sir.

The **Soldier** *salutes the* **Sergeant** *and climbs upstairs to speak with* **Rasha** *and her mother.*

Soldier   Thank you both, and sorry to bother you.

Rasha   We'll always remember you. Thanks to your superiors, who understand our desperate situation, and we're sorry we put you in such a difficult position.

Soldier   Don't be sorry. I should thank you for saving my life.

Rasha   You're welcome, but you don't have to thank us—we're grateful that you're allowing us to save our home.

The **Soldier** *takes off his goggles.*

Soldier   I regret to inform you that this house no longer belongs to you.

Rasha   What?

Soldier   The greater good requires that you both vacate the premises. Your lives are in danger. We want to protect you. This house is threatened from every quarter. It is our duty to protect you.

Rasha   But where will we go?

Soldier   We'll provide you with a tent in a safe place.

The mother *stops feeding the birds.*

The mother   What did he say? Why are you angry? Speak!

Rasha   Let me finish. (*To the* **Soldier**.) So, you haven't come to say goodbye?

Soldier   Yes. Goodbye. I will go back to the base, and you to your tent.

Rasha   Thank you. As I said before, dialogue is impossible between the branch and the bullet.

The sound of an explosion. The birds fly away. Curtain.

Notes

1   In Iraqi popular perception, keeping and/or breeding birds is a suspect pastime associated with burglary. The birdkeeper, on his rooftop, is ideally situated to spy on his neighbors.
2   *Halal* refers to what is considered permissible according to Islamic scripture.
3   A jerboa is a small, hopping desert rodent. The Mother's insult is comparable to calling the soldier a rat.

4   *Kafir* translates as "unbeliever" or "infidel." The word is commonly used to refer to non-Muslims, although in a broad sense it applies to anyone who rejects God. Whether or not it encompasses Christians and Jews (People of the Book) is disputed by Islamic scholars. Here it is used as a derogatory term.

5   In 622 CE, Mohammed and his followers fled Mecca for Yathrib, which would become known as Medina, to escape persecution by the Quraysh. The year of this migration, or *Hijrah*, would later be designated as the first of the Islamic calendar.

6   The Khan Jighan was a popular inn in Ottoman Baghdad. It was established in 1592 by the Wali (Governor) of Baghdad, Jighala Zada, and was also used as a grain storehouse. The Mother alludes to the open character of the inn, which was available to all travelers and allowed all manner of behavior, even licentiousness. In contrast, in Arabic and Muslim tradition, the home is considered a sacred, bounded space, deserving of respect.

7   Juha is a figure from Arabic folklore. In one story, he sells his house on the condition that he retain ownership of one nail. With ever greater frequency, he insists on visiting his nail, night and day. Finally, the new owner and his family move out in frustration and Juha reclaims possession of the house.

8   A *mujahid* is one engaged in *jihad.*

9   Plural of *mujahid.*

10 God willing.

11 "*Yalwalad yabni*" translates as, "oh, my child." "*Dililol*" is a nonsense word, perhaps derived from the English "lullaby." The repeated "l" sounds are intended to have a soothing effect.

12 Under sanctions and occupation, and even continuing after the withdrawal of US troops in 2011, tea was rationed.

13 Lut is the Arabic spelling of the Old Testament figure Lot. As related in the Quran, his wife was damned for refusing to believe that he was a prophet.

14 According to the Quran, one of Noah's sons perished in the Flood.

Introduction to *Cartoon Dreams*
Kareem Sheghaidil

I always think of how I might contribute toward making Iraqi theatre which conveys a humanitarian message, and which confronts the bitter reality within which my people exist; how to make a true theatre, in which the audience is faced with its own situation and is provoked to change. The theatre audience is shrinking in Iraq. They are offered only two types of theatre: firstly, farcical, shallow productions which lack intellectual content and artistic presentation, and secondly, "serious" plays. These serious productions are sunk by overly literary language that is both vague and delusional, and further hampered by a gloomy and exaggerated acting style. I have been looking for something in between these two, a theatre that attracts the audience with its moderate language, deep ideas, moral message, and authentic characters that represent the various classes of society; a theatre that interacts deeply with reality.

The current state of affairs in Iraq, since the fall of the dictatorship, with all its struggles, newfound openness, contradictions, and extremism, has produced new problems on a daily basis. The dream many have to travel has been oppressed and postponed for years, extending even to the mere thought of entering an airport. It has been exceptional, for an Iraqi, to even just possess a handful of dollars and a passport. The impractical intellectuals, frustrated soldiers, oppressed artists, and the extremists who declare themselves the guardians of thought and morality, all of them have contributed to the state and deepened the divisions within it, leaving the citizens to an unknown fate, tossed around by bloody conflict. Such a situation is ludicrous. Wobbly foundations are easily demolished. The Iraqi audience needs a space in which it can see what is hidden. We need to analyze the distorted version of humanity which emerged between the eradication of the oppressive regime and the establishment of a new, weak democracy, which was built on what was left. All of that inspired me to bring together a group of characters who are distorted in some way. I mean distortion here in a cultural sense. I bring them together to uncover their warped perceptions of themselves and others, and send them back to their past frustrations, after their flight collides with reality. I strip the veneer away from what happened and happens on all levels: political, social, and cultural.

For years, I have been engaged in conversation with various Iraqi actors and directors about these ideas. The concept for this play emerged in a café. The director Kadhim al-Nassar and I made plans for writing an ideal theatrical show, a black comedy or a political cabaret that would penetrate the surface of our confusing reality and reveal the source of its deterioration. Soon after, I wrote the script and shared it with al-Nassar, who responded enthusiastically. With his input, I revised it to arrive at its final version. Here it is in the hands of various readers, who may find our local problems to be of interest.

Cartoon Dreams was first produced in 2014 at the National Theatre in Baghdad and at the Jordanian Theatre Festival in 2015.

Cartoon Dreams

Kareem Sheghaidil

Characters

Singer, *female*
Soldier, *male*
Radical, *a radical, religious male*
Intellectual, *male*
Flight attendant, *female*
Captain, *captain of the airplane, heard over the PA*
Mysterious man
Voice over the PA, *in the airport*

The characters occupy an airport waiting area, which transforms into an airplane during the characters' collective dream. A spotlight illuminates the face of each character in turn as they dream, individually at this point in the play, of flying.

Singer   Aaahhh, if only I could fly.

She looks around at the others.

Everyone wants to forget everything, to leave it all behind and fly away.

Soldier   My bag . . . my passport . . . Yes . . . I'm going to fly! My bag is the most important thing. I have to make sure it doesn't get lost. Why am I carrying such a big bag, anyway?! No, no, it's important. Just shut up! Aren't you tired yet of carrying your soldier's duffel bag?! Oh man, just fly free. You've spent your entire life carrying a bag on your back. Leave everything behind and fly!

Intellectual   Aaahhh . . . I can't believe I am in the airport! I want to breathe pure air, free from smoke and pure. I want to fill my chest with high-altitude air, pure air, not polluted by anybody's bad breath. But you're not allowed to open the airplane window. Oh man! Fly first, breathe later!

Radical   I think they're all thinking of flying. *La hawla wala quwata illa billah.*[1] The situation is getting out of control. May God protect us! If everyone wants to fly, who will stay on the ground?

Singer   They say that there is music, dancing, partying, and lots of night clubs over there. Fun all night 'til morning. But so what! My voice is gone and my face has been invaded by wrinkles. Even my fans have forgotten me. Ah . . . my time is past. There's nothing we can do. I just want to fly. I can't believe I'm going to fly.

Soldier   I hope I can get a job, refugee status, anything. At least I'll live the rest of my life as a human being.

Intellectual   Everyone dreams of flying. We've spent our lives dreaming. Even dreaming was forbidden. We dream silently, and we don't share our dreams so we won't be punished. The time of the proletariat has passed, along with hanging on hooks. Now is the time to fly.

Radical   I might go on foot, or maybe by car. Yes, that would be better. All those people want to fly. Oh, how cheap you are! Always like that. You're used to riding the Tata,[2] which shakes like a train on uneven tracks. Oh come on, a man dies only once. Put your trust in Allah and fly like the others. So what if the plane crashes, we're all going to die someday. (*Mumbling in fear.*) I bear witness that there is no God except Allah, and Muhammad is the Messenger of Allah. I seek forgiveness from Allah. We surely belong to Allah and to Him we shall return.

Singer   Is it a big deal for someone to travel?! Female artists like me are always on the go, flying all the time, videotaping their songs while in the air. They aren't like me. Even when I get upset I can't croon even to myself, I'm afraid of being heard. Let me fly and I'll record my old songs. Oh my . . . I'm going to be famous again. Even if the song is trivial, it becomes original when it grows old. I have to become a star again. I will be the top story in the news. Men will tear their shirts off at the very sound of my voice.

Intellectual   Finally, I will travel, even though it's late. Never mind. The important thing is, I will wander through the great cities of culture, art, and literature. I will see all kinds of people, airports, cities, historical places, libraries . . . Aahh, I have spent my life in prison.

From the depths of my despair, I find it hard to believe that I'm in the airport now. I hope I can keep flying all my life. I want to go to an air-conditioned movie theatre, with a beautiful woman on my arm. I'm a bit old now for such things . . . then we leave the cinema to sit in a casino by the sea . . . aahh . . . we sip juice and I quietly reach for her hand, and no one interferes. Simple dreams. Daydreams that make up for years of deprivation. Even the cinemas are closed down, used as storage bins for scrap metal.

Radical   I am not sure whether it's *halal* or *haram* to embark on a plane.[3] Oh what the heck, we have no choice. Am I fortunate enough to fly and escape this heat and dust and to be treated for my asthma? And I can also have surgery on my eyes before I go blind. Where would I go if I became a blind man here? I would wander the streets aimlessly. I have seen the worst and I still have some sight left. Man, there's a paradise out there! I'm jumping out of my skin to see a plane, and to see how a passenger gets into a plane to begin with. If I were born there, I would have been an inventor of a plane, of a missile, or even an engineer or a physician. They have invaded the universe, and we are still arguing over what is *halal* and what is *haram*. In the end, *halal* is not *halal* and *haram* is not *haram*. Anyone can say that is *halal* or this is *haram*, as they wish. I seek forgiveness from Allah. Is it true that I'm going to fly?

Soldier   Hmmm . . . An old dream. How long have I dreamt of flying? From the moment I started to understand life, I hoped to travel, to fly with two wings. It doesn't matter where, the important thing is to fly. At least I can see the sea, I can walk without watching my back, and nobody will ask for my ID. Nobody will say "this is not allowed" anymore. All people dream of flying. Every one of us has been packing up his dreams in suitcases for years. Catastrophes delay our lives. Nothing is left. What is left is the smell of a helmet. Even travel has lost its taste. Oh, how we have dreamt of flying! But our heads hit the roof of the bomb shelter. Just forget everything and fly. Fly up high with your dreams.

The scene changes. The characters are sitting as if they are ready to fly in an airplane. The **Flight attendant***'s voice comes over the PA, as she demonstrates the safety procedures and welcomes the passengers aboard.*

Flight attendant (*over the PA*)   Ladies and Gentlemen, welcome aboard our flight, Happy National Airlines Flight 013.

There is a commotion among the passengers over the unlucky number 13.

Flight attendant (*over the PA*)   In order to ensure your safety, please fasten your seatbelts and tighten them over your laps. In case of an emergency, a life vest can be found under your seat. Please wear it. If an oxygen mask should fall, put it on. The emergency exits are located there, and there. In case of an emergency that requires evacuation, please proceed to the exit nearest you.

The **Radical** *jumps up in horror.*

Radical   Stop, stop! What's going on? Where are we?

Intellectual   Sit down, *yem awed!*[4] What's the matter with you?

Radical   Look, she's talking about emergency evacuations! What are we gonna do? Where are we gonna go?

Intellectual   This isn't new to us. We've passed our entire lives in a state of emergency.

Singer   Oh, poor man. It seems this is his first time on a plane.

Intellectual   Oh, as if *we* took a plane every time we traveled.

Radical   Didn't you hear what she said?

Intellectual   Brother, fasten your seatbelt and relax. Nothing will happen, don't worry.

Radical   Should I go back? I seek refuge from Satan. *La hawla wala quwata illa billah.*[5]

Soldier   The plane is taking off. Don't move!

Radical   Oh my God, my brain is shaking! Ohhh!

Intellectual   Brother, this is normal. It's the air pressurizing.

Radical   Pressure? Oh, father![6] My eyes are already ruined by diabetes, and now my blood pressure is rising. People, please, let me out of here! I've changed my mind.

Singer   This isn't a swing that you can jump off of.

Radical   Oh people, my head is going to blow up! My ears are blocked! Oh, my heart is going to stop! My sight is blurred. Oh people, I can't see! I'm going blind!

Singer   Someone help him! We have an emergency!

Intellectual   What emergency, for God's sake?! His blood pressure just went down a little. The flight attendant will give him some juice and he'll be fine.

Singer   Poor man, he's pale.

Soldier   Great, his heart might stop beating and we'll have a real problem here.

Intellectual   I told you that his blood pressure went down a little.

Soldier   And what are you, a physician, that you know this?

Intellectual   No, you don't need to be a physician to tell.

Soldier   Who told you that he has low blood pressure? He might have high blood pressure!

Singer   Ask for someone to come and check his blood pressure.

Soldier (*referring to the* **Radical**'*s condition*)   This isn't blood pressure.

Intellectual   What is it, then? A car bomb exploded next to him?

Singer   Shh! Be quiet!

Radical   Oh my God! What's this? A bomb under my seat?

Soldier   Dear God! There might be a bomb hidden on this airplane. (*Trying to calm the* **Radical**.) Sleep, sleep.

Singer   Please, don't turn the other passengers against us.

Intellectual   Can we just change the subject, please!

Soldier   It follows us, wherever we go.

Singer   Even when we're in the sky, it chases after us.

Soldier   We'll find them there having lunch in Paradise.

150   Kareem Sheghaidil

Intellectual   Of course! But we won't be allowed to sit with them. We'll be kept waiting at the door.

Soldier   Yes, because we weren't invited. If we go, there won't be any place for us at the table.

Radical (*jumping up*)   Where are we? Where are we? Have we arrived yet?

Captain (*over the PA*)   Ladies and Gentlemen, good morning to you. We are currently at 36,000 feet and at a safe cruising altitude. You may remove your seatbelts. The crew of Flight 13 wishes you a safe and comfortable trip.

Radical   Oh my God! 36,000 feet?! *Allahu akbar, Allahu akbar, Allahu akbar!*[7]

Singer   From the very beginning, I knew we were doomed. Yes, it's too high, 36,000 feet. Oh God, protect us.

Radical   What if he just descends a little bit and reduces speed?

Soldier   It's not a fighter jet, that can descend a little bit at will. Guys, just enjoy the flight. Don't wake us from our dream.

Intellectual   Yes, in 1963 I was thinking of travelling to Moscow. In fact, I was given a scholarship. They told me that Moscow was all snow, but it didn't work out. Those people came into power and spoiled our dreams. I should have gone then, but now I live in a different world. At least I could have become a translator. After that I was thinking about moving to Germany, after the fall of the Berlin Wall. I could have moved to Czechoslovakia, but it was ruined, too. Where could I have gone? To Darfur or Somalia?

Singer   No, don't go to Moscow. God only knows, the cold might have killed you. Even Germany, they say, is no good. And Czechoslovakia had its share of war and hardship. It's good you didn't go there, either. Darfur has nothing to offer, either, but Somalia! You could go there for the bananas. But they say that death walks in the street.

Intellectual   Well, I didn't go, anyway.

Singer   Oh no, why would anyone go there just to be killed?

Soldier   As if we are alive. You know, we're alive only by chance.

Intellectual   Yes, by chance we are still alive.

Singer   Our lives still have value.

Radical   Yes, we are valued by Allah. Oh, may God protect us . . .

Intellectual   Our life is but rented, and we are hiding from our landlord. We're meant to be here still.

Soldier   And by accident, the bullets didn't find our hearts. We're bleeding all over, but for what? The war grew up with us and made us old, but she never gets any older. She feeds on our flesh, and it keeps her young.

Singer   Forget it, leave the past behind, focus on the present.

Soldier   It's impossible to forget those black days.

Intellectual   Forget, *yem awed*, just forget!

Soldier   How can I forget? Can I forget the shrapnel buried in my body? Or the sound of the bullets still ringing in my ears?

Intellectual   I tell you, just forget it!

Soldier   How can I forget? Can I forget my friends who were buried alive? Or those whose limbs were scattered in the mud?

Singer   We beg you to forget, just forget!

Soldier   How can I forget? Why should I forget? We should not forget! We must always remember so we don't repeat the same disaster.

Intellectual   Who can say that it won't happen again?

Singer   And now we don't understand anything? It's the same death that's chasing us wherever we go.

Soldier   They're the same people who killed us before, and came back to kill us again.

Radical   What the hell are you talking about? What you're saying will make the pilot fly off his course.

Soldier   The executioner is always an executioner, but the victims forget.

Radical   And who sent you to war?

Soldier   Where have you been living, *yem awed*?

Radical   What do you mean?

Soldier   I hope you're not a captive from the First World War. I mean, where have you been living?

Radical   Where have I been living? In this country!

Soldier   No, I don't think so.

Radical   I was released from the army because of my bad health.

Soldier   Oh, you missed it, you poor bastard. You know, if you'd been in the army, we'd probably still be fighting.

Radical   And who says it's done?

Soldier   I mean that we were supposed to be victorious.

Radical   And who says we won't be?

Soldier   Victorious over who?

Radical   Over them. In the name of God, we will scatter their skulls across the field of battle.

Intellectual   Come on, people, let's change the subject. Let's discuss dialectics . . . the clash of civilizations . . . globalization . . . the Apocalypse.

Radical   This is the end of the world. Where are we now? We are in the sky, high above the clouds. Anytime now, the plane could crash. Isn't this the end of the world?

Intellectual   Forget about the end of the world for now—how about a song?

*The **Singer** goes to the corner and start singing.*

Singer   *Lefendi, lefendi . . . ayuni lefendi . . .* [8]

Intellectual   Back then, nobody went to bed without a book in hand. We had to leave very early in the morning just to get a newspaper. Even an old newspaper. The important thing was that we had traditions. In the evening, we went to the theatre, to the cinema at night, and in the afternoon we wandered the libraries. We used to draw, act, and write poetry and songs. We protested and demonstrated and fought until the sun came up.

Radical   Why did you fight?

Intellectual   No, we discussed. My friend, what's wrong with you? Is everything in your life a fight?

Radical   Life is an endless war.

Soldier   Of course! You don't care, it's always as if you're losing something. Only the poor are victims.

Singer   What good were your wars?

Intellectual   The cold war was . . .

Singer   What about it, did things warm up?

Intellectual   The strategic equation in the Middle East . . .

Soldier   We're fed up with this stuff. What good came from any of your wars?

Singer   All of the soldiers were wearing berets.

Intellectual   Yes, true. The phase required . . .

Singer   Nooses were hung everywhere in this country. People watched while bodies were dragged in the street. Not only were they watching, but they were singing, dancing, and cheering. Have we forgotten?

Intellectual   No, we haven't forgotten. Everything was confusing and unstable.

Soldier   Nobody could do anything.

Singer   Anybody who had come, we would have welcomed him hand-in-hand and hoped to get rid of the problem.

Soldier   Anybody who had come, we would have believed in him.

Intellectual   We were deceived and cast as victims. We have been well-trained in that role.

Soldier   People were applauding the executioner.

Intellectual   Applauding the victims, too, so that the executioner would stay the executioner, and the victims stay victims.

Radical   Could someone check where we are we now?

Soldier   There's a screen in front of you. (*Teasing.*) I wish we were in the Bermuda triangle!

Radical   Why do you hate me?

Singer   Oh my, the Bermuda triangle? They say it has swallowed a lot of ships and airplanes. Someone tell him to go around it!

Soldier (*still teasing*)   Oh, sweet. Now we're heading straight for the Bermuda triangle.

Intellectual   How many triangles and squares of death are there? And how many circles? This is death-engineering, and death-technology.

Soldier   Are we above Chechnya?

Radical   Oh God, Chechnya with its massacres and civil war?

Intellectual   No, guys, I think they've resolved their conflict.

Radical   How was it resolved?

Intellectual   Everyone picked a side.

Radical   And do you hate me, too?

Singer   I love you, my darling. I would die for you.

Radical   I seek refuge in God.

Singer   Why do you say that? Am I Satan?

Radical   Please, all of you, please! Our situation is critical. We are neither in Heaven nor on Earth.

Soldier   We have spent our entire lives hanging in between.

Intellectual   No, there's a big difference! We are now hanging between Heaven and Earth, and even though the skies are not clear, the path ahead of us is.

The flight encounters some minor turbulence.

Radical   What's that?

Soldier   Don't worry, it's just a little bump.

Intellectual   We're going to feel a lot of bumps. Before, not only were we hanging in limbo, we were also hostages.

The characters have various reactions to hearing the word "hostages."

Radical   True, we are being held hostage.

Singer   Oh my god, what will we do now?

Radical   What are they going to do to us?

Intellectual   They'll negotiate a ransom. We're just a commodity to them.

Soldier   We're stuck on an airplane in flight. No security, no safety, we don't have weapons to defend ourselves, and we can't jump from the airplane and escape.

Singer   They will surely slaughter us one after another.

Soldier   We have to be calm and clear-headed so we can negotiate with them.

Intellectual   Talk to them?

Soldier   We're innocent civilians. What did we do?

Radical   God, protect us from Hell's fires.

Soldier   Don't worry, they'll give you a ticket to Heaven.

Radical   They can't find another plane to hijack? Is it because I'm on this plane?

Singer   No, this is my bad luck!

Radical   What did I get myself into? I knew from the very beginning that we were doomed.

Singer   What are we going to do now?

Soldier   There might be a bomb on the plane.

The characters panic and start shouting.

Yem awed, where are they?

Intellectual   You can kidnap us now, and me, I could kidnap you. Anyone could kidnap anyone. Turbulence, turbulence, don't be afraid!

Soldier   I'll ask you a question, hypothetically. What if they were to tell us that the airplane would crash unless someone jumps out?

Singer   What are you talking about?

The **Intellectual** *laughs loudly.*

Soldier *(referring to the* **Intellectual***)*   Not him! He would jump with a parachute, and rely on his good luck.

Singer   What about you? You're a soldier and a hero. None of us can do it.

Radical   I can't, for health reasons.

Intellectual   Me neither. I'm above the legal age.

Singer   Me neither, I'm an artist. I can sing a patriotic song for you. *(She sings.) Ahne misheyene, misheyene, lel'harub . . . Ashigk' I daffe min adjil mahbubte.*[9]

Soldier   The war lasted for a very long time, and we got bored. We kept thinking it would end soon, but it went on forever so I started to fake injuries to get sick leave, and even injured myself just to get out of the war. In the end, I escaped.

Radical   Didn't they cut your ear?

Soldier   No, they needed us for the next war, so they gave us amnesty. And then I was actually wounded.

Singer   And then what happened?

Soldier   I was released. I couldn't believe that I was a civilian again. No beret, no boots, no orders. I could sleep as much as I wanted and I stopped having nightmares about death.

Singer   And then what happened?

Soldier   What happened? Another war. If I had run away this time, they would have executed me and charged my family for the bullets.

Singer   What happened after that?

Soldier   Then I was captured, and then released. Then poverty killed me. I worked any job just to survive, and I was degraded, humiliated.

Singer   Now you're turning your story into a Bollywood movie. Then what happened?

Soldier   I was taken hostage like you are now.

Radical   Kidnapped? I knew it from the beginning. Oh people, I can't see. I am blind!

Intellectual   We were taken hostage.

Radical   No, no, now we are hostages.

Soldier   People, we were born in chains, so we live poor and we die poor.

Radical   Oh people, I'm thirsty. My lips are very dry.

Singer (*singing*)   *Bithniyene ideye, ta'a'tesh wesher bak'mai bithniyene ideye.*[10]

Radical   I seek refuge in God. Could someone check where are we right now?

Soldier   Kandahar.

Radical   Please, watch your mouth.

Intellectual   He didn't say anything. He just said Kandahar. Don't you know Kandahar, Afghanistan?

Radical   Of course!

Intellectual   This is Kandahar. The tourist capital of Afghanistan.

Singer   Kandahar? Sometimes they call it Deathistan.

Radical   Now you've all become geniuses. I'm the only idiot here. My bad luck brought me here with you. Why are we going to Kandahar, anyway? I told you, we've been kidnapped!

Intellectual   It seems we have been kidnapped. What's below us? A desert? I'm afraid they'll drop us here, and we'll be eaten alive by wolves.

Radical   What did I say to you?

Singer   Oh, my God! Don't say that! Let me have just one more party before I die.

Soldier   Oh, what terrible luck if that happens.

Intellectual   Oh, kidnapped, hostages, whatever. What have we got to lose, anyway? Just the few years left of our lives.

Radical   Don't give up.

Soldier   What will we do?

Radical   Fight!

Intellectual   But what are we fighting?

Soldier   Okay, we'll fight, but under one condition: you must lead us.

Radical   Yes, yes, I'm ready. But the problem is I am unarmed and disabled.

Singer   I'm ready, too! I can sing patriotic songs for you all night long.

Radical   I seek refuge in God. I will pray for you two to win.

Soldier   The pilot isn't defending his own aircraft! How can we defend him? We're the passengers. Let's try another approach.

Intellectual   Let's negotiate with the kidnappers and come to an agreement.

Radical   That would be a surrender, a defeat. I reject that!

Singer   I'll dance to folk music.

The **Radical** *is horrified by the turbulence.*

Radical   They're coming to get us!

He tries to hide behind the seats. The **Intellectual** *holds him back.*

Intellectual   Where are you going, *yem awed*? It's just turbulence. Turbulence! Look, we might be victims of a conspiracy. We must identify the enemy.

Soldier   Is it a must to always have an enemy?

Intellectual   Even if there isn't an enemy, we must create one in order to remain vigilant at all times.

Soldier   So we can't even take a quick nap?

Intellectual   Governments create enemies to keep us busy. That's why they sometimes call you a traitor, sometimes a spy, and sometimes a collaborator.

Singer   In the name of the people, and in the best interest of the nation, we have made a revolutionary decision to protect the principles of the nation, and the decision is this: To execute the traitors, conspirators, spies, and cowards. And this decision represents the will of the people. And there will be no lamentation for the traitors.

Soldier   The prisons are full of people, kept there to protect the state. Genocides are carried out for the good of the nation. Torture . . . patriotic torture in chambers provided with the latest tools, made in the East and West, such as shackles, gags, cages, tasers, mass graveyards from the East to the West, wars, security, intelligence and special forces, guards, informants, spies, everything . . . everything! National security is at stake.

Radical   The most important thing is security.

Soldier   Of course, security! Security. All the young people fighting on the battlefield: let's congratulate them while the old ones wait quietly for their sons to be brought back to them dead, wrapped in a flag. Security . . . happiness . . . the lips of our old women have dried out, praying for their sons to come back safe or even to be captured rather than killed. Or even to come back as amputees. Security . . . happiness . . . There aren't any Iraqis walking on Rashid street now.[11] Only foreigners. They speak different languages. I looked for an Iraqi, but didn't see even one. Security . . . happiness . . .

Radical (*interrogating the* **Intellectual**)   Answer me quickly. Who are you working for, and who do you report to?

The **Intellectual** *does not respond.*

Radical   Your silence won't help you. You work against the best interests of the nation. Traitors, spies . . . We must liquidate you one after another, to rid ourselves of your evil.

Intellectual   But I haven't done anything.

Radical   Haven't done anything? I'll teach you a lesson. What about the books that we found in your house?

Intellectual   Those are old. They belonged to my older brother, may God rest his soul. We kept them in his memory.

Radical   Cut the baloney. We have information indicating that you're working with the enemy.

Intellectual   I'm being set up, sir. I'm a simple man. I come and go the same way every day.

Radical   How many times have you been imprisoned?

Intellectual   Before? I was imprisoned twice.

Radical   There you go! It seems that you've been a troublemaker for some time.

Intellectual   False accusations.

Radical   And you're still alive?

The **Intellectual** *laughs loudly. The* **Radical** *laughs as well. The two men shake hands.*

Intellectual   By God, I don't how we've stayed alive so long.

Radical   Our turn is coming.

Soldier (*to the* **Radical**)   Come here, come here. Why do you go to the mosque every day?

Radical   What mosque?

Soldier   Who do you meet every Friday?

Radical   Sir, I'm a drinker. What am I going to do at the mosque?

Soldier   Look, I've been told that you go to the mosque every day.

Radical   No, no, I go there to sell things.

Soldier   What do you mean? Are you begging there?

Radical   No sir, I sell rosaries and other religious items.

Soldier   So when do you go out drinking?

Radical   After I pray, right?

Soldier (*seriously*)   Speak the truth, you!

Radical   Do you want the truth? Sometimes when I'm broke, I go there to steal the shoes of the faithful.

Soldier   Which means you're a petty thief.

Radical   No, but I steal when I have no other options.

Soldier   What are you implying, that the government isn't taking care of you?

Radical   No, the government has nothing to do with it. It's just that I'm a bad person.

Soldier   Are you trying to say that, while the people are starving, the government is taking away our rights?

Radical   I swear to God, I didn't mention the government. I hold the government in the highest regard.

Soldier   Then why do you steal the shoes of the faithful? Is there no sanctity, not even in the mosque?

Radical   No, I don't pray and my reputation is quite impressive.

Soldier   Do you mean to say that the government is anti-religious? Oppressive? And preventing you from praying and fasting? Don't you pay alms? Apostate! Are you Arabophobic?

Radical   Do I have money to eat, that I would have extra for alms?

Soldier   Do you mean that the government is starving you?

Radical   The government has nothing to do with this.

Soldier   Listen, do you know how many charges we have against you right now? First, you're a petty thief, the punishment for which is execution. Second, you're attacking the government, which means you're offending the sovereignty of a nationalistic and patriotic country, and the punishment for this is also execution. Third, you're accused of agitating people against the government, which is high treason.

Radical   This is the Mother of all Executions!

Soldier   Shhh . . . Fourth: The country is at war, and you galvanize the people against the government, so you are accused of weakening the morale of the soldiers in this war, which is being fought for dignity and honor.

Radical   But the war is over.

Soldier   Which brings me to the fifth charge! How dare you say the war is over? Our war with the enemy of the nation continues.

Radical   I swear to God, I didn't know! I was released because of my bad health. I'm disabled.

Soldier   This is your sixth offense! You deserted during wartime.

Radical   Ok, I'm going to shut up now.

Soldier   And this is the seventh offense, idiot! Are you making fun of authority? Are you mocking the government?

Radical   *Yem awed*, just execute me already! When I pray, I'm a suspect. When I drink, I'm a suspect. And when I steal, I'm a suspect. So just tell me where I have to go.

Soldier   Look, you reap what you sow. So, you intend to leave the country? Ooohhh, I've got you now. You won't get away! Where do you plan on going? Who is your contact and who is funding you?

The **Intellectual** *takes a place at the center of a table, as if sitting as a Judge, the* **Soldier** *takes the spot of Prosecutor, and the* **Singer** *plays the role of the Defense Attorney.*

Soldier (*as Prosecutor*)   Listen, there are eight charges against you! Even if you're found innocent of one, you'll be found guilty of another. But . . . in accordance with international law, the court has appointed you a lawyer. So how could anyone accuse us of breaching your human rights? (*To the Defense Attorney.*) Please proceed.

Singer (*to the Judge, speaking as the Defense Attorney*)   Your Honor, I'm ashamed to defend this traitor and coward. This spy. I would rather ask that Your Honor apply the severest penalty for these crimes, so that he might serve as an example for others. And let me add to the charges a ninth. He now holds a grudge against us and expresses feelings of hatred in his heart toward us and toward this just and honorable trial. And we represent the people and the sovereignty of the law, which means that he hates the people and he doesn't respect the law. Look at him, Your Honor: Sadness holds his body and soul in a vice. Which means he harbors doubts about your jurisdiction and, in turn, he harbors doubts about the nation's competence and sovereignty. This is the tenth charge. *Wa salaam u aleyukum.*[12]

Intellectual (*as Judge*)   In the name of the people, we have reached a verdict. For the first crime, he will be hung by the neck until dead. As for the other charges, we reduced the punishment by executing nine of his family members.

The **Intellectual**, *as Judge, hits the gavel to mark the end of the trial. Silence. Funeral music fades in.*

Intellectual   Can you imagine we were living like that? Oh, father!

Radical   We're done with that past. We're past it now. Why do you want to drag us back?

Intellectual   Our past is unforgettable.

Soldier   We must remember it every day in order to keep it from returning.

Singer   Nobody will believe us.

Intellectual   People learned to tiptoe inside the walls. What was important was only to eat, drink, and sleep.

Singer   They didn't want to get involved with what was happening around them.

Radical   I suggest we confront the pilot, and ask him where he's taking us.

Intellectual   And who says it's in the hands of the pilot? Maybe the kidnappers are holding a gun to his head. And he's just following their orders.

Soldier   Maybe they pushed him aside and one of them is flying the plane.

Radical   It's not a Tata that anyone can drive.

Singer   But it doesn't even require a driver! Anyone can fly it. See how the pilot is swerving.

Soldier   There might be potholes or maybe checkpoints.

Radical   Checkpoints? I hope I didn't forget my military service documents.

Soldier   Wait a minute. Swerving? Since when has the sky road been paved?

Singer (*to* **Radical**)   And you, how long did it take you to set up checkpoints on those roads?

Soldier   To protect you.

Intellectual   It's one of two things: either the pilot is sleeping and the airplane is on autopilot, or he's tied up and they're driving.

Soldier   How do you know if the pilot is with them?

Radical   I suggest . . .

A **Mysterious man** *enters and scrutinizes all of the characters. He exits.*

Radical   I suggest that everyone sit in his seat and be quiet.

The passengers are quiet for a moment and then start speaking, one over the other in a panic.

Passengers   What happened? Who was that? Are we hostages?

The murmurs continue for some time.

Soldier   It seems that they are terr—

*The **Intellectual** covers the **Soldier***'s mouth.*

Intellectual   Shhh . . . Don't get yourself in trouble.

Radical   It seems that they are in control of the situation.

*The **Singer** puts on a* hijab.[13]

Singer   *La hawle wella quwete illah billah.*[14]

Radical (*referring to the* **Mysterious man**)   We don't know. He might be the person who will save us.

Soldier   I doubt it.

Singer   His face is scary.

Radical   At least we saw one of them.

Intellectual   And then?

Radical   Let's join him.

Soldier   What?!

Radical   Those people, they control everything.

Singer   We don't even know him.

Radical   He looks like the leader of the group.

Intellectual   You must be kidding. And everyone stay calm . . . this could be dangerous.

Soldier   What do you mean, dangerous?

Intellectual   We're in danger.

Radical   Do you mean that there's something wrong with the plane?

Singer   Do you mean we won't get to where we want to go?

Soldier   I feel as if the plane isn't moving.

Radical   Do you mean that it's broken?

Intellectual   What's broken is us, not the plane.

Radical   It would be best to join them.

Intellectual   This is the malfunction.

Singer   Now what are we going to do, people? Is there anything we can do? As for me, I'm an artist, a singer. I'm forced to do that. I'm forced to call out the names of fans so that they'll throw money at me on the stage.

Intellectual   This is the malfunction.

Soldier   We don't have a choice. Let's go with the flow.

Intellectual   This is the mal—

The **Mysterious man** *enters, and then exits.*

Intellectual   This is the right thing to do. (*To the* **Soldier**.) You know we can't depend on you anymore. War has exhausted you. And me, I was destroyed at the detention center.

Soldier   Then . . .

Intellectual   Then we wait.

Soldier   Again, wait?

Singer   Only waiting destroys us.

Radical   Waiting for the hour of salvation.

Soldier   But the airplane might have stopped. I don't feel it moving.

Radical   Tell me, does it run on benzene?

Intellectual   No, it works on oil.

Radical   White oil?

Intellectual   There's no such thing as white oil. It's all black.

Soldier   The world is begging for just one drop of oil, while we sit on a lake of it. But what's the use?

Intellectual   A dark predicament.

Soldier   We're like a rich person with a gambling problem. Having lost his fortune, he puts a lien on his house and lets his family go, banking everything on winning the next hand.

Intellectual   The gambler doesn't care, as long as he's playing, he thinks that he's going to win. Even if he destroys the world completely along the way.

Soldier   They're all gambling with our lives. We are what's at stake. If any one of them loses, another comes. Anyone who joins the table will win the first time, they will make sure he wins, until he is full of pride and becomes a cartoon hero that destroys all of us. Once his part is finished, they will tear him to pieces and throw him in the garbage.

Intellectual   It feels like we're living in an animated movie.

Radical   What does that make us?

Intellectual   Cartoons.

Singer   People, why talk about such depressing things? This is the best night of our lives. Would you please stop talking about politics? Tragedy is for losers. Can't we sing some more?

Soldier   Yes, indeed. A house with music cannot lose its joy.

Intellectual   A head without music? Cut it off.

Radical   Oh my god! Now we're cutting off heads!

Intellectual   *Yem awed*, it's just a proverb. How can we trust you if you don't trust us?

Soldier (*whispering into the* **Radical**'*s ear*)   Don't trust anyone.

Radical   There is no trust.

The **Singer** *takes center stage and the others put on* sidayer.[15]

Singer (*singing*)   Leffendi, leffendi ayuni leffendi . . .

The **Singer** *suddenly switches from a beautiful, traditional melody, to an upbeat, modern pop sound. The dancers throw down their* sidayer.

Singer (*singing*)   Hella billillab jobi, ennob ennob ennob.[16]

They are interrupted by the **Mysterious man***. He shoots a gun in the air and exits. The passengers hide behind their seats and we return to the scene inside the airplane.*

Radical   What were we doing? What happened?

Singer   Yem awed, we have been kidnapped!

Intellectual   It's just turbulence. What's the matter with you?

Soldier   You don't know that we fell into a hole.

Intellectual   This *arak* is tainted.[17] It's making us dizzy.

Singer   Arak? Or maybe the *jobi* is making you dizzy! It was just two shots in the air. He was trying to get you riled up.

Soldier (*swaying*)   You are the best singer in the world.

Singer (*swaying*)   You are the best at standing up and falling down.

Intellectual (*swaying*)   You know what? I'm just thinking, it's not appropriate for us to discuss this. But you know what? We were comfortable and having a good time. Let's discuss this later . . . You know the historical determinism affirmed by the bitter reality that we occupy. But this doesn't mean that there are no historical mechanisms crystallized in the concept of awakening. Which determines the paths of dialectics. And in turn the logical result . . .

He continues muttering to himself apart from the group, then realizes that he is talking to himself, but continues anyway.

Stop. Stop. Stop chattering. Just words, words without action. But what has passed is past. Now, what we have to do now. An embellished speech we learn from books and newspapers. It's useless. Where's the action? We couldn't, or haven't been able to, stop the bleeding and solve the problem. And we are still confused and spinning around. We don't know where to go. Enough.

Radical (*mumbling to himself*)   Qul' authu birab al'fellaq.[18]

Soldier (*mumbling to himself*)   The wealth of the nation . . . defeat . . . the enemies of the nation . . . the guaranteed victory . . . spies . . . traitors . . . long live the people . . . long live the President . . . long live the nation . . . and then what? What did we get? Look. This is the result. Let's consider the past dead. Shall we bury it and start again? We should not stay wounded and sorry for ourselves. We should think about what we have to do. How will we start over? Enough!

Singer (*singing*)   Hella billillab jobi, ennob ennob ennob. (*Speaking.*) That's where my problems started. I learned music and the *maqamat*.[19] And I dreamt that I would express myself through art. Lovely songs. Happiness and peace. But then I discovered that songs are burdened with sadness. And poetry flows from anguish. And step by step, songs became hard for me. Like a broken drum that gives you a headache. Enough. We shouldn't sing for just anyone. We have to warn the listener. Don't be kidnapped by fate. What have we done for the people? Sometimes we numb them. Sometimes we drive them crazy. And sometimes we make them kill each other. Where has goodness gone? Where has love gone? Enough. We have to wake up and escape from the past.

Confusion dominates the scene. The **Mysterious man** *enters and exits. An expectant silence.*

Radical   Where are we now?

Soldier   Wherever we land, let it be.

Singer   Has the airplane stopped? Or is it still moving?

Intellectual   What's the matter with you? The sky is cloudy. It's rainy and stormy. Please be quiet. I think we're in trouble.

Radical   Why not just admit it: we're hostages!

Soldier   Now it's clear, we are hostages. But we want to know: what will be our fate?

Singer   At least we know what to do.

Intellectual   I think this man works for airport security. And he's become suspicious of us.

Soldier   Why? What have we done?

Intellectual   They think we're going to hijack the plane.

Radical   What's wrong with us hijacking the plane?

Singer   You've made me feel uncomfortable, from the very beginning. Let's help the passengers. We can't be terr—

The **Intellectual** *covers the* **Singer**'s *mouth to stop her.*

Intellectual   Shhh . . . their suspicion will grow.

Soldier   I'm okay with hijacking, if that's what you want.

Radical   Bravo!

Intellectual   No! Our condemnation is now assured.

Singer   Are we going to start this again?

Intellectual   Let's say we hijack the plane. Then what?

Radical   Divide the shares.

Intellectual   What do you mean? Like everyone take a wing?

Radical   We'll sell it.

Soldier   *Yem awed*, are you serious? Where are we going to sell it? In the Thieves' Market?

Intellectual   You're officially all insane. Don't you see that once we're in the airport, they will arrest us for planning to hijack the plane? And the case against us will be irrefutable.

Singer   Yes, they will show us on TV and I will become infamous.

The **Singer** *assumes the role of a TV reporter.*

Singer   As the airplane was preparing to land, an armed group consisting of three men and a woman hijacked and diverted the plane. This is part of a worldwide series of hijackings. Accordingly, all airports in the world have shut down and are tightening security measures. Breaking news: Our sources report that the hijackers have not decided as of yet to which airport to divert the plane. Some sources indicate that there is a famous female artist on the flight. She was on her way to host one of her famous parties, held in capital cities from East to West.

Intellectual   Breaking news: It is reported that on that flight, there is a group of crazy people that will be delivered directly to a mental institution.

Soldier   Breaking news: The official spokesman for the hijackers reports that they have not yet settled on how to divide their shares in the hijacked plane. The analysts predict that the parties will not reach an agreement, and they might blow up the plane.

Radical   Breaking news: Reports indicate that the hijackers are supported by regional and international organizations. Many groups support their cause. In addition, some parties have expressed their willingness to negotiate the opportunity to refuel the airplane while in mid-flight.

Singer   On the other hand, other parties have expressed their eagerness to negotiate the purchase of the plane, and provide the hijackers with a crew of assistants and technicians, but the hijackers insist on reaching an agreement on how to divide the airplane between themselves before they reach their destination.

Intellectual   What kind of fate awaits all of us?

Singer   So, if the airplane has not been hijacked yet, must we do so? Haven't we said enough?

Radical   *Yem awed*, we've been working hard and making sacrifices to plan this.

Intellectual   So, since we've come this far, I want my share. But may I ask you a question first? When will we stop being hostages?

Soldier   Good question. But tell me this first. How will we carry out the hijacking?

Radical   We need weapons.

Soldier   Don't worry about weapons. That part is easy.

Intellectual   Easy. All you need is a razor. But tell me, where will you fly the plane to? Where will we land? And with whom will we negotiate? What are our terms? What about the other passengers? What will we do with them?

Radical   Anyone who opens his mouth—

Soldier   Easy man, easy. We haven't started yet.

Radical   Just make me the leader and you'll see what I'm capable of.

Singer   Oh, here we go again. Anyone can show up and stand on our shoulders and call himself a hero.

Soldier   *Yem awed*, that's enough. Let's stop this. Let's stay kidnapped. It's better than becoming hijackers.

Radical   (*scared*)   Oh man, where are we now?

Soldier   What's wrong with you?

Radical   Nothing.

The **Singer** *approaches the* **Radical** *and whispers in his ear.*

Singer   There's a group here who has smuggled weapons with them, but they want their share.

Radical   OK, we can split with them. Just introduce me to them. Our people are useless.

Singer   Listen, if you betray them, they'll blow up the plane. Don't go thinking that they're easy!

Radical (*to the* **Soldier**)   Listen, don't think that I'm alone here. Half of the people here are with me, and we have weapons.

Soldier   OK, go ahead, take the flight deck and take it away. What's stopping you?

Radical   But we already agreed on the shares. We'll live or die together, as you like.

The **Mysterious man** *enters and the* **Radical** *changes his tone.*

Radical   I will go with you to any place you want.

Singer   I'm with you. Don't forget me!

Intellectual   Don't forget that we were kidnapped.

Radical   Don't you remember what happened, or did you sleep through it?

Intellectual   Ok, I'm going back to sleep. It will take a long time.

Soldier   Until when? We're waiting.

Radical   People, where are we now?

Singer   Does this mean that we're going to sing again?

Intellectual   The historical determinism behind the fall of capitalism and the emergence of a new dawn of pro-literate and in accordance with the historical dialectics and the struggle of binaries and in consequence the result is civilized struggle ending in including the working class which will utilize the national economy and cultural capitalism (*He continues spewing illogical thoughts.*) Here we go, back to chattering. Enough. We have to know where we're going after we land at the airport.

Radical (*praying*)   Oh God, forgive us, have mercy on us, give us good health and abundance. And protect us from Hell's wrath. Forgive us, for you are the most merciful, the most forgiving . . .

He reads from the Quran. *Suddenly, he stops.*

Enough! Has everyone come here to control us? Enough!

Soldier   The interest of the nation, the enemies of the nation, I don't understand anything. What else can happen to us, worse than this? Let's stop and think about where we're going. Everything comes to an end. We shall not hold ourselves hostage. Enough.

Singer   What? We haven't learned anything from the past. What have the bureaucrats done for us? Those with the *sidayar* and Parker fountain pens. What have the berets done for us? Some were killed, some ran away. What have we understood of our lives? Look at what happened to us. Everyone is hiding in his cubby. We have broken the skin of the drum and we have stopped singing. We have forgotten music, the calm, gentle compositions. Our singing has been replaced with sad groans, and noise. For how much longer? Noise. Enough noise! We have to know what to do. We won't be held hostage until Judgment Day.

They talk to each other, but the discussion escalates between them.

Intellectual (*shouting*)   Enough! The nightmare has passed. Let everyone come back to his reality, and to himself. And see what he has done during this flight, and what he should do after it ends.

All the passengers quiet down and fasten their seatbelts. An announcement comes over the PA in the airport.

Voice over the PA   Attention please, attention please.

The passengers awaken and return to their places from the first scene.

Voice over the PA (*continuous*)   Attention please. Happy National Airlines Flight Number 13 has been cancelled and delayed indefinitely due to security concerns. We apologize to all passengers, and look forward to serving you the next time you fly Happy National Airlines.

The characters argue amongst themselves, becoming more and more physically agitated as they do so.

Curtain.

Notes

1   "There is no power except through (in) Allah." This saying is used to express discontent and to indicate that the situation is beyond one's control.

2   Tata is an Indian auto manufacturer. In Iraq, buses manufactured by Tata are employed for the cheapest available public transportation, used only by the poor and underprivileged.

3   "Allowed" or "forbidden" according to Islamic law.

4   *Yem awed* is an Iraqi expression that conveys a number of meanings, including, "you who have been and will be generous" and "you, for whom the years have passed but left you well." It is used in informal contexts to convey trust and, furthermore, it implies a certain level of intimacy based upon a shared Iraqi identity.

5   "There is no power except through (in) Allah."

6   "Oh, father!" is a common expression of dismay among Iraqis.

7   "God is the greatest."

8   The Singer begins to sing an Iraqi folk song that starts with, "The gentleman, the gentleman, my eyes are on the gentleman. . . ."

9   This is from a popular, patriotic song that was broadcast during the Iran-Iraq war. The verse translates as, "We are marching to war, as a lover defending his beloved."

10   From a traditional Iraqi song: "I'll cup my two hands to quench your thirst."

11   Rashid Street is one of the main thoroughfares in Baghdad.

12   "And peace be upon you." The Islamic greeting may also be used to indicate the end of a speech.

13   The "veil" worn by Muslim women. In Iraq, this is traditionally a scarf that covers the hair but not the face.

14   "There is no power except through (in) Allah."

15   The *sidara* (pl. *sidayer*) is a traditional Iraqi hat worn by educated men, mainly in Baghdad. It dates back to King Faisal I, who introduced it to Iraqi society, where it was taken up especially by those in government service.

16   The lyrics translate as, "Welcome to the dancer who dances the *jobi*, dance, dance, dance." The *jobi* is a traditional Iraqi folk dance, referred to here in an upbeat popular song. This reference indicates some ways in which music and dance in Iraq have changed in recent years. Originally, men only

danced the *jobi*, as a display of masculinity. Later, women joined in, especially at parties, thereby encroaching on, and altering, a traditionally male practice.

17 *Arak* is a Middle Eastern alcoholic beverage.

18 From the Quran: "I seek refuge in the Lord of dawn."

19 The *maqamat* refers to the melodic system of Arabic music, which consists of individual *maqama*, which are roughly analogous to modalities in Western music.

Introduction to *The Widow*
A. Al-Azraki

"The fault, dear Brutus, is not in our stars, but in ourselves . . . ."
—William Shakespeare, *Julius Caesar*

A belief in the humanistic and interventionist role of theatre leads me to focus, in my plays, on a crucial issue, that of the oppression of women in Iraq. *The Widow* is based on a true story of a relationship between a war widow and a young university professor who got her pregnant and ran away, leaving her to endure the awful consequences. Like many other victimized Iraqi women, she had to keep her mouth shut; to pursue justice in a society dominated completely by men would have been pointless. Instead, she struggled to overcome her haunted past by existing in a state of denial.

The Widow addresses an essential and substantial issue: the subjugation of widows in Iraq. In that country, one can uncover countless stories about violations against widows and divorced women. This play depicts the perilous social status conferred upon widows, who are victimized by practices embedded in patriarchal structures, and shaped by traditional biases and religious prejudice. In this regard, *The Widow* destabilizes the concept of *ghira*, which serves as a central pillar of the belief system of many Arabs, and Iraqis in particular.

Although the word *ghira* literally means "jealousy," it can also be translated as "chivalry," which connotes nobility, courage, honor, and morality. It is associated with masculinity, patriarchy, and male-centricity, and may refer to defending one's country, home, and honor, and to helping the needy. However, the most common usage of *ghira*, in Iraq in any case, refers to a man's obligation to defend and protect a woman's honor at any cost. An apocryphal event from Arab history serves as the exemplar of this. An Arab woman, held captive in Amorium, cried out the name of the Abbasid Caliph al-Mu'tasim bi'llah. Upon hearing of her plea, he mobilized his army and freed her from the Romans. Whether or not this story has any historical basis, it functions as a primary impetus for *ghira* in the Arab, and particularly Muslim, collective memory.

On the contrary, one can see that many women, especially after the Iraq War in 2003, are frequently harassed, abused, or sexually exploited. What kind of *ghira* allows men to target divorcées and widows and exploit them? What kind of *ghira* allows female students to be blackmailed by their "boyfriends," who threaten to post their naked pictures or videos online if they try to break up with them? Where is the *ghira* when hundreds of displaced women are begging in the streets and being sexually abused by men? What kind of *ghira* allows for the assault of hundreds of fleeing Romani dancers on a daily basis in Syria (prior to the civil war), Jordan, Lebanon, and the United Arab Emirates? Where is the *ghira* when thousands of Iraqis (men and women), living in the West, dance and party while singing "*Ehna Ahl al-Ghira*"—"We are the people of chivalry"—while their country is bleeding and in urgent need of their help?

I would like to conclude by recounting an incident that occurred following the production of *The Widow*. A female Syrian director came to me and asked, "Why did you show them our shit?" By "them" she meant the Western audience, and by "our" she meant that which belongs to Arabs. Another Arab critic noted that my play reinforces the stereotypical image of the Arab man. Although I disagree with his observation, if a realistic representation is seen as equivalent to the stereotype, then overlooking it is even worse. The play is based on a true story, of a kind which is imposed on women in Iraq every day. Whether or not I am reinscribing the stereotype, what matters most is that I am revealing the truth.

The Widow premiered on 7 August 2014 at SummerWorks Festival, Scotiabank Studio Theatre, Toronto, Canada.

The Widow

A. Al-Azraki

Characters

Nour, *the widow*
Hatem, *her deceased husband*
Hadi, *a professor*
Mother, *Hadi's mother*
Father, *Hadi's father*
Ali, *a student in Hadi's class*
Ahmed, *Hadi's friend*
Two Gunmen

Prologue

In the opening darkness, sounds of battle—aircraft, explosions, heavy weapons. As sounds fade, the figure of a man appears, in military uniform, heavy-set, with a beret like the one Saddam Hussein used to wear, mainly in silhouette. Light slowly rises on **Nour**, *veiled in the Iraqi* abbiya, *as she addresses the silhouetted figure. She speaks haltingly, with pauses.*

Nour   It's nearly two years, my darling. So much has happened. Terrible things. Can you see us? Can you see your beautiful daughter? Do you even know about her? I have missed you so much, Hatem. You were so loving to me. (*Pause.*) You said you were the lucky one, to find a beautiful, young, second wife. And I thought so too. But I was the lucky one, Hatem, to find a man so kind and loving. You were so kind to me and so patient. And I came to love you very much. Did you know that, Hatem? Did I let you see that? I was always a bit shy with you, I'm afraid. And then you were killed. (*Long pause.*) Hatem, I have to tell you . . . that I want . . . that I want to be loved again. It's been two years, and I've been faithful to your memory, but there is a young man that I like, he teaches at the college where I'm taking night courses again, like you wanted me to. And I think he likes me. I make him nervous. He's so young. He thinks I'm "an Older Woman." (*Pause.*) Would it make you very sad?

The silhouetted figure rises, kisses her on the forehead, and exits. Lighting change. An overlapping, brief scene reveals **Hadi** *in the closing moments of a lecture. He holds up a text and addresses the audience as a class of students.*

Hadi   So for next time I want you to read the play *Nine Parts of Desire*, by the American-Iraqi playwright Heather Raffo. Be prepared to talk about how she represents the situation of Iraqi women, and whether, in your opinion, that representation is truthful and appropriate.

He crosses to the area indicated as his office.

Scene One

Hadi's *office.* **Nour** *is standing in front of* **Hadi**, *who sits at his office desk, looking busy.*

Nour   Good afternoon, sir. May I speak to you for a moment?

Hadi (*uncertainly*)   Oh, yes? Come in. It's . . . Nour, isn't it? How can I help you?

Nour   Well, you see . . .

Hadi   Won't you sit down?

Nour   Thank you, sir.

Hadi   So?

Nour   It's about your class.

Hadi   The drama course?

Nour   Yes. (*Pause.*) I'm having some difficulty . . .

Hadi What sort of difficulty?

Nour I have difficulty taking in what you're saying.

Hadi Am I talking too fast?

Nour No, it's just that . . .

Hadi What then?

Nour I just want to tell you that I can't understand you in class because I am distracted by my feelings towards you.

Hadi What? Are you out of your mind?

Nour I have to tell you that I find you very attractive. Sir.

Hadi Oh my God!

Nour I've been wanting to let you know for several weeks.

Hadi You have to leave my office. Please! Go!

Nour Don't be nervous, sir.

Hadi Now!

Nour *exits. Now at home, she picks up the phone to call her sister.*

Nour Rana? It's Nour. Rana, I went to his office today. Don't you remember? My handsome and intelligent man! My professor, the man of my dreams, Hadi. I went to his office to meet with him. He tried to keep a distance and not look me in the eye. He was so scared, I wanted to laugh! He tried to be really angry and proper, but I know he likes me, really. Guess what? I think he's a virgin. Oh Rana, don't be such a prude!

Scene Two

Hadi *and* **Nour** *at Hussein's place.*

Nour Whose place is this?

Hadi My friend Hussein's.

Nour Does he know?

Hadi Not really.

Nour Does he?

Hadi Yes.

Nour What did you tell him?

Hadi That I was bringing . . . a friend.

Nour A friend. And what did he say?

Hadi "Be careful."

Nour Ah yes. You must. Of course. (*Pause.*) Now what?

Hadi   Are you shy?

Nour   No. Are you?

Hadi   Of course not. (*Pause.*) I thought you weren't coming.

Nour   It wasn't easy getting out of the house.

Hadi   What did you tell your family?

Nour   I told them I'm going to bring my daughter home from day care.

Hadi   You must see me differently now.

Nour   In some ways.

Hadi   How?

Nour   Yes, in class you're really different. Trying to be strong and intelligent.

Hadi   "All the world's a stage, and all the men and women merely players."

Nour   "And one man in his time plays many parts."

Hadi   Very good! My teaching hasn't been in vain.

Nour   I remember everything you say. (*Pause.*) But being a player doesn't make you sincere.

Hadi   Sincere about what?

Nour   About our relationship.

Hadi   We haven't started yet.

Nour   I'm here, aren't I? (*Pause.*) I need to know: are you a serious man or a player?

Hadi   Love does not come that fast.

Nour   Maybe a player.

Hadi   Let's just have fun.

Nour   Fun?

Hadi   Well, you know . . .

Nour   Sex, you mean.

Hadi   Why not?

Nour   Yes, why not? I'm a widow. Not a virgin anymore.

Hadi   What do you mean?

Nour   You know what I mean. Yes. Why not? "Just have fun."

Hadi   You know I can't promise anything.

Nour   I'm not asking you for anything.

Hadi (*uneasily*)   I think perhaps we should go.

Nour   Wait! (*She holds his hand.*) I need you.

Hadi   Why?

Nour   Everyone is against me.

Hadi   How?

Nour   Being a widow . . . you know . . . Men look at me differently when they know I'm a widow. They think widows are only good for sex. I just want to live my life! Like any other woman.

Hadi   Successful and happy. And free.

Nour   Exactly.

Pause.

Hadi   Not possible in Basra, I'm afraid.

Nour   Saddam's regime was more supportive of women in some ways.

Hadi   Saddam was a killer!

Nour   And now we have many killers. Every day the body of a woman thrown into the river. Rumours spread: indecent, prostitute, a traitor working for the occupation, honour killings. Saddam's time was better.

Hadi (*angrily*)   Better?! Seriously! Better! How? Wars, mass graveyards, ethnic cleansing . . . That was better? Young men were begging in the streets, widows selling themselves, while the President and his family enjoyed the most extravagant life by stealing the wealth of the country. And feeding the people patriotism. If the Americans hadn't invaded, we'd still be living in misery.

Nour   We still are.

Hadi   Not the same way.

Nour   The Americans killed my husband.

Silence.

Hadi   I'm sorry.

Nour   That's alright.

Hadi   I didn't bring you here to argue about politics.

Nour   No. (*Pause.*) So why did you "bring me here?"

Hadi   You know why.

Nour   So tell me.

Hadi   Well . . . to . . .

Nour   To have sex with me? (*Pause.*) It's alright. I want that, too.

Hadi   Tell me why you chose me?

Nour   I think you can make me happy.

Hadi   Are you unhappy?

Nour   I just want to feel safe again.

She cries.

Hadi   No, please don't cry! Do you know that song?

Nour   Sorry, which song?

Hadi   "Don't Cry!" Guns 'n' Roses. (*Sings.*) "Talk to me softly, there's something in your eyes. Don't hang your head in sorrow, and please don't cry."

Nour   Can I trust you?

Hadi   Yes. Yes, you can.

Nour   Hadi . . . Is this your first time? Have you never had a woman? Don't worry. Come. Undress me.

Scene fades to black. Music: "Don't Cry" by Guns 'n' Roses.

Scene Three

Hadi (*on the phone*)   She did everything I wanted . . . everything. Thanks for the place, man. I gotta get your keys back to you. When are you coming back to town? OK. Yeah, yeah. I don't know, thirty maybe? In love? Are you serious?! I told you, she's a widow with a two-year old daughter. Maybe I feel sorry for her. What? No, no, I am so careful, man! Anyways . . . yeah, ok. Will see you then. OK bye.

Nour (*on the phone*)   Yes, Rana we are, and I don't care what you think, so don't start lecturing me. Because I want to. Because it's been two years. *Two years!* Well I'm sorry, and that's too bad. (*Pause.*) Is that so terrible? (*Pause.*) You're saying that if Karim died, God forbid, you would never want to be with a man again? (*Pause.*) And if you died, you would expect Karim . . . ? *Why is it different?* Why, why is it different? (*Pause.*) Yes, of course I know that. Everything is controlled by them. (*Pause.*) Yes, Rana, we are in love. How do I know? I know, alright? We spend hours talking on the phone, and we see each other at least twice a week.

Longer pause. **Nour**'s *sister asks whether* **Nour** *thinks her illicit lover will marry her.*

Nour   Yes, I think he will. I do, Rana. He's an honorable man.

Scene Four

Corniche al-Basra, a street that runs along the Shatt al-Arab.[1] *Music.* **Nour** *and* **Hadi** *walking.*

Nour   If anyone of my family sees me, I'll be in a serious trouble.

Hadi   It was your idea that we go out together.

Nour   Better than skulking around in your friend's house all the time. Like criminals.

Hadi   Criminals?

Nour   This way feels like we're a normal couple, not guiltily hiding our love.

Hadi   Do you like it here, by the river?

Nour   I love it.

Hadi   Haven't you ever been here before?

Nour   Not for a long time.

Hadi   My dad used to bring me here when I was a child. We would always visit the statue of al-Sayyab, and my dad would tell me about his life, and recite these poems: (*In Arabic?*) "Your eyes are two palm tree forests in early light,/ Or two balconies from which the moonlight recedes."

Nour   "When they smile, your eyes, the vines put forth their leaves,/ And lights dance . . . like moons in a river."

Hadi   Oh my God, you know them, too!

Nour   Of course.

Hadi   Childhood full of paradoxes: sadness and happiness, wars and killings on the one hand, and love and poetry on the other. Like the whole history of this sad country.

Nour   My dad brought the whole family twice to Shatt al-Arab. We were children, riding the boat, singing and clapping. Seems so long ago, but what is it? Fifteen years? And we grew up so fast, and everything changed. Nobody sings or claps anymore. Not even children.

Hadi   Look at the river. So beautiful, huh?

Nour   Yes. Even though it's polluted by the oil tankers, and full of sewage.

Hadi   One of the oldest civilizations on earth and we're still so far behind. Worse than that, everyone here is blaming the Americans and the invasion.

Nour   It's an essential factor. You can't ignore it.

Hadi   I don't ignore it. I just don't think you can use it to explain everything that's wrong with this country—the corruption, deceit, killings, divisions . . .

Nour   Good people are either silenced or have escaped the country. Meanwhile, hypocrites have seized the chance to take power. This used to be a secular society. Now suddenly religion has become fashionable again. Fundamentalism has become mainstream.

Hadi   God, it's too depressing. Let's change the subject. (*Pause.*) Do you know what I wish now?

Nour   What do you wish, my love?

Hadi   I wish we were in America or Europe, so I could kiss you in public.

Nour   You are a romantic, *habibi*.[2] Do you think about leaving?

Hadi   All the time. I'm going to do it, sooner or later.

Nour (*teasingly*)   Will you take me with you?

She looks at her watch.

Habibi, it's almost nine, I must go home.

Hadi   You go ahead and I'll keep you in sight.

Nour   "Goodnight, goodnight. Parting is such sweet sorrow,/ That I shall say goodnight till it be morrow."

Nour *kisses him quickly and discreetly and then leaves.* **Hadi** *watches her go, and then follows.*

Scene Five

A classroom. **Hadi** *addresses the audience as well as* **Nour** *and* **Ali**.

Hadi   Good afternoon. Thank you for all being here—and on time. I take it as a compliment. Alright. Let me see a show of hands. How many of you managed to read *9 Parts of Desire* by Heather Raffo? (*Seeing a good number of hands.*) Good! That's excellent. So today I'd like to hear what you have to say about the play. As an Iraqi reader, living in Iraq, do you *respect* the play, as a depiction of life in this country? What are the strengths and weaknesses of the play? Do you find it interesting, clichéd, realistic, idealistic, and how? Who will start us off? Anyone?

Nour *puts her hand up.*

Hadi   Nour?

Nour   I think the play is far from being authentic. Who is Amal? When I read her story, I had to laugh because it was so extremely far-fetched: a Bedouin marrying an Iraqi man, then leaving to London where she catches him with another woman? Then she leaves for Israel and becomes a second wife? Really? Then she comes back to Baghdad, where she begins a phone relationship with a friend of her ex-husband, then meets him in Dubai? Then she leaves for London again? Like what . . . ? Like she's Sinbad? Maybe this is believable for an American audience but for us it's absurd. She ignores the majority of the Iraqi women who suffer unbearable conditions, and focuses on an artist, whose past is suspicious at best, on a drunk communist in exile, and on a totally inconceivable character like Amal.

Hadi   Well, that's a pretty severe judgment! Anyone else?

Ali *puts his hand up.*

Hadi   Ali?

Ali   I kind of agree with Nour. I think her representation of Iraqi women is too selective. She tries to challenge the stereotypical, orientalist image of the Iraqi woman, but it's not an accurate portrayal.

Hadi   I'm really impressed by your critical opinions about the play! After all, what makes a literary work successful are the diverse interpretations and perspectives it provokes. Good texts are always open to independent interpretations.

Ali   Including sacred texts?

Hadi   Yes, even sacred texts.

Ali   Like the Quran?

Hadi   Exactly! We have to have the freedom to interpret it according to our best judgment.

Ominous pause.

Ali   But sir, this is blasphemous. There can only be one truthful interpretation of the Quran.

Hadi   What about the different interpretations of the Quran by the Shia and Sunnis?

Ali   But they agree on one truthful interpretation of the essentials. Especially about Heaven and Hell.

Hadi   Well, let's look at that. How do you understand the accounts of Heaven and Hell in the Quran?

Ali   I believe that there will certainly be Heaven or Hell, for the righteous and for sinners when we die. Don't you, sir?

Hadi   Not in the way described in the Quran, no.

Ali   So, you don't believe in the truth of the Quran? Sir.

Hadi   I believe in the human values incorporated in the Quran, but not in the literal description of Heaven and Hell. For me, the Prophet . . .

Ali   Peace be upon him.

Hadi   . . . created these descriptions as a strategy, either to intimidate or seduce Arabs who lived in the desert, to make them believe in God and leave their savage manners and pagan beliefs.

Nour   I agree! I think belief in Hell contradicts the main foundation in Islam, which is Divine Justice. How can a person be tortured in Hell for eternity because he commits, for example, adultery or sodomy or even stealing or lying? A punishment must fit the crime . . . an eye for an eye. This is justice, not to be burned in Hell forever for something so trivial. I mean, where is justice in that?

Ali   You call adultery and sodomy trivial? Trivial? Shame on you!

Hadi   Even Heaven, look at the descriptions! Rivers of wine and honey, untouched virgins, fruits of every kind. The Prophet . . .

Ali   Peace be upon him!

Hadi   . . . appealed to those poor desert Arabs with things they could only dream of. They lived in an arid environment, a desert, where honey, wine and women were their utmost wishes. For people of our era, the descriptions are childish.

Ali   So you're insinuating that the Prophet, peace be upon him, "created" the Quran? Made it up?

Hadi *becomes suddenly guarded, realizing that he's in dangerous territory.*

Hadi   Well, no, certainly, I mean, I'm not saying that.

Ali   Sir, this is very shocking.

Hadi   Listen, it's my interpretation. I could be wrong. It is just my perspective. Nietzsche says, "There is no such a thing as a truth, there is only perspectivism."

Ali   Excuse me sir, but you are interpreting the Quran by applying Western theories. This is a fallacy.

Nour   He is trying to rationalize it.

Ali   Oh yes, we know that you're always taking his side. Western thinking has poisoned our spirituality and faith.

Nour   The West is far ahead of us intellectually, hundreds of years.

Ali   This is not true! Look at America now! What do you see? Poverty, unemployment, and violence. Their life is merely sex, drugs, and guns.

Nour   You are talking as if we don't have any problems in our society.

Ali   No, I just disagree with you; they are neither ahead of us nor better than us.

Nour   You always disagree, just to show . . .

Ali   And you! You're always agreeing with his immoral, atheistic ideas. Yes, and we know why, don't we! You should be ashamed. You are an immodest woman.

Nour   How dare you speak to me like that!

Ali   We all know what we know.

Hadi   Please, please. Enough. I'm going to have to call a halt to this discussion for today. We are straying too far from our original topic.

Scene Six

Hadi's *house, the kitchen.* **Hadi**, *his* **Father**, *and his* **Mother** *sitting around a table, having dinner.*

Father   So Hadi, how's the teaching going?

Hadi   It's going well, I think. I hope.

Mother   I'm so proud of you, Samouri. My son, the professor!

Father   The English professor! What English are you teaching, exactly? My colleagues keep asking me, and I'm never sure what to say.

Hadi   Shakespeare and Modern Drama.

Father   Well. I will tell them. And as your mother says, we're very proud.

Hadi   Thanks, Dad; I hope you feel that your efforts have paid off.

Mother   So. Now you need to complete the other half of your life and religion.

Hadi   I know what you're saying, Mom. But I think I'd rather wait for perhaps another year or two.

Father   Don't wait too long! You know what they say: Get a life, get a wife.

He laughs.

Hadi   I know, I know. One step at a time!

Mother   You're not a boy anymore. I want to see your children before I die.

Hadi   God forbid. You'll see them, and you'll raise them up in this house.

Mother   That's my son.

Father   Sure, but why not now? You have a permanent job and . . .

Mother   Maybe he hasn't found Mrs. Right.

Father   What do you mean? He teaches at the university! He can pick the prettiest woman, and she won't say no to him.

Hadi   I can't marry a student.

Mother   What about Mariam? She's gorgeous, and she'll be a doctor soon.

Hadi   She's my cousin! And she's still a student.

Father   So wait until she graduates.

Hadi   I need to be in love before I get married.

Father   Sure, sure. Like father, like son.

Hadi   Exactly. You chose mom yourself. It wasn't an arranged marriage, was it?

Father   Oh no! We were in love before we got married.

Mother   Are you going to tell the story again?

Father   Why not? Your mother feels shy whenever I mention our love story.

Hadi   I want to hear it again.

Father   She was gorgeous.

Hadi   She's still gorgeous.

Father   I agree.

Mother   Oh come on, you two!

Father   I used to wait for her in front of her high school. I was handsome . . .

Hadi   You're still handsome.

Mother   I agree.

Father   Back then I was really handsome.

Mother   Listen to him!

Father   I used to wear my suit and walk her as far as Abu Ahmed's shop, which was close to her family house.

Mother   One day, my father, God bless his soul, saw him following me, and—(*She laughs.*)—your father ran away like a deer.

Father   Man, I was scared.

Mother   My father asked, "Who is he?" I said, "I don't know. I can't help it if he follows me."

Father   He came to my father and said, "If I see your son following my daughter again, I'll break his head open."

Hadi   So what happened?

Father   My dad took me to his room and asked me, "Do you love her?" I said, "Yes, I do." And then he asked, "Does she love you?" I replied, "Yes, dad, I think she does." "Then let's go and ask for her hand!" I couldn't believe it. I thought he was joking.

Mother   When I opened the door to them, I was really shocked! I thought something horrible was going to happen. Then a crowd of women came. Your dad smiled and said,

Mother and Father   "Just say yes when they ask you."

Father   So we got married, and we went to Istanbul for the honeymoon.

Hadi   Wow!

Father   Everything was so different then.

Mother   People have changed. Everyone has become so intense and violent.

Father   Like a nightmare.

Mother   War after war.

Father   You know, if I could have seen what was coming, I would have taken your mother and gone to live somewhere else.

Hadi   Maybe you should have. Even the University, which is supposed to be a place of intellectual freedom, has been taken over by a bunch of religious maniacs.

Father   Which is why I always say to you, "Be careful!" Don't criticize anything related to religion or politics. Stick to your Shakespeare. I'm serious.

Mother   Yes, son, be careful.

Hadi   I am careful. Don't worry about me.

Scene Seven

Nour *and* **Hadi** *in Hussein's place.*

Nour   Look, I bought something for you.

Hadi   Really? What?

Nour   Something you'll really like!

Hadi   What is it? Tell me.

Nour   I got you this.

She gives him a wrapped copy of Romeo and Juliet.

Open it, Professor.

Hadi   What is it? A book. Is it . . . ? Oh!

He finds the passage that has been marked and reads.

"If I profane with my unworthiest hand/ This holy shrine, the gentle fine is this:/ My lips, two blushing pilgrims, ready stand/ To smooth that rough touch with a tender kiss."

Nour *takes the book.*

Nour   "Good pilgrim, you do wrong your hand too much,/ Which mannerly devotion shows in this;/ For saints have hands that pilgrims' hands do touch,/ And palm to palm is holy palmers' kiss."

Nour *gives the book to* **Hadi**. *They embrace.*

Nour   Mmmmmm.

Comfortable pause.

Baby?

Hadi   What, sweetheart?

Nour   How long will we go on like this?

Hadi   For as long as you like.

Nour   No, I mean seeing each other secretly, as if we were committing a crime.

Hadi   What are you talking about?

Nour   When will we be able to be together like a normal couple?

Hadi   Not possible here in Basra, I'm afraid. You know that.

Nour   Hadi?

Hadi   What?

Nour   Do you really love me?

Hadi   Of course I do.

Nour   Then why don't we get married?

He draws away from her.

Hadi   What? I can't get married.

Nour   Why not? Why can't you?

Hadi   I said, right at the start . . .

Nour   Hadi, I've given you everything I have. I've trusted you. I've put my whole life at risk for you. Why can't we get married?

Hadi (*with rising panic*)   I'm not ready.

Nour   What do you mean?

Hadi   It's not the right time.

Nour   I can wait.

Hadi   Please don't.

Nour   Why? Don't you love me? Is it all just words?

Hadi   Why do you always think of marriage as your ultimate goal?

Nour   Why not?

Hadi   You've already been married.

Nour   So what?

Hadi   Well, I mean . . .

Nour   Does that make a difference to you?

Hadi   It's not the right time. My current situation is not . . .

Nour   Are you saying it might get better in the future?

Hadi   We can't get married.

Nour   Why? Tell me why?

Hadi   Because . . . because . . .

Nour   Because what? Huh? Because I am a widow with a daughter. Is that the reason? Tell me!

He doesn't respond.

Why are you silent?

She collars him and shakes him angrily.

Is that the reason, Hadi?

He doesn't respond.

Hadi   I can't . . .

Nour   Because Mister Professor has to have a virgin for his wife? Is that it? Is that it? Are you just like all the others? What am I? Some kind of a used car? Good enough to make use of, to drive around in? But when you actually get a car of your own, it's got be shiny, untouched, new? Mister Professor Hadi can't be seen with a second-hand wife? Is that really what it's about? Hadi, I love you and you love me. We're both educated . . . It's better than marrying a stranger, someone your parents arrange for you. What do you expect from a wife? I mean what do you want? Care? Sex? I can do both better than any new wife. Talk to me . . . So you don't want to talk . . . OK, then listen! I've been going through hell for our relationship: lying to my family, risking my reputation and life, endangering my daughter's life, enduring awful gossip about me, never mind my sincere feelings that you hurt deeply. Has it just been all about sex? I'm not a prostitute to desire whenever you need sex and have a place to take her to. I will give you some time to think about our relationship. Remember, I don't need a sexual partner. I need a man who can love me, and protect me, and be a safe haven for me and my daughter in this bloody country. If you are willing to be that man, then call me.

She leaves.

Scene Eight

Hadi *and* **Mother** *in living room. An envelope is slid under the door.* **Mother** *picks it up and pulls out a letter and a bullet.*

Mother   Hadi, what is it?

Hadi *holds up the bullet.*

Mother   What—who's out there? Who delivered that? Mohammed! Mohammed!

Father   What is it? What is that?

Hadi   It's a note.

Mother   Who's it from? Go outside! They're probably still there!

Father   Calm down! Please calm down! We can't think if you don't calm down. Hadi, read it.

Hadi   What for?

Mother   You know who it's from?

Father   Just read the note!

Hadi   Alright! (*He reads.*) "In the Name of Allah, the Most Gracious, the Most Merciful . . . " They misspelled . . .

Father   Just read the damn thing, OK?

Hadi   "Those who turn their back as apostates after Guidance was clearly shown to them—the Evil One has instigated them and busied them up with false hopes." This is bullshit.

Father   Just finish it.

Hadi   "They really wish that you should also become disbelievers, as they themselves are, so that both may become alike. So you should not take friends from among them unless they orient themselves in the way of Allah." These people are so childish! I can't read this!

Father   Give it to me, then! (*He picks up the reading.*) ". . . orient themselves in the way of Allah. And if they do not, then seize them wherever you find them and slay them."

Hadi   They left this bullet in the envelope.

Mother (*crying*)   What are we going to do now, Mohammed? We have to do something! Go to Syria or Jordan. You must get out of Basra by tomorrow morning.

Father   Calm down! Hadi, did you speak about religion in your class?

Hadi   Not really.

Father   Did you?

Hadi   Yes, I did.

Father   And what did you say?

Mother   You can go and stay with your brother. We'll borrow the money.

Hadi   They'll never give me a visa.

Father   Did you insult Islam in any way?

Hadi   No, not at all.

Father   You must have said *something*. What did you say?

Hadi   I said that I don't believe in the literal reality of Heaven and Hell.

Father   For God's sake! Why would you say something like that in your classroom?! Are you insane?!

Hadi   You don't believe in these things yourself, do you? Do you?

Father (*fiercely*)   That's not the point!

Mother   Do you think one of the students is involved in this?

Hadi   I don't know.

Father   You must disappear for a few days till we figure out who is behind this.

Mother   Yes. Yes. Listen to your father!

Father   Hadi, you will go with your mother to my brother's farm in Abu al-Khasib. The place is safe and secured by guards. Go tonight, go before dawn. Do you understand? No argument. Do as I say.

Hadi   What about my job?

Father   I'll take care of that. I'll talk to the Dean. Right now your "job" is to get away from here, while we figure out a longer-term plan. You may call them childish but these people are dead serious. You wouldn't be the first to be found floating in the river.

Scene Nine

A public street. **Hadi**, *with hat and sunglasses.* **Nour** *waiting for him.*

Hadi (*in a conspiratorial tone*)   Nour! Nour!

Nour (*not recognizing him*)   What? What do you want?

Hadi   Nour, it's me.

Nour   Oh my God! You scared me. I didn't recognize you.

Hadi   I don't want to be recognized.

Nour   What's the matter? I've been calling you for days. Why are you ignoring me?

Hadi   Keep your voice down. People are watching. What do you want?

Nour   I was worried because you didn't show up for class. You haven't been answering your phone. What's going on, Hadi?

Hadi   Just tell me what you want.

Nour   Hadi, you know I love you. You know that. You told me that you love me . . .

Hadi   I don't want to talk about marriage right now.

Nour   It's not about marriage.

Hadi   Then what's it about?

Nour (*trying to hold back tears*)   Hadi, listen to me. I'm . . .

Hadi   What the hell's going on?

Nour   You told me you would never leave me.

Hadi (*trying to be patient*)   Nour, what's the matter?

Nour   You promised that you wouldn't let anyone hurt me, and that you would always be there when I needed you. Don't you remember that?

Hadi (*realizing*)   Oh my God. No, not now! No, oh my God! This can't be happening. Are you . . . .?

Nour *nods, cries.*

Nour   Please help me, Hadi. Please. I have no one and nowhere to go. If my family finds out they'll kill me. To hell with me, I don't care, but my daughter, Hadi . . . my daughter . . .

Hadi   Nour, I'm leaving. I'm leaving Iraq. Very soon! Maybe even tomorrow.

Nour   What?!

Hadi   I'm leaving this bloody country!

Nour   You are leaving *me*?!

Hadi   I can't help you. I have to get away from here.

Nour   Leaving me like this? It's your child, Hadi!

Hadi   Keep your voice down, for God's sake!

Nour   It's your child!

Hadi   Get an abortion! I've got enough problems to deal with.

Nour   Abort your child! What are you saying? Where and how?

Hadi   I don't know! I can't think. My life's fucked up!

Nour   My life, too . . . Hadi, honey, you can't just leave me in this situation.

She kneels before him.

Please, you have to help me.

Hadi   What're you doing? Stand up! People are looking.

Nour   I'll abort the child, if that's really what you want. But please help me. I can't tell anyone about this. You're the only person who can help. My life is in danger.

Hadi   So is mine. I received a threatening letter, with a bullet inside.

Nour   What?! When?! Why didn't you tell me?

Hadi   I can't answer a lot of questions right now. I have to flee the country, or they'll kill me!

Nour   Take me with you.

Hadi   Are you crazy? I don't know what I'll do myself. I don't even know where I'm going. I can't take you with me. What about your daughter?

Nour   I'll leave her with my parents.

Hadi   No! I'm telling you, no! I have to go now.

Nour *holds his hand.*

Nour   Please Hadi, my darling, don't give up on me.

Hadi   Nour, if I don't leave soon I'll be dead. These people aren't joking.

Nour   Where can you go?

Hadi   To Syria, Jordan, any country that accepts me without a visa.

Nour   What about me? What am I supposed to do? What about your child?

Hadi   I've told you, get an abortion.

Nour   I don't even know how! Hadi, if you don't help me I will go to your family and tell them. It will be a huge scandal.

Hadi   Don't ever tell anyone about this, OK?

Nour   Then you must help me.

Hadi (*in desperation*)   I'll do my best. I promise I'll do my best.

Nour   Thank you, baby, thank you. Please remember that I love you. Do you know that?

Hadi (*painfully*)   Yes, I know. And I . . . I love you, too. Yes, I do. Please don't cry again! I have to go. I'll be in touch.

He squeezes her hand and leaves hastily.

Scene Ten

At home. **Hadi** *and his* **Mother.**

Hadi   Mom . . . can I talk to you?

Mother   What's wrong, what happened? Did they threaten you again?

Hadi   No, I . . . my . . .

Mother   What? Tell me!

Hadi   My girlfriend is pregnant.

Mother   What?!

Hadi   Yes, my girlfriend.

Mother   I don't understand . . . You got her pregnant! A virgin!

Hadi   You wanted to know. And now you know. And now we have to think.

Mother   Think! Now you want to think! Oh God, Hadi! Oh God!

She wanders vaguely around the room.

How are we going to get out of this disaster?

Hadi   Mom . . .

Mother   Shut up! Don't say a word! You're not my son! My son does not fuck a virgin and get her pregnant! Shame on you! Shame on us! You're a disgrace! You . . .

Hadi   Mom, please let me explain . . .

Mother   Explain what? What is there to explain?

Hadi   She's not a virgin.

Mother   What?

Hadi   She's a widow. It was a temporary marriage, *mutaa*.[3]

Mother   What? A temporary marriage! *Mutaa*! Are you insane?! How will you explain to her family that you had a temporary marriage?

Hadi   I didn't intend . . .

Mother   *Mutaa*? I can't believe my son could do such a thing! It's another word for prostitution. For people who can't face their filthy reality. No family would let their daughters get married as *mutaa*.

Hadi   Mom . . .

Mother   Don't start making excuses for your horrible actions. You could have married instead of getting us involved in this mess.

Hadi   She can abort the child, before her family finds out.

Mother   I can't be part of this, killing an innocent human being. You have to get married.

Hadi   I can't get married.

Mother   Why not? You have to get married eventually.

Hadi   She has a two-year old daughter.

Mother   Oh my God! Yours too, I suppose.

Hadi   Of course she's not mine.

Mother   Why "of course"? How would I know?

Hadi   She's not mine.

Mother   You have to get married to this woman.

Hadi   No, I can't. I won't. You know I have to leave the country, and she will have to abort the child.

Mother   Hadi, you are a bastard! A monster!

Hadi (*wretchedly*)   I am sorry, Mom.

Mother   You are not my son.

Hadi   I am really sorry, Mom. Sorry to you. Sorry to her. Sorry for everything.

Mother   Why, Hadi?! Why? Why did you have to . . .?

She tries to slap his face but stops and embraces him.

Hadi   Do we have to tell Dad about this?

Mother   It's better if he never finds out. I don't think he could deal with this.

Hadi   So you won't say anything to him.

Mother   No. It stays between us.

Scene Eleven

Mother *and* **Nour** *in a park.*

Nour   Are you Hadi's mother?

Mother   Nour?

Nour   Why do you want to see me?

Mother   Listen, Nour . . .

Nour   Where's Hadi? Where is he?

Mother   Calm down and listen to me.

Nour   Is he still hiding? Tell me where he is.

Mother   He's safe. Out of the country.

Nour   What do you want?

Mother   I know what has happened to you.

Nour   What do you mean, exactly?

Mother   I know you're pregnant.

Nour   What?! Who told you that?

Mother   Are you really pregnant?

Nour   Are you serious?

Mother   Answer my question!

Nour   Yes, I am pregnant.

Mother   Is it my son's child?

Nour   What do you think?

Mother   Answer the damned question!

Nour   Yes, it's your son's child.

Mother (*sighs*)   Oh God!

Nour   Where's Hadi?

Mother   Forget about Hadi. We need to work out a solution for this!

Nour   There isn't any but to have an abortion.

Mother   You can't keep it and look after it? My grandchild.

Nour   Can you?

Hadi's mother *thinks about it.*

Mother   No. Impossible. My husband would never agree. He would be ashamed.

Nour (*with bitter irony*)   *He* would be ashamed?

Mother   Then you must have an abortion. (*Pause.*) How far along are you?

Nour   Two months.

Mother   Oh God! I will be burned in Hell for this!

Nour   What about me? No one here cares about me! What if I die during the abortion?

Mother   To hell with you! Who told you to have sex with my son? You should have been careful!

Nour   How dare you! You come here and insult me, without even showing any compassion. Your son should have been careful, not me!

Mother   You have no idea what I've been going through! NO IDEA! (*She cries.*) I'm sorry.

Nour   Don't be sorry. I understand.

Mother   Me too. Forgive me. I understand what you're going through. I am really sorry that my son . . .

Nour   I love your son. I love him.

Mother   He doesn't deserve your love . . . Come here.

They hug each other.

Nour   I'm scared. Many women die during abortions.

Mother *holds* **Nour**'s *hand.*

Mother   You'll be fine. You're a strong woman. I'll go with you and be there.

Nour   But suppose . . .

Mother   You'll be fine.

Nour   If anything happens to me, will you take care of my daughter?

Mother   Nothing will happen to you . . .

Nour   But if it does . . .

Mother   I will see that she is looked after.

Scene Twelve

Toronto, Canada, Tim Horton's coffeeshop. **Hadi** *and his friend,* **Ahmed**, *having coffee, wrapped in heavy winter coats.*

Hadi   I'm fed up man. I can't stand it anymore.

Ahmed   Relax man, relax. You been what? Three months in Canada?!

Hadi   Three months not doing anything. So boring! And frustrating! My money's running out.

Ahmed   I told you to go on welfare, but you got mad at me!

Hadi   Yeah, I did. I can't take that money. I should find a job.

Ahmed   OK, good luck with that.

Hadi   What do you mean, "Good luck with that?"

Ahmed   For refugees, getting a job here is like chasing a crazy chicken in a football field.

Hadi   What? What do you mean?

Ahmed   I mean look at me! Been here almost a year and a half, and still working in an Arab restaurant.

Hadi   OK, but how about Jamal?

Ahmed   Who?

Hadi   Jamal, our friend from Diwania, the doctor. I heard he's working in a pharmacy.

Ahmed *laughs.*

Ahmed   Who told you that? He works in a gas station, man.

Hadi   What?! Seriously?!

Ahmed   You want more? Remember Rasha, our friend from school?

Hadi   Rasha?

Ahmed   Tall. Big tits.

Hadi   Right, the lawyer. She's in Canada now?

Ahmed   Yup. Works at Subway in Home Depot. Listen, man. You need to pass a whole lot of exams to get re-qualified to work in Canada. And then they say you have to have Canadian experience. Hah. You can't get a job without experience, and you can't get experience without a job. You're fucked, man.

Hadi   But I can't work in a restaurant! I was a university professor, and now I'm a waiter?

Ahmed   That's if you're qualified to work as a waiter.

Ahmed *laughs.*

Hadi   Wow.

Ahmed   It's tough, my friend.

Hadi   Do you ever think of going back?

Ahmed   You crazy? To get killed? At least I'm safe here, man.

Hadi   Even if you're stripped of your dignity?

Ahmed   Dignity is a relative term. I want to be able to walk the streets without being afraid that I'm going to be abducted and shot. If not worse. We're lucky to be here.

Hadi   Doesn't feel lucky to me.

Ahmed   Listen, forget you were ever some kind of a university professor. Face reality. This is it. This is where you live. Tim Horton's. Get used to it.

Hadi   I can't. I just can't. I can't work in a gas station or a donut store!

Ahmed   A lot of people do. A lot of Canadians do. (*Silence.*) You want another coffee?

Hadi   No. Thanks.

Ahmed   You still thinking about that woman?

Hadi   What woman?

Ahmed   The one back home. You told me her name. The one you . . .

Hadi   Nour? Yeah, I still feel guilty about her.

Ahmed   What could you do, man? Really?

Hadi   I just ditched her. Left her in the dirt. Just ran away.

Ahmed   Why don't you go back, then? Get married and bring her with you.

Hadi   It's not that easy. I was a total shit, man.

Ahmed   Yeah, probably. We all are. But if you can't do anything about it, you're going to have to forget her. You want to know how? There's an Iraqi party tonight at the Zanoubia night club. A lot of gorgeous women, lots of booze . . . You want to come? We'll forget our problems and have fun. What do you say?

Hadi   So you work your ass off, then go and spend the money on drinking and partying?

Ahmed   You got a better idea? Huh? Save money? (*He laughs.*) You can't save money in this fuckin' country, man! So dance, have fun, get drunk. Maybe get laid.

Hadi   OK. I'll come tonight.

Ahmed   That's the man! OK, gotta go to work. Get fired if I'm one minute late. Nine o'clock.

Hadi   Alright.

Scene Thirteen

Hadi's *house.* **Nour** *and* **Mother** *having tea. Iraqi music.*

Mother   I was so happy when you called and told me you were coming.

Nour   I've missed you.

Mother   Me too. It's been a long time . . . How are you? How have you been?

Nour   I'm . . . alright. Better, thanks to you. I can't thank you enough for . . .

Mother   Please! Don't say another word. Tell me, how is Yasmine?

Nour   She's started kindergarten.

Mother   Already?

Nour   She's very precocious. She's doing well so far. She says she wants to be a lawyer.

Mother   A lawyer?!

Nour   Of course she doesn't know what it means. But she says it's so that no one can hurt me.

Mother   She's a brave child.

Nour   Yes, but I worry about her.

Mother   Why?

Nour   I just worry about the world she's going to be growing up in. So many dangers. For girls, especially.

Mother   It's true.

Nour   Even in the daycare center where I was taking her, it came out that the janitor was luring one of the children to his room with candy, and . . .

Mother   Oh my God!

Nour   It could have been my own daughter! (*Pause.*) I feel so alone, you know.

Mother   Since you moved out on your own?

Nour   I couldn't stay at home anymore. It was just too painful.

Mother   How's the new place?

Nour   Well, it's a really small apartment, but it's our own, at least. It's lonely, but more peaceful.

Mother   Do you miss Hadi?

Nour   And I got a job interview!

Mother   He always asks about you whenever he calls.

Nour   Aren't you going to ask me about the interview?

Mother   Of course I want to know how it went. But I just want to say forgive and forget, Nour. I know you're still mad at him, and I know he still feels guilty. (*Pause.*) So, tell me about the job.

Nour   So, I had an interview at the one of the big oil companies.

Mother   That's great! What's the position?

Nour   I'm not even exactly sure! It involves some translating and office work. It's nothing very grand—but it's a *job*! If I get it, I'll be earning money and supporting myself and my daughter.

Mother   And how do you think it went?

Nour   I think it went well. Though you never know. The boss seemed very kind and thoughtful. He was really sympathetic when he found out I was a widow with a daughter—which was something I'd been worried about, because, you know . . . But he actually said, "Consider yourself hired."

Mother   I am *so* happy for you, Nour!

Nour   Well, I don't know. It feels like a fresh start, you know . . .

Mother   So when will you begin?

Nour   He said probably as soon as next week. I'll be assigned to one of the departments, as a trial.

Mother   Wonderful! Let's celebrate!

She turns the music up and grabs **Nour**'s *hand.*

Mother   I love this song. Let's dance.

Nour   Um Hadi! Are you serious?!

Mother   Come on! Let's be a little crazy. Let's dance and have fun.

They dance. **Nour**, *isolated in a spotlight, removes her headscarf and shakes out her hair.*

Scene Fourteen

The scene dissolves to the Zanoubia nightclub in Toronto. Music even louder. **Hadi** *is quite drunk and is dancing with* **Nour**, *who is gyrating quite seductively.* **Ahmed** *is applauding and encouraging* **Hadi**.

Ahmed   Yeah, yeah, yeah, yeah! Way to go, Hadi!

Hadi *stumbles and nearly falls.*

Ahmed   Whoa! Steady, my friend. Here, have another one!

Ahmed *gives* **Hadi** *another bottle of beer.* **Hadi** *seizes the bottle as if it is a microphone. He climbs onto a chair and speaks into the "microphone," addressing the crowd aggressively.* **Nour** *disappears.*

Hadi   Good evening, ladies and gentlemen. I hope everyone is having a good time!

Ahmed   Oh boy! Here we go!

Hadi   I'd like to make a toast . . . But before I do that I want to introduce myself.

Ahmed   Hadi, come with me, you're drunk!

Hadi   No no no, I'm totally sober, man. Just let me give a toast. OK?

Ahmed   Hadi, you are totally wasted.

Hadi   I am not! Ladies and gentlemen, listen! Are you listening? Is this working?

He taps the bottle.

Ladies and gentlemen, I am going to give a toast. You have been dancing and singing, I should say we . . . we have been singing patriotic songs about Iraq—(*Perhaps he sings a couple of phrases in Arabic.*)—while living magnificently, MAGNIFICENTLY, seven thousand miles away, seven thousand miles away, from that wretched land and that wretched people . . . So I say . . . So I say, let's drink Cabernet France and Pinot Noir and Molson's Canadian, and cheer for our country . . . Ladies and gentlemen . . . To Iraq! The cradle of civilization. The richest land, inhabited by the most miserable people!

Ahmed   Hadi, please get down . . . you're drunk and you're making a fool of yourself.

Hadi I told you I am sober . . . And I can't make a fool of myself, because I'm a fool already. Folks, I have a confession to make here. Please listen to me! Are you listening? My name is Hadi, a new member joining your worthless existence. I just want to say that I am a bad person, OK? Very, very bad person. And you know why? I'll tell you why. Because I disappointed my girlfriend. And I disappointed my family . . . And my country . . . And came here to Canada, to be a worthless piece of shit!

Crowd booing.

A stranger with no job, who begs from the government to . . .

Ahmed *takes away* **Hadi**'s *"microphone," forces him to step down, and takes him away. Music back.*

Hadi Yes . . . go on and dance! Dance on the bleeding body of Iraq! Hypocrites!

Scene Fifteen

South Oil Company. Manager's office. A 65-year-old manager sits behind a fancy desk while **Nour** *stands in front of him. If possible, it should become apparent only gradually that the manager is* **Hadi's father**—*whom* **Nour** *has never met.*

Father (*genially*) Ah, Nour! Good, good. Come in.

Nour You wanted to see me, sir?

Father Yes, I do. In fact, I want to talk with you about your promotion.

Nour A promotion?! I've just started working last month.

Father Please have a seat.

She sits.

It's not really a promotion; it's more of a, shall we say, a gesture of appreciation. You are a very good employee. I've heard a lot of good things about you.

Nour Thank you, sir. I try to do my best.

Father I'm sure you do. I know it's not easy for you. You're a widow, with a daughter. I understand your situation. I'd like to help you.

Nour Thank you, sir. I really appreciate your kindness.

Father Not at all. I've decided that you should work here in my office. As my secretary, as my personal assistant, really. That way you can go home early, arrange your hours of work to suit your own circumstances. What do you think?

Nour I don't know . . .

Father I'm offering you an excellent opportunity.

Nour Of course I really appreciate that . . . But I'm really happy with my current position, sir. My colleagues are really nice to me. I feel very close to them.

Father That's wonderful. And I want you to feel close to me, too.

Nour How do you mean?

Father   I mean close, you know? Comfortable.

Nour   But why?

Father   Because I . . . like you.

Nour *is beginning to see where this is going.*

Nour   Oh. I think I'm going to go now.

Father   Wait, Nour. Please. Don't misunderstand me . . . I find you very attractive.

Nour   Please, I have to go.

Father   I'm not trying to take advantage of you. We can get married.

Nour   What? You're already married.

Father   That doesn't mean that I can't feel attracted to you. We can still get married.

Nour   How? What are you talking about?

Father   A temporary marriage. *Mutaa.*

Nour   What? Are you out of your mind? No! Of course not! How dare you? You are *Haji*, for God's sake![4] How could you even suggest such a thing? I am not a prostitute.

Father   Please! Calm down, and lower your voice.

Nour   I am a woman with honor. Do you understand?

Father   I understand, yes. All I'm suggesting is a temporary marriage, according to the Sunnah of our Prophet. I will be your husband. I will take care of you and your orphan daughter.

Nour   You want me to be your mistress! Hah! You can't fool me! *Haji*? *Haji*?

She laughs.

Mutaa is another word for prostitution, and I am not a prostitute! Not for you. Not for anyone!

She leaves.

Scene Sixteen

Hadi *and his* **Mother** *over the phone.*

Mother   We all miss you, my son. How can you think we don't? But you can't come back now.

Hadi   I've bought a ticket.

Mother   Cancel it. Change it. We can come and see you in Amman or in Dubai.

Hadi   You don't understand. I can't stay anymore. I can't bear it. I'm sorry. My doctor says that I suffer from depression. If I am destined to die in my country, then let it be. I don't care. At least I will die among my family, not alone in a foreign country. (*Disconnected*) Hello . . . Mom . . .?

Mother   Hello . . . Sami? . . . Are you there?

She tries to call him again but can't get through.

Oh God.

She calls **Nour** *but doesn't get an answer.*

Mother   Come on! Answer. Please, God!

She texts **Nour***, spelling out the words.*

Mother   Call . . . me . . . back. Now. (*Into the phone.*) Be there. Please!

Her phone rings.

Hello?

Mother *and* **Nour** *over the phone.*

Nour   Hi, Um Hadi. Is everything alright?

Mother   No, it's not alright. He's coming back.

Nour   Who?

Mother   Hadi. I just talked to him.

Nour   Wow! Well, that's good news, isn't it?!

Mother   No, it's not good news! If he comes back he'll be killed. I tried to tell him, but he wouldn't listen.

Nour   I don't know what to say . . .

Mother   Nour, can you call him and tell him not to come. He loves you. He'll listen to you.

Nour   But I haven't talked to him since he left.

Mother   Please, Nour. Do it for me . . . please.

Nour   What am I going to say?

Mother   Just tell him, "Don't come. Not now."

Nour   I don't know.

Mother   Nour. Please. We're talking about his life.

Nour   Well, OK, I guess. Text me his number.

Mother   Thank you, Nour. Please call him as soon as possible.

Nour   I will, I promise.

Mother   Thank you, thank you. I almost forgot to ask about your job. What happened with that asshole? Excuse my language.

Nour   He issued an order sending me to the farthest location in the desert of Basra, Majnoon oil field.

Mother   Where?

Nour   The Majnoon field. But I don't see how I can manage it. It's almost three hours there and three hours back.

Mother   Did you say Majnoon?

Nour   Yes, and there's nothing I can do about it. I can't complain to anyone. He's the personnel manager.

Mother (*suddenly alarmed*)   Which company did you say you are with?

Nour   It's called Erfat, but it's really a subsidiary of Southern Oil.

Mother *realizes that* **Nour**'s *boss is almost certainly her own husband.*

Mother   Oh my God.

Nour   Anyway, don't worry about me. Let's deal with Hadi's problem now. I'll let you know how it works out. (*Pause.*) Um Hadi? Are you OK?

Mother   Please just call Hadi.

Nour   OK, I will.

Mother   Thank you. Goodbye.

Scene Seventeen

At **Hadi**'s *house.* **Mother** *and* **Father** *together.*

Mother   There's no news. Nobody has been able to get through to him, for two whole days.

Father   What's the big deal?

Mother   I'm so worried. I can't think straight.

Father   I'm sure he's fine. The trouble with you is you worry too much.

Mother   Don't tell me what my trouble is! You have no idea . . .

Father   What? What is it?

Mother   I don't want to talk to you right now.

They are silent and tense. Suddenly **Hadi** *enters, with suitcases.*

Father   Hadi!

Mother   Oh my God.

Father   My son, my son! Come here!

Father *embraces* **Hadi** *fervently.*

Father   We were so worried. You know how your mother is. How was the flight? Are you tired? Are you hungry? Do you want you something to eat?

Hadi   Dad, I hate to do this, but could you pay the taxi-driver? I don't have any money, and he can't take a card.

Father   Of course, of course! I'll be right back.

Fath3er *goes out briefly.*

Hadi   Mom? Aren't you glad to see me?

Mother (*almost breaking down*)   Oh Hadi! Hadi! Of course I'm glad to see you! But why did you have to come? I'm worried sick.

Hadi   Mom, I told you. I couldn't stand it. I was so lonely. And it was getting so cold! You can't imagine.

Father (*coming back in*)   You should have called from the airport.

Hadi   I wanted to surprise you.

Mother   Well, you certainly did that.

Father   Are you tired? How was the flight?

Hadi   Really long. Eight hours waiting in Istanbul.

Mother   Are you hungry? Shall I get you something to eat?

Hadi   I'm fine. There was a meal on the flight.

Mother   You were saying it was so cold in Canada.

Hadi   Cold like you can't believe! And it keeps getting worse.

Father   A nice plump Canadian girl-friend, that's what you need. To keep you warm? Eh?

Mother   Don't . . . say that.

Father   What?

Mother (*fiercely*)   Don't say that!

Hadi   It's OK, Mom, he's joking. You know what Dad is like.

Mother   Do I?

Father   I'm going to call your sister. She'll want to see you right away.

He goes to make a call.

Hadi   Mom! Have you heard anything from . . .?

Mother   Not now.

Hadi   But is she . . .?

Mother   Later.

Hadi   Dad still doesn't know, right?

Mother   I said later!

Scene Eighteen

Dusk. By the Shatt al-Arab. Sounds of waves and seagulls. **Nour** *and* **Hadi**.

Nour   This better be important . . .

Hadi   That's all you have to say? No "hi?" No "I've missed you?" No "happy to see you back?"

She stares at him. He falters.

You look nice.

Nour   Thanks.

Hadi   Just thanks?

Nour   What can I do for you, Hadi?

Hadi   I can't believe you are so cold towards me.

Nour   I can't believe that you would have the nerve to ask to see me, after you dumped me and left me helpless. By the way, people are asking about you.

Hadi   What people?

Nour   Just people. That boy from your class . . . Ali?

Hadi   What did you tell him?

Nour   Nothing. I have nothing to say to him. He's gone all religious.

Hadi   Did you tell him I was back?

Nour   He seemed to know already.

Hadi   I came back for you, Nour.

She laughs mirthlessly.

Nour   Oh sure. Don't even try to . . .

Hadi   Honestly, I came back to see you.

Nour   Oh! I believe you. Try another one.

Hadi   Are you still single?

Nour   Single?

Hadi   Do you have . . .?

Nour   Do I have what?

Hadi   You know what I mean. A man.

Nour   What do you want, Hadi? What is this about?

Hadi   I want to apologize.

Nour   Apologize?

Hadi   To tell you that I'm sorry.

Nour   You flew seven thousand miles to apologize.

Hadi   My conscience . . .

Nour   Oh, you have a conscience? Really? I didn't know.

Hadi   Yes, I do. That's why . . .

Nour   That's why you left me hopeless and helpless after you got me pregnant.

Hadi   I am sorry, Nour. I am so sorry.

Nour *is silent.*

Hadi   Before I got to Canada, I couldn't imagine how much I would miss . . .

Nour   What? Sex. Yes, I'm sure.

Hadi   I missed *you*, Nour. You have to believe me.

Nour   Do I? Do I have to believe you?

Hadi   Do you still love me, Nour?

Nour (*angrily*)   Why are you asking me that? What do you want from me?

Hadi   I just . . . I don't know anymore . . . I came back for you, Nour, and I don't know . . .

Nour   Have you come back to get me pregnant again and run away?

Hadi   No. I came back to ask your hand in marriage.

Nour   What?!

Hadi   I came back so we can get married. Properly. A permanent, public, normal marriage.

Nour   What would your family say?

Hadi   It's not their business. It's mine. Yours and mine.

Nour   Your father? Would he be happy to see his precious son marrying a widow with a child?

Hadi   When he meets you, he will love you, too.

Nour (*after a pause*)   Are you serious about this, Hadi? This is not just because you got lonely and scared in Canada?

Hadi   I'm serious. I want to marry you. And be a father to your child, if you will let me. And have children of our own.

Nour   I can't believe that . . . you came all this way to marry me?!

Hadi   I love you, *habibti*! I do. I know it now.

Nour   Your "used car."

Hadi   Don't say that.

Nour   I'm teasing, my darling.

Car headlights sweep the stage. Sound of a car screeching to a halt. **Two Gunmen** *get out of the car and rush at* **Hadi***. They try to take him. He struggles, while* **Nour** *tries to defend him.*

Gunman (*pushing her violently*)   FUCK OFF, BITCH! I DON'T WANT TO HURT YOU!

Several shots ring out. **Hadi** *falls dead in slow motion. The* **Gunmen** *exit. Sound of car doors slamming and car roaring away.* **Nour** *embraces* **Hadi**'s *dead body. Sound of waves* *and seagulls. After a while,* **Mother***, veiled in mourning, comes forward and silently sits on a bench.* **Nour** *rises, stands behind her, puts a hand on her shoulder. The two women are silent.*

Notes

1   The Shatt al-Arab is a river that forms where the Tigris and Euphrates join.
2   *Habibi* is a term of endearment that translates here as "my darling." *Habibti* is the feminine form.
3   *Nikah al-mutaa* is a form of temporary marriage allowed in Twelver Shia Islam. It is contracted in private, with duration and dowry specified in advance.
4   A *Haji* is a Muslim who has made the pilgrimage to Mecca.

www.ingramcontent.com/pod-product-compliance
Ingram Content Group UK Ltd.
Pitfield, Milton Keynes, MK11 3LW, UK
UKHW020734280225
455688UK00012B/644